A Guidebook to

in Georgia, North Carolina and Tennessee

ATTRACTIONS, SCENIC TOURS, OUTDOOR ACTIVITIES,
PARKS, WILDERNESS AND RECREATION AREAS
LODGING, DINING, SHOPPING

Compiled and written by
Rusty Hoffland

Fifth Printing, Revised Edition
Copyright 1984, 1985, 1986,
1988, 1990
On the Road Publishing
2870-I Twin Brooks Road, NE
Atlanta, Georgia 30319

ISBN 0-9616316-1-9

Graphic design:
Monica Hall

Cover photo:
Anthony Lampros

This book is dedicated to
Tallulah Falls School,
its faculty and staff,
and members of the
Georgia Federation of Women's Clubs
for their commitment to keeping
"The light in the mountains"
at Tallulah Falls, Georgia.

Enjoying the view from a mountain trail

Contents

Photo: Diane Kirkland

Notes from on the road . . .

I n the high country, there's a plaque on a broker's desk which reads, "The first person to make a mountain out of a molehill was a real estate salesman." *I* may have been the second. On a rainy, foggy night, Chattanooga's Mounteagle Mountain, while not exactly a molehill, was a terrifying Mount Everest to this Wisconsin woman taking her first trip over *any* mountain. Nearly two decades and countless mountain miles later—through northern Georgia, western North Carolina and eastern Tennessee—that fear has given way to pure exhilaration.

In this book I'd like to share with you some of that exhilaration . . . and a few favorite places to go, things to see and do. This is not meant to be, could not be, a comprehensive guidebook—the magnitude of my enthusiasm is in no way a measure of my knowledge of this area. Instead, consider this a book to encourage exploration throughout this region where going there can be as enjoyable as being there.

Around any curve, down into any gorge, up over any summit, mountain roads reward the traveler with scenes captured for a lifetime without benefit of camera—an entire mountainside strewn with rhododendron . . . "quilts for sale" flapping in the breeze on a country clothesline . . . a white goat in front of a weatherbeaten barn . . . children splashing in the mini-rapids of a mountain stream.

This is the place to rediscover the reality of change. What were clearly three commonplace mountaintops across a valley in the early evening become three mysterious islands at daybreak, their summits floating on an ocean of low-lying clouds. A summer green ridge line changes to a deep, luminous blue in the late afternoon sunlight. On a splendid October day, a mountaintop is a canvas of brilliant autumn colors; in the midnight starlight, it becomes a magnificent cathedral.

Considering the dramatic visual changes which occur in one place in one day, the seasonal changes here seem hesitant, procrastinating, dillydallying around. Spring starts early but takes its own slow, sweet time—putting out some buds here, some blossoms there, then splashing mountainside and valley with wild plum, redbud and dogwood, and finally beginning a lengthy experiment with several thousands shades of green.

Summer generally makes daytime visits only, staying for the night occasionally in July and August, and always lingering for the evening concert of katydids, crickets and other creatures that go singing in the night.

The autumn leaf show is at least a six-week-long performance, traveling from the higher elevations to the lower . . . a show that always plays to a full house and brings the curtain down for those who never venture to the mountains after the end of October.

But it is not yet winter, and November may be the nicest month of the year. The earth is red and golden with leaves that rustle underfoot on hoarfrost mornings, leaves that no longer hide the shape of things. Visible now are silver-barked trees silhouetted atop ridge lines, and cliffs, bluffs and huge, lichen-covered boulders, brooks and streams, even waterfalls which were only glimpsed or heard through summer's thick covering. Except for the highest elevations, winter comes late and exits early. Christmas-card scenes of snow-blanketed country churches, log cabins and split rail fences will sparkle only a few hours under the winter sun. Seasons. Scenes. Definable details. Things we can name. Trees of the forest. Identifiable temporary parts of an inexplicable, eternal whole. Touchstones. Reassurances. No less significant because of our projection of significance. Simple entities of Now, discovered in a Forever landscape of mysterious blue ridges. The ultimate ambiguity, these mountains. The perfect paradox. Here we can lose ourselves, or find ourselves, or free ourselves from doing either—enjoying the journey for its own sake, learning not to make mountains out of molehills.

Rusty Hoffland

About the Cover Photo & Photographer

A View from Whiteside Mountain was photographed by Anthony Lampros. This view includes Rocky and Chimneytop Mountains with Toxaway Mountain in the distance. Whiteside Mountain is located between Highlands and Cashiers, North Carolina (see table of contents).

Anthony Lampros is park superintendent of Black Rock Mountain State Park between Mountain City and Dillard, Georgia. (Another of his excellent scenic photographs is used with the listing of that park — see table of contents). He is a graduate of the University of Georgia and has been with the Department of Natural Resources since 1982. Outdoor photography is a natural branch of his other hobbies which put him in places with beautiful scenery — hiking and snow skiing. Anthony and his wife, Sharon are both natives of Rabun County, Georgia and consider themselves fortunate to be working and raising their three children, Ryan, Everett and Lindsey in their home county.

NATIONAL LANDS

Photo: Courtesy Georgia Department of Industry and Trade

Trout fishing is available in miles of streams in the southern mountains' national forests and national parks

National Lands

Hiking Across the Smokies

The Great Smoky Mountains National Park

T his national treasure, divided almost equally·between North Carolina and Tennessee, has over eight million visitors each year—more than any other national park in America. Yet even during summer vacation and autumn leaf seasons those who seek solitude can find it in the 800 square miles of forested mountains, many rising to over 6,000 feet. There are over 900 miles of hiking trails, both backcountry and self-guiding nature trails, to enable almost everyone to enjoy the park's natural wonders. Within the 514,093 park acres there are over 125 species of native trees and 1,200 of flowering plants; 300 species of birds and wildlife not including the 70 species of fish.

The visitor centers are located at Sugarland, just inside the park at the Gatlinburg entrance, at Oconaluftee from the Cherokee entrance, and at Cades Cove off Tennessee 73 which enters the park at Townsend. Stop at the centers for free maps and information and natural history exhibits.

Accommodations and Camping

The only lodging within the park is at LeConte Lodge, accessible only by trail, and at rustic Wonderland Hotel. (Both are listed under Gatlinburg.)

There are 10 developed campgrounds in the park, with picnic tables and grills, bathrooms with cold water and flush toilets (no showers). There are some RV sites, some dumping stations, but no hookups. Three of the campgrounds accept advance reservations for May through October: Cades Cove (near Townsend), Elkmont (near Gatlinburg) and Smokemont (near Chero-kee). Reservations by mail: Ticketron Reservation System, P.O. Box 2715, San Francisco, CA 94126, or in person at nationwide Ticketron walk-in outlets. No phone reservations accepted. All other campgrounds operate on a first come first served basis. Most campgrounds are open year round. Call the visitor center for more information.

Scenic Roads & Side Trips

No commercial vehicles are allowed on the few roads within the park, and the speed limit is 45 mph or lower. There are no gasoline or automobile services. The only road all the way across the park, connecting North Carolina and Tennessee, is scenic Newfound Gap Road (US 441), a paved winding two-lane, with frequent scenic overlooks, quiet walkways, wildflower displays and various exhibits along its 33 miles.

Just south of Newfound Gap where the road crests at 5,048 feet at the North Carolina/Tennessee state line, is a 7-mile spur to Clingman's Dome, at 6,643 feet, the highest point in the park. On a clear day, when there is no haze, there are maginificent panoramic vistas from the road and from atop the observation tower.

The Little River Road (TN 73) between Sugarlands Visitor Center and Townsend, Tennessee, is beautiful, rain or shine, in haze, fog or whatever. Its 18 miles through the park climbs no mountains; it follows the little River's course most of the way, passing whitewater rapids, clear pools, rocky basins, and paths to nearby waterfalls. Laurel Creek Road, off the Little River Road about a mile inside the park from Townsend, connects with Cades Cove, the park's most visited area. An 11-mile paved loop road encircles this beautiful valley, with stops to tour various community buildings and the actual home-steads and farms of those who last lived in the cove. The loop road is closed to automobiles at certain times during the vacation season, and used for walking and bicycling only. Check with the visitor center.

Two gravel roads lead from Cades Cove. Parson Branch goes one way south to connect with US 129; and Rich Mountain Road, a one way north to US 321 about five miles from Townsend.

The Roaring Fork Motor Nature Trail and Cherokee Orchard Road is a five-mile scenic loop beginning off Airport Road in Gatlinburg. Also from Gat-linburg, the Greenbrier Road leaves US 321 (about six miles east of its junction with US 441) for a four-mile unpaved country drive leading to a trail to the Ramsey Cascades, the park's highest waterfalls.

For a lovely solitary side trip to the park's least visited areas see Cataloochee Valley listing under Maggie Valley, North Carolina.

Balsam Mountain and Round Bottom Roads are reached via the Blue Ridge Parkway, about 11 miles from Cherokee. Balsam Mountain Road re-enters the park after another nine miles. The reward for this trip, other than camping or picnicking at Balsam Mountain Campground, or access to several hiking trails, is the wonderful Heintooga Overlook, one of the best places in the mountains to watch a sunset. If you don't care for narrow gravel roads, take the same route back. For the more adventuresome, the Round Bottom Road is scary looking but offers a perfectly safe 27-mile tour, some parts gravel, some paved, some one way, some two way, through mountain forests, leaving the park for a few miles, junctioning with the US 441 Parkway again near the Oconaluftee Visitor Center.

Hiking

Whether it's a short stroll along one of the paths marked "Quiet Walkways," a scenic day hike or a backcountry backpacking trip (permit required for this;

check at visitors centers), or a stint on the Appalachian Trail (which crosses the summit of the Smokies almost following the North Carolina/Tennessee line), hiking is a favorite activity here. Free trail maps are available at the visitors centers where you can also buy hiking guidebooks. A good day hike book is *Hiking the Great Smokies* by Carson Brewer, with descriptions of over 60 trails, mileage, points of interest, directions and some maps. The 11th printing was priced at $2.50. If you only do one hike, and it's when the wild azaleas are blooming, consider Andrews Bald. It's an easy two miles down, and a moderate 2 miles back up. The trail starts on the Appalachian Trail (south) at the Clingman's Dome parking area, and is well marked where it turns to Andrews Bald.

Bicycling, Horseback Riding, Skiing, Fishing, Picnicking & Tubing

Bicyling in the Smokies is not for the round-the-neighborhood level of rider with the exception of Cades Cove, where you may rent bicycles and ride on a level loop road, with certain times closed to auto traffic. Bicycling the park's other roads requires excellent bikes and excellently conditioned riders, who are brave (or foolish) enough to get out there on narrow hairpin turns with all those cars and RVs. No off-road bicycles or other vehicles are allowed on park trails.

Horseback riding stables are located in or near the park but bridle trails within the park are limited and horses must be kept on those specific trails.

Cross-country skiing, weather permitting, is open on Clingman's Dome Road and other park roads closed to winter traffic.

Fishing requires either a North Carolina or Tennessee license for anyone over 16. Check regulations first, as there are several off-limit streams and various rules regarding bait.

Tubing is popular in several areas and is not illegal although it is not encouraged by the park rangers as it can be dangerous. The most popular spot is near the Deep Creek Campground—see listing under Bryson City, North Carolina.

Picnic areas throughout the park have water, picnic tables, grills and restrooms. Alcoholic beverages are allowed in picnic areas but not at campground sites.

Scheduled Activities

During the summer, various programs are scheduled in different locations throughout the park. These will usually include hikes and nature walks lead by park rangers, and slide presentations. Occasional special events such as music and story telling evenings may be scheduled. Check the activity schedule at the visitors center, campground office or ranger station.

Tremont Environmental Education Center

Summer camp for children, a family camp week, Elderhostel weeks including one with the grandchildren, and teacher and naturalist weeks are scheduled at this institute in the park. Programs are conducted by the Great Smoky Mountains Natural History Association in cooperation with the National Park Service. Tremont facilities include comfortable dormitory lodging and a dining hall for up to 100. For information on Tremont, call 615/448-6709.

About the Bears

The symbol of the Smokies is the black bear, and the park's population is estimated at 400 to 600. Fewer and fewer are seen alongside the road, as the old time "panhandlers" have been moved deep into the backwoods. The shy creatures do have voracious appetites, however, and will sometimes wander out of the wilderness in search of more food. Feeding bears violates regulations and can be dangerous to you and the bears who become trusting of people and easy marks for poachers. If bears are along the road, stay in your car with the windows closed. They can be dangerous, especially if there are cubs involved. If bears are near trails they will generally pick up your scent and avoid you.

Additional Information

More information on two of the park areas is included in other sections of this book; Cataloochee Valley, the park's least visited and most remote section is listed under Maggie Valley, North Carolina and the Deep Creek area, a popular spot for tubing, with campground, hiking and nearby waterfalls, is listed under Bryson City, North Carolina.

For additional information by phone or mail, a park map and trail maps, contact Great Smoky Mountains National Park, Gatlinburg, TN 37738; phone 615/436-6516.

Blue Ridge Parkway

T his is more than a 469-mile scenic highway. It is also a 469-mile-long national park, offering accommodations, camping, hiking, biking, attractions, craft centers, scheduled activities, and more. About 250 miles of this mountaintop highway follows the crest of North Carolina's highest mountains, from it's terminus at the Great Smoky Mountains National park to the Virginia state line. From there it continues to Skyline Drive and the entrance to the Shenandoah National Park. There are no commerical vehicles and no billboards — the parkway was built solely for leisure use.

Numbered mileposts simplify locations, and exits to nearby towns and highways are clearly marked. The road itself is a beautifully engineered and maintained two-lane, with occasional spurs to attractions, overlooks or parkway facilities. It is often lightly traveled, but can be heavy during peak vacation periods, especially the autumn color season. Generally quite safe, there are

Photo: Hugh Morton
Courtesy Grandfather Mountain

The Blue Ridge Parkway's Linn Cove Viaduct glides gracefully across the side of Grandfather Mountain near Linville, NC, giving drivers access to some of the most rugged terrain in the Blue Ridge Mountains

sections which can be totally fogged in during the evening, early morning or rainy weather. Extreme caution should be used in winter, and some sections in the higher elevations are closed for the season.

Whether you use the parkway and it facilities as a vacation destination, for scenic day tours from wherever else you are vacationing, or just as a route to get you to somewhere else in the mountains, there is so much to see, so many attractions to visit, so many trails to hike, you'll wish you had more time, and will want to return often. As you travel, stop at campgrounds or other ranger offices for information and any scheduled activites in that area.

(Several of the parkway's attractions are covered in more detail and listed under nearby towns.)

Camping and Lodging Accommodations

There are five developed campgrounds with tent and RV sites along the North Carolina portion of the parkway. Campgrounds have dumping stations but no electrical or water hookups. There are flush toilets, cold water and no showers. Sites have picnic tables and grills. Evening programs are often scheduled and may include naturalists' talks, slide presentations, maybe a "night prowl," and occasionally there will be music or story telling. No reservations are accepted. (If campgrounds are filled, there will usually be sites available in private campgrounds in nearby towns and villages.)

Lodging accommodations, operated by private concessionaires liscensed by the park service, are available at two of the following campground areas which are listed from south to north.

Mount Pisgah: Hiking to Mount Pisgah's observation tower makes camping or lodging at this area extra special. Many of the 70 trailer and 70 tent sites offer better than average privacy and convenience to vehicle parking space. There is a picnic area, store, gas station, and Mount Pisgah Inn for lodging, breakfast, lunch or dinner with a view. On a ridge at 5,000 feet it is some view! Good food, reasonable prices and rates. Usually busy, and lodging reservations are a must during the busy season. Milepost 408.6

Linville Falls: Linville Gorge, waterfalls and wilderness are the attractions here (see more information under Linville Falls, NC) where there are 55 tent sites and 20 trailer sites, and a large picnic area. Milepost 316.3.

Julian Price Memorial Park: There are 100 picnic sites here which gives you some idea of its popularity. One reason is the trout stocked lake. There are 68 trailer and 120 tent sites on this beautiful 3,900 acre park located at milepost 294.1.

Doughton Park: There are 20 miles of trails through thickets of laurel, rhododendron and azaleas, beautiful wildflower meadows, and great rocky bluff formations in this 6,430 acre park at an elevation of 3,850 feet. Certainly one of the most beautiful areas along the parkway, Doughton Park offers picnic areas and camping in 26 trailer and 110 tent sites. The Bluffs Lodge has 24 comfortable rooms. There is a service station, a gift shop, plus a coffee shop and restaurant. The absolutely excellent food is equalled only by the sincere friendliness of the staff. Open for breakfast, lunch and dinner. Prices and rates are very reasonable. Milepost 241.1.

Crabtree Meadows: Crabtree Falls drop for 80 feet and are reached by an easy 1.6 mile hike from this 253 acre park with picnic area, 71 tent and 22 trailer sites. Milepost 339.5.

Special Points of Interest

Following are only a few of the sights to see, stops to make, hikes to take, and places not to miss along the parkway from south to north:

Richland Balsam at milepost 431.4 where there's a short hike to the highest point on the parkway—6,410 feet; The Folk Art Center at milepost 382, (see listing under Asheville); Craggy Gardens at milepost 363, a visitor center and nature trail on a great heath bald covered with crimson and purple rhododendron; Mount Mitchell State Park (not exactly on the parkway, but can only be reached by a five-mile spur off the parkway) at milepost 355.4 offers camping and hiking on the highest mountain in the eastern US—6,684 feet above sea level; Museum of North Carolina Minerals at milepost 331 displays samples of minerals mined in the area; Linn Cove Viaduct at milepost 300, an astonishingly beautiful piece of construction in a snake-like bridge resting atop 7 tiers, 150 feet apart, and following the contours of this magnificent mountain, believed to be one of the oldest in the world; the Tanawha Trail which begins at the viaduct and takes hikers up on Grandfather for a *real* view; Moses H. Cone Memorial Park, milepost 293, a grand estate with a mansion housing North Carolina crafts and 25 miles of bridle trails—no horses but great hiking; Northwest Trading Post at milepost 258.5 is a great old mountain cabin chock full of co-op members' crafts and gifts; Cumberland Knob, the last stop in North Carolina is a 1,000 acre park with a picnic area, and trails through galax and laurel.

There is much more to see and do; the scenery changes constantly with the weather, times of day and the season. Take a picnic and watch a sunset; better still, take a breakfast basket and watch a sunrise. Stop at the first visitor center or campground for a list of trails and mileposts, and go hiking on dozens of trails along this great national scenic highway and park.

For a fold out map of the park's total 469 miles, and for further information, contact Superintendent, Blue Ridge Parkway, 200 BB&T Building, #1 Pack Square Asheville, NC 28801; phone 704/259-0779.

Big South Fork
National River and Recreation Area

Big South Fork of the Cumberland River in the Big South Fork National River and Recreation Area

Photo: Courtesy National Park Service (BSFNRRA)

O pened by the National Park Service in 1986, this new national park includes over 80 miles of the Big South Fork of the Cumberland River, and over 100,000 acres, mostly in wilderness backcountry, and mostly in Tennessee's Cumberland Plateau, with some of the park extending over into Kentucky.

Hundreds of miles of hiking and horseback riding trails were planned and developed by the Army Corps of Engineers to include awe-inspiring views and overlooks. Many lead to great natural sandstone bridges, spanning treetops over several dozen yards. Others lead into the river gorge, a place of unspoiled natural beauty. (An excellent hiking and interpretive guide to the area is *Hiking the Big South Fork* by Brenda D. Coleman and Jo Anna Smith. The 221-page book includes maps, difficulty ratings and good directions.) The river and gorge remain untouched except for these trails, and a limited number of access points for canoeing, kayaking and rafting. The river and streams are open for fishing; smallmouth bass, rock bass and bream are abundant. Hunting is allowed during the season in this new new national facility, one of the reasons it is technically not a national park, but a national recreation area.

No permits are required for backcountry campers, who need only be sure their campsites are at least 300 feet from the trail. Bandy Creek Campground is a beautiful new facility, with 200 campsites for tents, RV's, and group camping, bathhouses with showers, picnic areas, nature trails, and the Visitor Center, where maps, information and programs are available year round. Bandy Creek is reached via the only highway through the park. Camping is also available at the excellent Pickett State Park and Forest which borders the park on the west, and can be reached via 154 north out of Jamestown. (See the table of contents, Tennessee.) This road also leads to the trailhead to the only accommodations within the park, which must be reached by foot or horseback; the Charit Creek Lodge (see table of contents).

The Blue Heron Community (located within the Kentucky section of the park) is a sort of ghost town, developed by the National Park Service at the Blue Heron mining community which operated between 1937 and 1962. The park has done an outstanding job in conveying a sense of what life was like for the familes in this remote, company owned mining camp. Ghost structures, lifesize black and white photograph "cutouts" and tape recorded "memories" of those who actually lived, or had parents and grandparents who lived in Blue Heron, are used effectively to create this unique place within the park. To reach Blue Heron, continue north from Oneida, Tennessee (see table of contents) on US 27, turning west, (left) on Kentucky 92 a few miles before reaching Sterns, and follow signs.

The Big South Fork National River and Recreation Area is serviced by Tennessee Highway 297, which connects with US 27 at Oneida, and with Tennessee 154 north of Jamestown. For more information on the area and towns surrounding the park, see the table of contents. For brochures, maps, and further information contact The Big South Fork National River and Recreation Area, Route 3, Box 401, Oneida, TN 37841; phone 615/879-4890.

Georgia:
Chattahoochee National Forest

Georgia's Blue Ridge Mountains have over 748,000 acres of this national forest, its coverage frequently divided by private lands, but generally ranging most of the way across the mountainous northern portion of the state. It has 12 wildlife management areas and over 500 species of wildife, over 1,000 miles of river and streams, and 10 lakes for trout, bass or catfish, boating, swimming and water sports.

Camping is plentiful in 19 developed recreation areas with over 400 campsites for tents and RV's, plus almost unlimted fee-free primitive camping, reached by forest service roads or hiking trails.

Over 430 miles of trails include wilderness areas, self-guiding nature trails, day hike trails, 79 miles of the Appalachian Trail, and the 53-mile Benton MacKay Trail.

Photo: Courtesy of Chattahoochee National Forest Service

Brasstown Bald Visitor Center
The Chattahoochee National Forest Visitor Center is located atop Georgia's highest mountain, 4,784-foot Brasstown Bald (see table of contents, Blairsville).

Seven scenic areas, picnic facilities, and a number of overlooks are served by hundreds of miles of US, state, county and forest service roads. The five mountain district offices are listed with address and phone numbers in the introduction to the Georgia section in this book (see table of contents.) Contact any of the district offices for maps and further information, or the Supervisor's Office, U.S. Forest Service, 601 Broad Street, Gainsville, GA 30501; phone 404/536-0541.

Tennessee: *Cherokee National Forest*

T he Cherokee National Forest is the only national forest in the state. All of its 604,000 acres follow the rugged mountain terrain along the state's boundary lines with the sections of Georgia and North Carolina covered in this book. The forest is split into two sections by the Great Smoky Mountains National Park.

There are over a thousand miles of streams and rivers in the forest, 105 hiking trails covering 540 miles, and 29 developed camping areas with 685 sites for tents and trailers (up to 22 feet long), with water, flush toilet facilities, grills and picnic tables. No hookups, and no reservations. Picnicking and scenic drives are good here, with 22 picnic areas, and 1,100 miles of roads with many scenic overlooks. There are boat ramps, beaches and swimming facilities, self-guided nature trails, horse trails, bicycle trails and motorcycle trails. No permits or check-ins are required.

Rafting on the Nolichucky
Photo: Courtesy Cherokee National Forest

For more information and maps, contact the Supervisor's Office, U.S. Forest Service 2800 North Ocoee Steet, Cleveland, TN 37311; phone 615/476-9700, or any of the six ranger districts: Hiwassee Ranger District, 1401 South Tennessee Ave, Etowah, TN 37331, phone 615/263-5486; Nolichucky Ranger District, 504 Justis Drive, Greeneville, TN 37743, phone 615/638-4109; Ocoee Ranger District, Route 1/Parksville, Benton, TN 37307, phone 615/338-5201; Tellico Ranger District, Rt. 3 Tellico River Road, Tellico Plains, TN 37385, phone 615/253-2520; Unaka Ranger District, Rt. 1, 1205 N. Main St., Erwin, TN 37650, phone 615/743-4452, Watauga Ranger District, Rt 9, Box 352-A, Elizabethton, TN 37643, phone 615/542-2942.

North Carolina:
Nantahala & Pisgah National Forests

Whiteside Mountain between Highlands and Cashiers
Photo: Courtesy National Forests in North Carolina

T hese two national forests are scattered over several tracts and thousands of acres in western North Carolina. The 516,000-acre Nantahala is located in the southwestern section; the Pisgah's 495,000 acres are generally to the east and southeast of the Great Smoky Mountains.

Camping, hiking, fishing, rivers, streams, lakes, even waterfalls seem endless here, and many of the campgrounds operated by the forest service have modern facilities, including hot showers, and some take a limited number of advance reservations during the busy season.

Attractions include the Roan Mountain Gardens, atop the mountain which straddles North Carolina and Tennessee. Acres of purple rhododendron cover the summit in June. Scenic NC 261 north from Bakersville offers great views and access to trails, including the Appalachain Trail which crosses Roan Mountain, after almost 200 miles across the state. The Craddle of Forestry in America, and a truely stupendous "sliding rock" recreation area, complete with bath house and viewing deck are both located off US 276 (See Brevard), and the Joyce Kilmer Memorial Forest and Slickrock Wilderness are loved by naturalists and all levels of hikers (see Robbinsville). For maps and further information contact the Supervisor's Office, National Forests in North Carolina, 100 Otis Street, Asheville, NC 28802; phone 704/257-4200, or one of the five district offices.

The Nantahala District Offices are as follows: Cheoah Ranger District, Rt. 1, Box 16-A, Robbinsville, NC 28771, phone 704-479-6431; Highlands, P.O. Box 749, Highlands, NC 28741, phone 704//526-3765; Tusquitee Ranger District, 201 Woodland Drive, Murphy, NC 28906, phone 704/837-5152; Wayah Ranger District, Rt 10, Box 210, Franklin, NC 28734, phone 704/524-6441.

The Pisgah District Offices are as follows: Pisgah District, 1001 Pisgah Highway, Pisgah Forest, NC 28768, phone 704/877-3265; Grandfather District, P.O. Box 519, Marion, NC 28752, phone 704/652-2144; Tocane District, P.O. Box 128, Burnsville, NC 28714, phone 704/682-6146; French Broad District, P.O. Box 128, Hot Springs, NC 28743.

GEORGIA

T | *he following map generally indicates only those towns under which information is listed in the book, and should be used in conjunction with a state map. The towns covered are not organized alphabetically, but as they appear along and off main travel routes, generally from south to north, then east to west, then south as follows: Dahlonega, Cleveland, Helen, Sautee, Demerost, Clarkesville, Tallulah Falls, Lakemont, Clayton, Mountain City, Rabun Gap, Dillard, Hiawassee, Young Harris, Blairsville, Blue Ridge, Ellijay, Chatswoth, Jasper, Tate.*

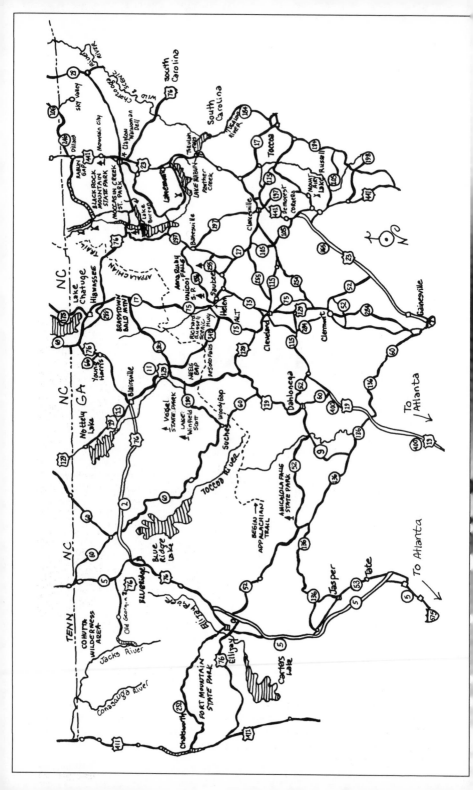

Georgia
· · · · · · · · · ·

Photo: Courtesy of Tourist Division, Georgia Department of Industry and Trade.

Georgia: *An Introduction and Sources for Additional Information*

From the Cohutta Wilderness to Lake Rabun's quiet waters, from 729-foot Amicalola Falls to the 1,200-foot depths of Tallulah Gorge, from the Chatooga's whitewater rapids to Brasstown Bald's breathtaking vistas, natural beauty and recreational resources abound in north Georgia's Blue Ridge Mountains.

Helen, Georgia is a Bavarian-Alpine-style village of shops, restaurants, lodging, attractions and four seasons of annual festivals including a hot air balloon race, Octoberfest and winter carnival.

Several state parks and the Chattahoochee National Forest offer developed and wilderness camping, and hiking on hundreds of miles of trails. The Appalachian National Scenic Trail begins in north Georgia and ends over 2000 miles later in Maine. Lakes and trout stocked mountain streams, gentle and wild rivers offer fishing, canoeing, rafting, tubing, and swimming.

Visitor accommodations ranging from log cabins to small luxury inns are available in dozens of small towns and villages. And food is any way you want it; from family style tables lighted with kerosene where fried chicken is still the king, to lace covered candle-lighted tables where fine wine is served with the nouvelle cuisine. And for in between snacks, there are roadside stands offering the Georiga classic: hot boiled peanuts.

Scenic touring is about any road you find yourself traveling. Especially recommended is Richard Russell Scenic Highway (GA 348) just north of Helen, offering 14 miles of mountain vistas at elevations up to 3,644 feet. GA 60, north from Dahlonega to Blue Ridge winds up through national forests passing scenic areas and overlooks. GA 180, between GA 60 and US 129, is Georgia's most winding road, paralleling the Appalachian Trail over Blood Mountain to Neels Gap. It passes Lake Winfield Scott, the Sosebee Cove Scenic Area and Vogel State Park along the way, and continues west to the road to Brasstown Bald before connecting with GA 17/75 south of Hiawassee. GA 197 north from Clarkesville ends a few scenic miles later at US 76 west of Clayton, after having crossed an "upside down bridge," followed several miles of the Soque River banked with laurel and rhododendron thickets abloom in spring, meandered 'round meadows and passed Lake Burton before heading up the mountain.

If you don't find the information you are looking for listed under the various towns on the following pages, good sources for further information include the following:

Georgia Mountain's Travel Association, P.O. Box 2553, Gainesville, GA 30503. Phone: 404/536-5209 and Northwest Georgia Mountain Association, 4 Depot Street, Marietta, GA 30060; phone 404/429-1115. The Georgia Department of Industry and Trade, Tourism Division, 285 Peachtree Center Ave, Suite 1000, Atlanta, GA 30301; phone 404/656-3590.

Maps of forest trails and recreation areas are available from the Chattahoochee National Forest, Supervisor's Office, 601 Broad Street, Gainesville, GA; phone 404/536-0541. District offices are located at: Brasstown District, US 19/129 South, Blairsville, GA 30512, phone 404/745-6928; Chattooga District, Burton Road, Clarkesville, GA 30523, phone 404/754-6221; Tallulah District, P.O. Box 438, Clayton, GA 30525, phone 404/782-3320; Toccoa District, Route 3, Box 3222, Blue Ridge, GA 30513, phone 404/632-3301; Chestatee District, 200 West Main, Dahlonega, GA 30533, phone 404/864-6173.

Hiking guidebooks are available at most bookstores, outdoor outfitters and mountain shops. One of the best is *The Hiking Trails of North Georgia* by Tim Homan.

Georgia Power Lakes and Recreation Areas is a free guide booklet available at the the Terrora Park and Vistor Center on US 441 in Tallulah Falls, or write for it to P.O. Box 9, Tallulah Falls, GA 30573.

Somethin's Cookin' in the Mountains, compiled and edited by John and Glen LaRowe is a cookbook/guidebook to the northeast Georgia mountains, featuring recipes of mountain residents and sketches by John Kollock. It is available at many book stores and mountain shops, and from Soque Publishers, Route 3, Box 83, Clarkesville, GA 30523.

Dahlonega
Gold Museum/Gold Rush Days/Visitor Center

F or many Atlantans this is where the mountains begin and end. This 19th century village is built around a public square and Georgia's oldest public building. Originally the Lumpkin County Courthouse, the 1836 structure now houses the Dahlonega Gold Musem. There is a minimul fee for a self-guided tour of the museum, which is operated by the state under the Historic Sites Division. A slide presentation outlines the history of gold mining in the area. Exhibits include old mining photos, a gold nugget weighing over four ounces, and coins minted in Dahlonega between 1838 and 1861 when the federal government minted nearly one and a half million pieces of gold here.

Surrounding the historic square are several interesting shops. "Gold panning" operations are often set up around the square, and there are several nearby "mines" for more gold panning. During Gold Rush Days, an event the third weekend in October, the square is as filled with tourists as it was with prospectors when gold was discovered here in the 1820's. The festivities include a parade with a Gold Rush king and queen, mountain music, crafts, more gold panning, and interesting contests such as pig calling, and liars competition.

The Visitor Center is located at the Chamber of Commerce, on a corner of the square. P.O. Box 2037, Dahlonega, GA 30533; phone 404/864-3711.

Dahlonega
Amicalola Falls State Park

G eorgia's highest waterfall, dropping in several cascades for 729 feet, is a major attraction for day visitors to this park, which also has vacation cottages, tent and RV campsites, and a beautiful picnic area. Activities nearby include fishing, boating and all levels of canoeing and rafting. Trails include the eight-mile approach trail to the "AT"—see following. Located about 20 miles west of Dahlonega on GA 52. Phone 404/265-2885.

Dahlonega
The Appalachian National Scenic Trail

T he "AT" is the longest hiking trail in eastern America. Beginning in the Georgia mountains, it follows Appalachian Mountain ridges across 14 states, ending over 2,000 incredible miles later on Mt. Katahdin in Maine. Starting at 3,700 feet on Springer mountain, northwest of Dahlonega, the trail drops below 3,000 only 10 times in its 79 miles across Georgia to the North Carolina border. Easy to follow, marked with white blazes (with double white and blue blazes indicating water, side trails, and confusing turns), the AT is heavily used.

A popular section is over 4,458-foot Blood Mountain between Woody Gap (on GA 60) and Neels Gap (on US 19/129), a little over 10 miles. For a leisurely day hike, you might consider the section from Neels Gap north to Tesnatee Gap on the Richard Russell Scenic Highway. It's a moderate 5.7 miles with several overlooks and great scenic vistas along the way. The "2,000 Milers" are those who have hiked the entire trail, usually leaving Georgia in April, and hopefully reaching Maine in September or October.

If you want to start at the beginning of the AT, you'll have a tough hike to start your hike. The strenuous 8.0 mile Approach Trail (blue blazed) begins behind the Amicalola Falls State Park Visitor Center. Various Appalachian Trail books, or hiking books which include the AT are available at most book stores and outfitters, including the Walasi-Yi Mountain Crossing shop where the AT crosses US 19/129 at Neels Gap. (See under Blairsville.)

Dahlonega
Appalachian Outfitters

Even beginners can take a self-guided, canoe trip from this outpost on the Chestatee River. Everything is furnished, including shuttle service back to your car, and the cost is quite moderate for a fun-filled adventure. For those with little or no experience, the most popular trip is an "easy section" of the Chestatee, requiring two to four hours of leisurely paddle time. Stretches of shallow rapids offer a little bit of excitement; others offer the opportunity to relax and take the time to look and listen to the magical sights and sounds of river and forest. For those who are ready for a bigger challenge, full day trips on tougher sections of both the Chestatee and Etowah Rivers are available.

The outpost also operates a year round shuttle service for area hikers and canoers, and offers rental equipment, instruction in various outdoor sports, and custom designed "adventure camps" for groups. The experienced staff includes owners and operators, Ben and Dana LaChance who've been providing outdoor adventures in these mountains for 10 years. Weather permitting, trips can be made (by reservation) year round, but the regular season is April through October. The outpost is located on Highway 60 & 19, one mile south of town. Appalachian Outfitters, P.O. Box 793, Dahlonega, GA 30533; phone 404/864-7117 or -3982.

Dahlonega
Gold City Corral: Trailrides and Campouts

David Kraft likes horses. He owns 29 of them. And he likes the forest trails. He has the use of about 50 miles of them adjoining his corral. He also likes to camp, and has established a site for campouts, complete with campfire ring, and enough firewood to last as long as riders can stay awake after the traditional trail cookout of steak with all the fixin's. All food, including a ranchhand size breakfast, all equipment and all services are furnished—riders don't have to lift a hand except to get food to their mouths, and perhaps their own beverages from their saddlebag. David's horses are suitable for all levels of riding experience, and rides, either the one hour or longer, and the camping trips are open to all. He's open all year, and located about 13 miles from town. Take Highway 9 & 52 west, stay on 52, watching for signs to Forrest Hills Mountain Hideway (the stable is near the entrance). Contact Gold City Corral, Route 3, Box 510, Dahlonega, GA 30533; phone 404/864-6456.

Dahlonega
Mountain Top Lodge at Dahlonega

In winter and early spring there's a 360-degree view of the mountains. In summer and autumn there's garden-like seclusion among towering oaks, pines and a profusion of dogwoods. Welcome to the Top—easy to reach, difficult to leave.

This two-level rustic lodge, wrapped with decks and porches, sits at the pinnacle of its own 40 acres of woods and pastureland, five miles from Dahlonega's courthouse square. Roughcut cedar timber, tongue-and-groove cathedral ceiling, sturdy beams and railing all combine for a feeling of warmth and permanence, creating a relaxed and casual atmosphere. The greatroom has a woodstove, color television, and the kind of comfortable furnishings that encourage good conversation. Downstairs there is a breakfast/dining room where a full country breakfast, prepared by host David Middleton, is served from colorful fiesta ware. Above in the loft is the library and card room. The eight guest rooms, each with private bath, are tastefully and individually furnished in interesting combinations of 1930's English furniture, unusual antiques, and flea market finds. Two of the rooms have sitting areas and private balconies. All have lovely views. Open all year. For rates and reservations, contact The Mountain Top Lodge at Dahlonega, Route 3, Box 173, Dahlonega, GA 30533; phone 404/864-5257.

Dahlonega
Forrest Hills Mountain Hideaway

T his is a "naturalist's retreat" environment with luxury amenities in contemporary rustic cottages, including honeymoon cottages with bedroom hot tubs, over-sized canopied beds, stereo, fireplaces, and color television. Other accommodations include two, three and four-bedroom cottages, each set in private woodland areas, and each completely furnished and equipped, from porch swings to fireplaces, TV, modern kitchens and baths. Complete breakfast and a hearty dinner are included with lodging rates. The small resort is secluded on 146 wooded acres, untouched except for bridle and hiking trails. It borders the Chattahoochee National Forest, and is four miles from Amicalola Falls State Park. On-premises amenities and activities include a swimming pool, tennis courts, dining room, activity center, craft shop, and the woodlands of pines and hardwoods, home to wildflowers, birds and small wildlife. Owned and operated by the Frank Kraft family. For rates and information, contact Forrest Hills Mountain Hideaway, Rt. 3, Box 510, Dahlonega, GA 30533; phone 404/864-6456 or 1-800-654-6313.

Dahlonega
Worley Homestead Bed & Breakfast Inn

R estored by the great granddaughter of its original owners, Captain and Mrs. William J. Worley, this 1845 home in downtown Dahlonega also has an adjacent guest cottage with two bedrooms and a fully-equipped kitchen. There are seven guest rooms in the main house, three with fireplaces, all with private baths, and each with its own individual charm. Both the cottage and the main house are furnished with antiques and accented with old photographs and other collectibles.

Breakfast (included for cottage guests also) is a big country affair, served family style in the dining room which features one of the inn's five fireplaces, or you may choose breakfast-in-bed.

The entire inn may be reserved for special occasions (a lovely place for a wedding), and special weekend packages for two and four couples are available. The latter includes a scenic mountain trail horseback ride, and a cookout with country music. (Two-hour trail rides can be planned for all guests, on request.)

The inn is located two blocks from Dahlonega's courthouse square, and is across the street from North Georgia College. Open all year, and featuring a Victorian Christmas during the month of December. Contact innkeepers Bill and Linda Green, Worley Homestead, 410 West Main Street, Dahlonega, GA 30533; phone 404/864-7002.

Dahlonega
Smith House Hotel & Restaurant

Dahlonega was made famous by its gold, but this landmark keeps it famous for something better: outstanding, downhome, all-you-can-eat, family style meals. This is the Georgia mountain's "pig-out heaven" closest to Atlanta (about an hour's drive), and the wait used to be forever—or so it seemed. No more. The dining room has doubled, then tripled, and while it's still crowded on weekends during the busy season, there is almost no wait.

Smith House tables are kept replenished with platters of marvelous fried chicken, maybe some baked ham or other savory meats, bowls of country vegetables, salads, homemade breads, relishes, beverages and desserts. All that, Tuesday through Sunday. On Friday and Saturday only, there's a Smith House "Special Feast" of boiled and fried shrimp, catfish, fried chicken, barbeques, all the above extras, and all served family style.

Saturday and Sunday there is a 15-item country breakfast buffet, plus fruit bar, guaranteed to fortify you for a mountain hike or a day of "gold mining." Breakfast is 7:30–10; lunch/dinner weekdays 11–7:30, until 8:30 weekends, with hours shortened a bit after December. The Friday and Saturday "Special Feast" hours are 4:30–8:30.

Accommodations at reasonable prices are available at the comfortable little two-story hotel, established in 1922. One of its sections was originally a carriage. This is a country inn atmosphere, with rocking chair porches and plenty of individual charm in the 16 guest rooms, each with a private bath. Located just off the square and open all year. Contact The Smith House, 202 South Chestatee Street, Dahlonega, GA 30533; phone 404/864-3566.

Cleveland

The welcome center here has a rather ironic home; the old White County Jail. Built in 1859 for $4000 and renovated in 1964 at a much larger cost. Located just off the square which surrounds another of the oldest public buildings in Georgia, the old White County Courthouse, constructed in 1859, mostly of brick made in the area by slave labor. Since construction of the new courthouse, this building and the archives have been maintained by the White County Historical Society, which offers regularly scheduled tours. For more information contact the Visitor Center, White County Chamber of Commerce, Cleveland, GA 30528; phone 404/865-5356.

Cleveland
BabyLand General Hospital

B abyLand General Hospital, in Cleveland, Georgia, is the only place in the entire world where you can watch a Mother Cabbage go into labor and deliver a lovable, huggable original Cabbage Patch kid, and then become an adoptive parent yourself—all in the same day!

Xavier Roberts, creator of the internationally famous Cabbage Patch Kids, brings fantasy to life for millions of people with his soft-sculpture babies, each individually hand-stitched to birth. In 1978, with the help of five college friends, Xavier renovated the former Neal Clinic, built in 1919, and opened BabyLand General Hospital. Doctors and Licensed Patch Nurses are on call for daily deliveries from Mother Cabbages at the Magic Crystal Tree birthing area, and are ready to offer assistance to prospective "parents." After taking an Oath of Adoption, parents receive an Official Birth Certificate and Adoption Papers. The fantasy continues with imaginative displays, a Christmas room, a pond, and BabyLand's gift shop offering a wide variety of Cabbage Patch Kids and accessories as well as many other unique items.

Visiting hours are Monday through Saturday, 8:30 a.m. to 5 p.m. and Sunday 1 to 5. (Closed January 1, Easter, July 4, Thanksgiving, and December 24–25) No admission charge. Bus tours welcome. BabyLand is located at 19 Underwood Street, Cleveland, GA 30528; phone, 404/865-2171.

Cleveland
Villagio di Montagna

V illagio di Montagna combines luxury with the tranquility of the Georgia mountains to rejuvenate and refresh the spirit. Xavier Roberts, creator of the Cabbage Patch Kids, extends his artistic talents into the design and development of European-style accommodations where guests enjoy the magic of the mountains in plush Palazza suites with private balconies overlooking the Tesnatee River. Villas in single or multiple bedroom units offer a secluded, sophisticated escape. Marble, glass and tile enhance this unique mountain getaway with individual fireplaces and Jacuzzi for pleasure and relaxation. Suites and villas have kingsize beds, service bar with icemaker, AM/FM stereo, tape deck and TV monitor system, plus hair dryers and lighted makeup mirrors for extra convenience.

Outdoor enthusiasts can explore trails cut in the beautiful woods at Villagio, take a dip in the Olympic-size swimming pool, relax in a rock grotto, refresh in the spa or sauna—and have a getaway or vacation where luxury truly is second nature! Villagio de Montagna is located one mile north of Cleveland on US 129, and is open year round. For reservations, contact P.O. Box 714, Cleveland, GA 30528; phone 404/865-7000.

Helen/Sautee
Alpine Helen

T his make-believe Bavarian-style village is known from Florida to Michigan, New York to California for its colorful shops and almost continuous festivals. Many who vacation in northeast Georgia—at least for the first time—go because of, or make a visit to, "Alpine Helen." Those few visitors who had not heard of Helen, and who discover it by chance while driving GA 75/17 must be utterly astonished to find an Alpine village in an Appalachian valley. Major annual events include the Hot Air Balloon Festival which kicks off the balloon race to the Atlantic Ocean, held late May into June; and the Oktoberfest which begins in mid-September and continues to mid-October. Approaching Helen from the east, visitors will drive GA 17 and GA 255 through the scenic, historic Sautee-Nachoochee Valley. The Helen Welcome Center is located just off the Main Street strip, (GA 75/17) on Chattahoochee Street. Telephone 404/878-2181.

Helen/Sautee
Unicoi State Park

North Georgia's most popular state park is located two miles northeast of Helen on GA 356. Facilities include a contemporary rustic lodge and conference center, restaurant, craft shop, two beaches, cottages and campsites, and a number of hiking trails. Many annual special events are scheduled; contact the information number for the calendar. One of the largest, attracting hundreds of visitors from throughout the region, is the Fireside Arts and Crafts Show held in the main lodge during the third full weekend in February. Located in the lodge and open year round is the Unicoi Craft Shop featuring a wide selection of authentic Appalachian handcrafts. Their quilt display is one of the largest in the country, all made by quilters in the surrounding area. Other crafts include weavings, pottery, rugs, dolls and wooden toys. The shop also stocks a good selection of informational and guide books to the area. The park offers craft and naturalist programs throughout the year, giving visitors a special look at mountain culture. For information call 404/878-2201. (For reservations only call 404/878-2824.)

Helen/Sautee
Anna Ruby Falls/Craft Shop/Smith Creek Trail

Surrounded by a 1,600-acre Chattahoochee National Forest Scenic Area, these twin waterfalls from Curtis and York Creeks drop side by side to form Smith Creek which flows through Unicoi State Park and forms Unicoi Lake. A paved .4 mile trail leads to the foot of the falls from the recreation area parking lot. It is steep, but there are benches along the way for resting. Wear proper shoes—the trail is sometimes wet and slippery. The falls can also be reached by the 4.8 mile Smith Creek Trail from the state park. Follow the blue blazes—the trail does not follow the creek most of the way. Fairly easy hike, with a couple of shallow stream crossings. A craft shop, operated by the Chattahoochee/Oconee Heritage Association, offers Appalachian arts and crafts, with emphasis on works of local people. Earnings from sales support interpretive programs and preservation of the forest. To reach the falls parking area take GA 356 into Unicoi State Park and follow signs. There is a small parking fee for cars and RV's, a larger fee for buses. For more information call the US Forest Service Office at Gainesville, GA, 404/536-0541.

Helen/Sautee
Sunburst Stables

Trail riding on over 25 miles of scenic, wooded trails is available year round at Sunburst Stables. Ride for an hour or two in winter, watching for deer in the open woods or taking in the bright, clear vistas of frosty mountain ridges. Enjoy an afternoon or full day in spring, riding on deep forest and steep gorge trails lined with rhododendron. Delight in the adventures of a two-day overnight ride, trotting and cantering through the forest and up ridge lines for breathtaking views, camping at night under starry skies. All you need for the camping trip is a sleeping bag—Sunburst provides all other equipment and fresh cooked meals. Experience the brilliance of autumn's cool crisp days, riding horseback on trails laced with leaves of red and gold.

Adjoining 7,000 acres of the Chattahoochee National Forest, Sunburst Stables is an 88-acre facility where Kevin Craig and Richard Hayes have over 10 years experience in making horseback riding dreams come true. In addition to the varied trail ride programs, Sunburst offers a full line of services including boarding, training, sales, tack store, and hauling. Located one and a half hours from Atlanta, six miles east of Helen on GA 255 in the Sautee Valley. For hours, rates and reservations contact Kevin or Richard at Sunburst Stables, Route 1, Box 1075, Sautee, GA 30571; phone 404/878-2095.

Helen/Sautee
The Old Sautee Store

Four miles from Helen, in the Sautee-Nacoochee Valley, is a country store museum over a century old. In back where the post office used to be is a Scandinavian gift shop with imports from Norway, Sweden, Denmark, Finland and Iceland.

It's an interesting combination. Country store memorabilia of old fixtures, posters and antiques (including a working nickelodeon), none of which are for sale, and a Scandinavian gift shop where the reasonably priced quality items go almost as fast as Norwegian-born owner, Astrid Fried, can import them. There are warm, bright ski sweaters, crystal, dinnerware, pewter, hand-wrought sterling, jewelry, embroideries, posters, books, even gourmet foods and hand-carved, handpainted storybook "trolls." Adjacent to the old store is Astrid's largest import—an actual Norwegian "stabbur" (storehouse) with sod roof, which she had shipped from Norway and reassembled here to house the large Christmas trim collection. Astrid also owns and operates the Old Norway Store in downtown Helen.

The Old Sautee Store is located at the intersection of GA 17 and 255. It is listed on the National Register of Historic Places, as part of the Nacoochee Valley District. Open all year, Monday through Saturday 9:30 to 5:30, Sunday 1 to 6. Mailing address is Old Sautee Store, Sautee-Nachoochee, GA 30571; phone 404/878-2281.

Helen/Sautee
Nora Mill Granary and Store

This 1876 mill is still grinding out grits, cornmeal, buckwheat and rye flour the old fashioned way—on 46-inch original French Buhr water-powered turbine wheels. On display, but not in use, are three antique roller mills. The granary and adjacent store—which features "Grandma's Famous Pies"—are open to visitors and shoppers year round. Custom grinding and special gift orders, packaged and shipped, are available. Located on GA

17/75 just south of Helen. Nora Mill. P.O. Box 41, Sautee, GA 30571.

Helen/Sautee
Betty's Country Store

T his is one of those places that fits the mountain saying, "If you can't find it here, it probably ain't worth having." In front there's an open shed filled with an unexpected variety of plump, fresh produce in season. In back there's a kitchen where homemade desserts-to-go—whole pies, cakes, loaves of banana nutbread, brownies and cookies—are baked fresh every day. And in between the front and the back, all through the original 1937 building, there's a variety of things to eat, use, wear, read, drink, give and play with. There's hoop cheese and pickled pig's feet, Moon Pies, health food and Haagen Dazs ice cream. There's the *Farmers Almanac,* barrels of gourmet coffee, comic books, coloring books, crayons, crafts, tee shirts, picnic supplies, notions, newspapers, cookbooks and guidebooks. There's an old time Coke cooler filled with cold wet bottles of "pop," there are big jars of "jawbreakers" and, in unusual old grain display cases, there's fancy candy by the ounce. Many of the old display bins, counters, cases and boxes in use here are from this original seed and general store or from Fain's Antiques located on the other end of Main Street. Betty's Country Store is near the north end of Main; phone is 404/878-2943.

Helen/Sautee
Mountain Valley Kitchen (and Gift Shop)

T his is the place to go in Alpine Helen when you want Georgia country cookin' at the most reasonable prices. This bustling friendly restaurant offers a bountiful buffet breakfast, or from the menu there are flapjacks, omelets and specialties like real country ham. Lunch and dinner offer homemade soups and breads, fresh vegetables and cobblers southern style, salad bar, steaks, trout, catfish and more. Bessie Trammell, who was born and raised in this area, is still the head cook after all these years.

Owners Joan and Richard Lundstrom, operations supervisor Tom Johnson, and a friendly staff keep things running smoothly in the dining rooms and still have time to greet guests from all across the country—and often from other countries too. The decor is warmly rustic with wooden booths and tables, and fireplaces in both dining rooms. An additional private dining room for up to 65 can be reserved for groups, and is a good place for bus tours which are always welcome.

The entire second floor is devoted to a really special gift shop, appropriately named Upstairs at the Kitchen. Don't miss this one if you enjoy browsing among really nice and unusual gift items. In case you do have a short wait for a table, browse a bit here; you'll want to come back after you eat. There is limited and free parking for restaurant guests at the side of the building. Located less than a block off Main Street, next door to the City Hall and Welcome Center on Chattahoochee Street. Open all year round, daily except Wednesday. Phone 404/878-2508.

Helen/Sautee
The Stovall House Country Inn & Restaurant

T his is the third role for one of the first residences in the Sautee Valley. Built a century and a half ago as a private home to a prominent attorney, it later served as the home, office and treatment center for an ex-Navy doctor who brought much needed medical care to the area. In the mid-1980's the historic building was restored, renovated, and refurnished with outstanding antiques from foyer through the five guest rooms, to become the valley's first bed and breakfast country inn.

The setting offers a true country experience, a sense of peace and quiet, with ever changing views of the surrounding mountains. Guest rooms, some with fireplaces, are beautifully appointed, cheerful with skylights and hand-stenciling. Two have a connecting bed-sitting room with a brass daybed. A continental breakfast is served to house guests.

The intimate, attractive dining room has a relaxed informal atmosphere. The seasonal menu reflects the emphasis on fresh, wholesome foods, delicately prepared, beautifully served and reasonably priced. There's also a porch dining area, perfect for summer evenings. Restaurant hours may vary with the season, but are generally 11:30 until 2 for lunch, 6 until 9 for dinner. Reservations are suggested. Lodging rates are moderate, and there is no charge for children under 12 in their parents' room (cots and rollaways are available). Located on GA 255, just north of the intersection with GA 17. Contact innkeeper, Ham Schwartz, The Stovall House, Rt. 1, Box 103-A, Sautee, GA 30571; phone 404/878-3355.

Helen/Sautee
Grampa's Room Bed and Breakfast Inn and Gift Shop

Bring the kids. This big old country home has welcomed four generations of children including the 14 grandchildren of hosts, Lib and Mack Tucker. Lib herself is the granddaughter of James Glen who helped build this house on the old Unicoi Turnpike, and purchased it on completion in 1872. The Glen-Kenimer-Tucker house has been in the same family since the original purchase.

It's the kind of place kids and grownups love to explore. There are lots of trees, swings, lawn tables and chairs, a garden, an old well, several outbuildings, and porches upstairs and down, front and back. You'll find no elegant interior decorating here, but the house is filled with antiques and family heirlooms, including books and magazines dating back to the late 1800's. There are three large and comfortable guest rooms (some with antique iron beds), and two baths to be shared by house guests.

A large side room attached to the lower level has been converted to a crafts, antiques and collectibles shop. Unique items featured include dolls, miniatures and fine Kershaw knives. House guests receive a 10% discount on purchases.

The inn is located three miles from Helen on GA 17. Open all year except during the holidays when all those grandchildren arrive. Moderate rates include a full country breakfast. Contact the Tuckers at P.O. Box 100, Sautee-Nacoochee, GA 30571; phone 404/878-2364.

Helen/Sautee
Lumsden Homeplace Bed & Breakfast Inn

Built in 1890 as the home of state senator Jesse Richardson Lumsden, the "Homeplace" Bed & Breakfast is operated by his great grandson, Mike Crittenden and his wife, Linda. Mike has converted closets to bathrooms, so each guest room has a private bath. Beds are twin or doubles, covered with white hobnail spreads or quilts. There are white lace curtains and lazy paddle fans, eight fireplaces, family heirlooms and period furnishings for warmth and charm, and 60 acres of family owned property, in and around this piece of the Sautee Valley, with plenty of mountain views and woodland paths.

Breakfast features such culinary delights as fresh ginger custard, cheese biscuits or cornmeal pancakes along with the ham or bacon and eggs. Listed on the National Register of Historic Places, and open all winter for warm, cheery getaways. Contact The Lumsden Homeplace, P.O. Box 388, Sautee-Nacoochee, GA 30571; phone 404/878-2813.

Helen/Sautee
Mountain Greenery Cabins

L ocated only ten minutes from Helen, these cabins with fireplaces, television, airconditioning and phonecard phones also offer country privacy on twenty-five wooded acres adjacent to the national forest. The one bedroom or two bedroom with two bathroom cabins also have sleeper sofas in the living room, and can accommodate two to eight. There are cozy comforters on the king, queen and double beds, carpeting on the floors and new appliances in the fully furnished kitchens. Firewood is supplied, so is fuel for the gas grill on the screened porch; bring your own charcoal for open deck grills. There is even a map in each cabin with directions and descriptions of several nearby hiking trails. Your host, Francis Forziati, is on the premises in case you could possibly ask for anything more. Contact him at Mountain Greenery, Route one, Box 1069, Sautee, GA 30571; phone 404/878-3442.

Helen/Sautee
Georgia Mountain Madness

T hese cabins are perfect for romantic getaways that aren't too far away. It's only one mile to Unicoi State Park and four miles to the Alpine village of Helen from these contemporary rustic cabins, secluded on 30 wooded acres bordering the Chattahoochee National Forest. Six of the nine cabins have indoor hot tubs. All have fireplaces, stereo and tape deck. No telephones. No television. How romantic can you get? How about a candlelight dinner prepared in the fully-equipped kitchen. Or steaks grilled on the deck for a moonlight picnic. In the winter there is electric heat as well as the fireplace (and free firewood). In summer there are ceiling fans in addition to air conditioning. All the linens for the queen-sized beds, towels, cooking utensils—everything you need is furnished. Some of the cabins have two bedrooms, including one with a 7×7 Continental Spa.

From Atlanta, Chattanooga or Asheville areas, you can probably get there after work in time for a walk in the park or a stroll down Helen's colorful streets. Your hosts, Pamela and Randall Rogus, are on the premises. They'll be glad to help you plan outings to nearby attractions, festivals, scenic road trips or antique shops . . . or activities like whitewater rafting, skiing in winter or hiking year round. A winter hike is especially fine when there's that fireplace and hot tub waiting for your return. For rates and reservations, contact Georgia Mountain Madness, P.O. Box 308, Helen, GA 30545; phone 404/878-2851.

Helen/Sautee
The Chattahoochee River Lodge

T he lodge is secluded on a paved road in the woods above the river, but is only a mile from downtown Helen. Hosts Mary and Bob Swift offer the hospitality and helpfulness of a small inn, the privacy of a motel, the convenience of kitchens in two of the four units, and the peace and quiet of the country.

Guest units have private entrances and private, modern baths, color television, brass beds, paddle fans and wood panelling. Two or three large windows in each double-insulated unit coax in the mountain breezes, but there is also air conditioning and heat when needed. The two smaller units are designed for couples, and the kitchen units can comfortably accommodate four people. A large ridgetop deck has a grill and picnic tables, and is a perfect spot for birdwatching. Over 30 species have been identified at the bird feeders around the lodge. If you get really lucky some early morning, you may see a deer wander across the yard on the way for a drink at the river. Spring is especially pretty here—lots of dogwoods and mountain laurel. Late summer and early fall weekends, units are usually reserved early by returning guests and honeymooners, so keep that in mind when making plans for reservations.

There is a special winter discount off the regular moderate rates, and always plenty of winter festivals, activities and holiday shopping in Helen. For further information, rates and reservations, contact The Chattahoochee River Lodge, P.O. Box 175, Helen, GA 30345; phone 404/878-3144.

Helen/Sautee
Hilltop Haus Bed & Breakfast

Frankie Tysor sort of evolved into being the proprietor of Helen's first bed and breakfast. When motels were filled, she was often asked to lodge the overflow on her hilltop home within walking distance of the heart of Helen. She liked the visitors. They liked her; came back again; sent friends and relatives. So with a passing nod to the Alpine theme, Frankie named her home Hilltop Haus and became an official innkeeper.

So much for titles and Alpine themes. . . . This big plain comfortable ranch style home could be in any Hometown USA. Coffee is always ready, a cake is usually in the oven or cooling on the counter in the family/room kitchen. The fireplace is surrounded by a clutter of TV, books, magazines and newspapers. There are four nice sized guest rooms with private and shared baths, and a suite with private entrance, fireplace and sleeper sofa in the living room, a double bedroom, bath and kitchenette. Guests are welcome to borrow the bikes and hiking gear in the carport, or to loaf on the deck or under the shady trees on the lawn above the Chattahoochee River. A country breakfast is included in the reasonable rates, which are reduced for winter getaways. Contact Hilltop Haus, P.O. Box 154, Helen GA 30545, phone 404/878-2388.

Clarkesville/Demorest

In 1983 Rand McNally voted this small, quiet and pretty county seat of Habersham County the third-best retirement place in the United States. In 1987 they voted it the second best. It just keeps getting better and prettier. No big-time tourist attractions here, and the mountains are more accurately gently rolling hills. Turn on US 441 Business so as not to miss the two or three blocks that make up downtown. It's small but has interesting shops, eateries, and is a nice place to visit as well as a nice place to live. The smaller town of Demorest is just south of the Clarkesville city limits. The County Chamber of Commerce phone number is 404/788-4654.

Clarkesville/Demorest
Panther Creek Trail

This four-mile (one way) trail is easy except for a couple of spots where huge bolders narrow the trail and force some to reach for a hand from their companions, or scramble up over the obstacles on hands and knees. The trail also seems to be deteriorating off the edge of the steep slope as it nears the falls; possibly from constant heavy use. This is a popular hike, and is well worth the few rough spots. The waterfalls are really the secondary attraction during the spring when wildflowers both common and rare are found in abundance. Save your sack lunch for the falls where you may sun yourself on huge flat boulder's, eat and dangle your feet in the cold stream. Park in the recreation area parking lot (there are restrooms here), and walk directly across the road (Highway 441) to the trailhead. Blue blazed. Located about 3 miles south of Tallulah Falls, 10 miles north of Clarkesville.

Clarkesville/Demorest
Moccasin Creek State Park/Lake Burton/State Fish Hatchery

Moccasin Creek flows into Lake Burton at this state park, popular with RV campers for fishing and boating. There are also tent sites, comfort stations with hot showers, fishing and boat dock, and picnic area. The creek separates the park from the state fish hatchery, open for public tours. A short section of the creek is heavily stocked with trout, and is open to fishing for those under 12 and over 65. The lake has 62 miles of shoreline, and is one of six Georgia Power Company lakes this area of northeast Georgia. No reservations are accepted at the campground which is located on GA 197, about 20 miles north of Clarkesville, and a few miles from Clayton via 76 west to 197. Phone 404/947-3194.

Clarkesville/Demorest
Habersham Plantation Market Place

In 1972 the Eddy family of Habersham County began handcrafting pine furnishings and accessories in a small home workshop. Making simple pine furniture was not unusual or new to the Georgia mountains. Pine was plentiful; money for furniture was not. Rural people often built their own, but pieces produced by the Eddy family were unusual. Meticulous workmanship, hand-rubbed finishes, handcarved designs or handpainted folk art set them apart from the simply functional. Carrying the Habersham Plantation signature, the first pieces were marketed in Atlanta. The rest is history. Habersham Plantation set the standard for the "country look" and is sold throughout the United States and featured regularly in decorating magazines.

The 18,000-square-foot showroom carries the original line plus all the new designs, woods and finishes. Visitors come for all over the country. Many come for the bargains; "blems" with slight variations in color, finish or design, or discontinued lines. Others come to order custom work. Others just to browse and shop for mountain crafts, imported dinnerware, baskets, hand-dipped candles, Capel rugs, handwoven and braided rugs in rounds and ovals, handknotted Chinese rugs in all sizes. And everyone comes for the two big sales each year, beginning around July 4 and Thanksgiving, when additional discounts are offered on hundreds of items.

Located just south of the city limits off GA 17; open Monday-Saturday 10–5. P.O. Box 786, Clarkesville, GA 30523; phone toll free, in Georgia 1-800-241-5232, from other states, 1-800-221-3483.

Clarkesville/Demorest
Mark of the Potter

One of the most picturesque places in the Georgia mountains is this studio/shop of potter Jay Bucek, housed in the Old Grandpa Watts Mill near the splashing shoals of the Soque River. There's a porch over the river bank where visitors may feed native trout that gather, almost like pets, as they once gathered for scraps of the corn being water-ground into cornmeal.

Built in 1915, the restored and preserved mill has been famous since 1969 as Mark of the Potter. Visitors can watch as Jay or artist-in-residence, John Scott Bailey, works at the potter's wheel, turning clay into functional and decorative pottery. The stoneware clay body is formulated to produce permanently beautiful, nonporous pottery that is safe for microwave and conventional ovens.

Over 45 other southeastern artisans are represented in the wide selection of pottery and other crafts in the showroom. Everything is handmade and original, including some exquisite jewelry, wood carvings, weavings and hand-blown glass. The shop also stocks the prints of John Kollock and a variety of regional books, including *Somethin's Cookin' in the Mountains*, a cookbook guide to northeast Georgia.

The shop is located 14 miles from Helen and 10 miles from Clarkesville on GA 197. Hours are 10–6 every day, closed only Christmas day. Contact Mark of the Potter, Route 3, Box 3164, Clarkesville, GA 30523; phone 404/947-3440.

Clarkesville/Demorest
Steffi's Store

S teffi Walker has created Demorest's most attractive corner on US 441 Business at Georgia Ave. A former art teacher with degrees in art history and interior design, Steffi has restored and transformed the historic Starkweather building into a place of on-going pleasure and excitement. Ruffled curtains and window boxes filled with bright blossoms through the changing seasons please the eye of every passerby and tempt the curious.

Nine rooms on the two levels feature the works of artists and craftspeople from across the US including over 60 potters. Steffi travels to exhibits and festivals from New England to New Mexico seeking out the best in the decorative and useful, selecting items ranging from designer quilts to hand-carved decoys, from unique jewelry to country pine furniture.

A work space in back of the store often draws visitors to watch the creative process, as Steffi and her staff create beautiful wreaths for every season, using all natural materials that lend themselves to a variety of shapes and sizes. The entire store offers a place to shop in the style rather typical of olden times, when friendly conversation and laughter were as important as the business of buying and selling.

A festival ushers in the holiday season at Steffi's, when bright, wreathed windows beckon shoppers into the store glowing with goodwill and Christmas cheerfulness. Even carved birds and porcelain cats wear ribbons and holly. The rooms sparkle with poinsettias and five gorgeous trees, each decorated in a different style, from old fashioned country to Victorian to shining modern. On the day of Open House—the first weekend in December—the festivities include unusual Christmas pastries and punch.

Open year round, 10 a.m. to 5 p.m. Monday through Saturday, and on Sunday 1 until 5 from October through the Christmas season. Steffi's Store,

P.O. Box 474, Demorest, GA 30535; phone 404/778-9128.

(You may now enjoy Steffi's of St. Simons, located at 2463 Demore Road #1, St. Simons Island, GA 31522; phone 912/638-1883.)

Clarkesville/Demorest
Habersham Winery & Tasting Rooms

When in the Demorest area, continue south on 441 to the 365 exit, then south another couple of miles to the Habersham Winery and Tasting Room. Established in 1980, the winery was the first in Georgia to win a gold medal in international competition. By the end of its first decade it had won a total of 70 national and international medals for its 15 different wines of which two-thirds are from its own 32-acre vineyard near Clarkesville.

But this is no place to get snobby. This is also for fun. Don't miss the Muscadines. The intensely fruity Georgia Muscadine, a two time gold medal winner, and the Granny's Arbor (with its outrageous Georgia Gothic label) are both nostalgic ways to put some south in your mouth. A sip or even a sniff is guaranteed to bring a flood of memories to every native (and even some transplanted) southerners. For more serious wine drinkers, the winery also produces Cabernets and Chardonnays from Georgia among its other fine wines.

Habersham wines can be purchased by the bottle or case, and cases can be mixed. Wines can be purchased seven days a week at the winery tasting room and gift shop where you will also find wine accessories and other gifts with a taste of the Georgia mountains.

The winery has three other tasting rooms—two in the mountains at Helen and Hiawassee and another (open daily) in Underground Atlanta. Address is Habersham Winery, P.O. Box 426, Baldwin, GA 30511; phone 404/778-9463. The corporate offices are located at 300 Northcreek, Suite 590, 3715 Northside Pkwy, Atlanta, GA 30327; phone 404/239-9463.

Clarkesville/Demorest
Adam's Rib

On Highway 441 Business at the south edge of Clarkesville, this long-time favorite of hungry travelers is the place to stop for a good breakfast, lunch or dinner at reasonable prices with no waiting. It has always been a popular stop for skiers, fall color watchers and spring flower hunters or just about any traveler taking this route through the Georgia Mountains, and local residents love it too—a good sign of good value. Breakfast bacon is sweet; there's country ham too, and homemade biscuits and gravy. The cafeteria at noon offers several meats or fish, hot vegetables and a salad bar. Or you may order from the menu at noon and evening; steaks, sandwiches and seafood, including boiled shrimp in the shell; try some steamed in beer. Good! The seafood is flown in twice weekly. Wine or beer is available with meals only. In the back dining room there's a large TV screen for major special events and sportscasts, all on satellite TV.

Next door there's a wine and cheese shop where you can stock your cooler in case your destination is one of many "dry" spots in the mountains. Adam's Rib is open 6 a.m. to 10 p.m. and closed Wednesdays. Telephone 404/754-4568.

Clarkesville/Demorest
Taylor's Trolley

In 1907 one of Clarkesville's main attractions was an elegant new soda fountain on the square at the trolley stop. Visitors gathered under the cooling ceiling fans to socialize and admire the latest in decor, the solid wood and brass fixtures and display cases. Eighty-odd years later about the only thing that's missing is the trolley, but there are lots of nice additions.

A lunch menu Monday through Saturday ranges from fresh and fancy soups and salads through substantial standards. Full-course dinners Thursday through Saturday include entrees like filet mignon with bearnaise sauce, prime rib, mountain trout and veal parmigiana. There are imported beers, wine by the glass, and oh yes, there is still the soda fountain. You can still get old fashioned sodas and sundaes, but you may be tempted to try some special delights—all homemade—like fancy flavored cheesecakes, warm crepes stuffed with ice cream and toppings, or a four-layer chocolate cherry torte with cream cheese filling.

Restauranteurs are James and Kathleen Taylor, Georgia mountain born and bred, big city raised, now happily and successfully downhome again in their very uptown restaurant. Taylor's Trolley is as popular with area residents as with visitors, so be prepared with reservations if you are in a hurry. But it's really best to just go, relax, socialize and enjoy the friendly atmosphere like visitors did back in 1907 when they arrived by trolley. You can drive up in your car and park it free on the square. For reservations phone 404/754-5566.

Clarkesville/Demorest
Glen-Ella Springs Inn

E ven most area residents were unaware of the existence of the 100-year-old Glen-Ella Springs Hotel until late 1987 when it was restored, refurbished and reopened by a Decatur, Georgia couple, Barrie and Bobby Aycock.

After all, who would expect to find a hotel at the end of a gravel road practically in the Chattahoochee National Forest? A fine hotel . . . or inn, as it is now called . . . with rockers and swings on two levels of porches, and a third floor "penthouse suite!" With a great stone fireplace in the parlor, cheerful with chintz, cozy with books and games. Who would expect to find 16 guest rooms and suites with private bath, phone, individual heat and air condi-

tioning, antique and locally handcrafted furnishings? And some with whirlpool bath, television and gas log fireplace! And would anyone expect to find classic American cuisine being served in a perfectly delightful dining room or on a patio under the grape arbor—beside a swimming pool?! Regional classics like Cajun sausage gravy and grits on the Sunday buffet brunch. Dinner specialties like fried Brie, chicken livers and mushrooms in Marsala wine sauce, mountain trout sauteed with lime juice and fresh herbs, fine aged beef, veal, grilled fish, and homemade breads and desserts.

Well, it's all there, right next to the forest. Part of the charm of Glen-Ella Springs Inn is its unexpected location, bordered by Panther Creek, surrounded by the hills of Habersham, serenely secluded on what feels like the beautiful middle of nowhere. Actually, it's only three miles—1.5 of it gravel—off US 441/23 between the community of Hollywood and Tallulah Falls. Watch for the sign just south of the Panther Creek Recreation Area. The inn's 17 acres include meadows, flower and herb gardens, trails through the national forest along the creek, and the original mineral spring which drew people to "take the waters" for health and vitality until after the turn of the century. The Aycocks' plans include rebuilding the spring house and adding a water garden and picnic area around the spring.

The inn is available for weddings, receptions, small conferences and other special events and is open all year. The dining room is open to the public during the winter for lunch Tuesday through Saturday, for dinner Thursday through Saturday, plus a big country breakfast on Saturday and the sumptuous buffet brunch on Sunday. During the travel season, beginning in June, dinner is served five nights a week. Reservations are suggested but not always required. A complimentary continental breakfast is available daily to house guests. Contact Glen-Ella Springs Inn, Route 3, Box 3304, Clarkesville, GA 30523; phone 1-800-552-3479.

Clarkesville/Demorest
LaPrade's Restaurant, Cabins and Marina

Tucked up on a sloping, wooded hillside adjacent to Lake Burton, LaPrade's Restaurant has four room-length, boarding-house-style tables, and the cabins have no phone or TV, but this is one of the most popular eating and getaway places in the Georgia mountains. The primary reason is the food. Other reasons (and their order of importance) depend on individual choices of recreation. There's the lake, with all kinds of boat rental at the marina across the road. The lake and nearby streams yield bounties of bass, pike and trout. Cleared trails and scenic roads offer hikers and drivers vistas and closeups of mountains, lakes, forests, small wildlife, wildflowers and foliage changes with the seasons.

But back to the food and those four long tables—where everyone sits elbow to elbow, passing heaping bowls and platters, morning, noon and night. It's family style, all you can eat and more than you should, but this is LaPrade's, so forget the calories and have a second or third helping. There are roasts, vegetables, fried chicken, slaw, dumplings, gravy, biscuits, cornbread, ham, sausage, eggs, cobblers, potatoes, rice, cakes, relishes, jams and jellies. Fresh? You bet! All the vegetables and most of the pork and chicken come from the 90% self-sufficient LaPrade's farm. Relishes and jams are "put up" in the LaPrades kitchen.

You have to be there at scheduled seating times to enjoy these feasts, so plan your time appropriately: seating for breakfast is 8 to 9, for lunch it's 12:30 until 2, and dinner is 7 to 8. No meals on Wednesdays. If you aren't a cabin guest, you'd be smart to make reservations—early. Before each seating, especially during weekends and the busy season, the rocking chair porches are lined with "summer people" from lakeside homes, with local year round residents, with cabin guests, hikers, bikers, hungry vacationers from all over, and with Atlantans who drive up just to eat at LaPrades.

If you are a cabin guest, three consecutive meals are included for about the cost of an ordinary budget motel. (Remember, no meals on Wednesday.) There is no charge for children under three; under 10 is half price. The spotless, rustic cabins are "early LaPrades" (this was a fishing camp for years) and basics include bathroom, screened porch, quilts, homemade furniture and linoleum-covered floors. There are no kitchens. For those who come just to eat, prices are typical for family style dining in the mountains.

The marina offers rental of fishing boats, canoes, rowboats, motors, and has all the necessary bait for the varieties of fish in Lake Burton. Just up the road from the marina is Uncle Tom's Craft Shop; a quaint cabin filled with mountain crafts. LaPrade's is open April 1 until December 1 (Weekends only in April and November—Friday supper through Sunday lunch.) Located on GA 197 about 18 miles north of Clarkesville. LaPrade's, Route 1, Clarkesville, GA 30523; phone 404/947-3312.

Clarkesville/Demorest
Laurel Lodge Restaurant and Cabins

To find this hidden-away getaway, take GA 197 north from Clarkesville for about 15 miles, or south from US 76 for about seven miles, watch for a sign near the Brooks Store, turn here and follow the hard-packed dirt road for another couple of miles. Eventually you'll come upon an 1800's log cabin, six rustic cabins from the 1940's, a large swimming pool (circa 1980's) and the Laurel Lodge Restaurant—all on 22 acres surrounded by national forest, lakes and mountains. The log cabin, built for the old Mt. Zion Church preacher (the old cemetery borders the property) now houses the office of Laurel Lodge proprietor, Ricky Ferguson. The other cabins are the original accommodations for a hunting/fishing camp. The pool was added after the weekend city visitors replaced the hunters and fisherman.

The restaurant has homemade wooden tables, ladder back chairs, plank flooring, ceiling fans, electric lanterns and a screened porch. It caters to cabin visitors, local people who know value when they taste it, summer people who have cottages on Lake Burton which borders the property (no access) and mountain visitors who have heard about the food and been smart enough to get directions. Meals are family style, all you can eat, usually featuring fried chicken with fixin's, lots of vegetables, biscuits or cornbread, iced tea and homemade cobbler. There is a catfish feast on Friday nights. The restaurant is open six days a week, June through August (closed Mondays except for holidays); Friday through Sunday evenings only during April, May and September through November 15. Reservations are not required, but are accepted.

The rustic cabins offer basic accommodations year round. Each has gas heat, modern bath, simple but comfortable furnishings (no TV or phones) and will accommodate up to eight people. Rates are modest and do not include meals.

Pets are not allowed. A separate section of the 22 acres also has group facility with a large dormitory which can sleep up to 50, an athletic field and covered pavilion. Contact Laurel Lodge, Route 1 Box 1338, Clarkesville, GA 30523; phone 404/947-3241.

Clarkesville/Demorest
Burns-Sutton House and Willow Tree Gift Shop

Innkeepers John and JoAnn Smith are also skilled craftspeople whose works can be found throughout this 14-room bed and breakfast inn. The stained glass windows, reverse stenciling, handwoven baskets, fabric art, decorator and functional pottery enhance the Smith's collection of fine period and antique furnishings.

The 1901 house, listed on the National Register of Historic Places, is itself an example of architectural craftsmanship, featuring intricate cutwork on the great stairwells, traditional wrap around porch railings, carved mantles and tongue-and-groove paneling. The Smiths have restored the house to its original Victorian elegance and added a few late 20th century comforts like air conditioning to assist the ceiling fans. There are seven spacious guest rooms; some are suites and some have private bath and fireplace. All are wonderfully inviting. Morning at the Burns-Sutton House begins with a complete breakfast of country ham, eggs, hot biscuits and coffee, seasonal fruit and other goodies.

After breakfast, if guests wish to see more of the Smiths' craft work, they may stroll a few blocks to the square and visit the Willow Gift Shop. JoAnn makes many of the items herself and prices are low, almost wholesale. The shop also features some carefully chosen antiques and pieces by other regional craftspeople. The Burns-Sutton House is open all year. Well behaved children are welcome. No pets or smoking. Located at 124 South Washington Street and US 441 Business. Address P.O. Box 992, Clarkesville, GA 30523; telephone 404/754-5565.

Clarkesville
The Charm House

A bed and breakfast inn is the sixth reincarnation of this 1848 Greek Revival mansion, listed on the National Register. It has also served as residence, hospital, tea room, clothing shop and restaurant without losing any of its dignity and charm. The enduring structure is made entirely of heart pine from floor to rafters. The great room, twelve-foot wide hallways, six guest rooms, parlor and dining room are all furnished with the antique collection of innkeepers Mabel Fry and daughter, Rhea Allen. The nine useable fireplaces still have their original mantels, and no two are alike. The wide verandas are shaded by stately oaks, and a magnificent pine tree. The entire inn can be reserved for weddings, receptions, small church clubs, family reunions and other special occasions. Open year round. Located on a hillside overlooking US 441 Business, a few blocks from the center of the village. For further information, contact The Charm House, P.O. Box 392, Clarkesville, GA 30523; phone 404/754-9347.

Tallulah Falls/Lakemont
The Town, Gorge, Point Overlook & Park Nature Trail

The best way to start your visit here is to pick up a $1.50 copy of *The Life & Times of Tallulah . . . The Falls, The Gorge, The Town*. This booklet, by John Saye, social studies teacher at Tallulah Falls School, is available at most places you'll want to visit here.

The gorge is two miles long, 1,000 feet wide and 1,200 feet deep. Before construction of the Georgia Power hydroelectric dam, it is said that the roar of the falls could be heard miles away. The river still drops 350 feet in the first mile of the gorge, and three of the four remaining falls are visible for most of the year from the Park Nature Trail along the gorge rim. (A small admission is charged.) The gorge (not the falls) can also be viewed from its highest point at Tallulah Point (no admission) There are free restrooms here, and rockers on a porch over the gorge, provided by the Tallulah Point Shop; a good stop for snacks, ice cream, gifts and film. Highway 441 was shifted a few hundred yards away from this scenic point in 1987, but watch for the scenic loop sign. Plenty of free parking is available at the Point. Near where the loop rejoins the highway is the Gorge Park and Nature Trail, and the following craft shop and gallery.

Tallulah Falls/Lakemont
Tallulah Falls School

This boarding school's only criteria for admission are a sincere desire to attend and a willingness to make use of the opportunities the school offers for academic development and personal growth. Scholarships based on need are available. All students, regardless of ability to pay tuition, are required to do an equal share of chores. Students cook, do dishes, clean classrooms and offices, and help with grounds work. The school is owned by the Georgia Federation of Women's Clubs, whose financial support also provides college grants for TFS graduates, based on academic achievement. Profits from the Tallulah Gallery and the Tallulah Gorge Park, part of the school's complex, are also used for scholarships. The school is located on a 600 acre campus adjacent to US 441. For an information package and admissions application, contact Director of Admissions, Tallulah Falls School, Tallulah Falls, GA 30573; phone 404/754-3171.

Tallulah Falls/Lakemont
Tallulah Gallery

The gallery is located in the large two-story frame house on the scenic loop just north of the junction with 441. Original arts and crafts include weavings, watercolors, oils, baskets, jewelry, photographs and pottery from Georgia's artists and craftspeople as well as others in the region. The gallery was established in 1973 as an educational and service project for Tallulah Falls School. All profits from sales go toward the school's scholarship fund. Open all year, seven days a week, 10 to 5, and during October until 8 p.m. Telephone 404/754-6020.

Tallulah Falls/Lakemont
The Co-op Craft Store

From the early 1900's to the 1960's the Tallulah Falls Station welcomed visitors who arrived by train. There is still a warm welcome at the historic old depot for those mountain visitors who want to browse and shop for locally made handcrafts and soak up a bit of history. The store in the old depot is one of two co-op stores regulated by the Georgia Mountain Arts Products, a cooperative formed in 1969 to increase the income of local people and help preserve the mountain crafts heritage. The other store is located at the "quick turn" on US 441 Business in Clarkesville. Both stores are filled to overflowing with authentic Georgia crafts at reasonable prices; quilts, soft sculpture, woodcrafts, toys, stained glass, pottery, pillows, jewelry and much more, by hundreds of craftspeople. The co-op fills mail and shipping orders from all over America and other countries too. They are open year round from

10 to 5, seven days a week. For more information, contact the Co-op Craft Store, Box 214, Clarkesville, GA 30523; phone 404/754-2244, or at Box 67, Tallulah Falls, GA 30573; phone 404/754-6810.

Tallulah Falls/Lakemont
Terrora Park, Visitor Center & Campground

On Highway 441 at the bridge, this park, operated by Georgia Power Company, offers a free picnic area and playground, tennis courts and lakeside trails. The Visitor Center has animated exhibits about the area's history and the power company's northeast Georgia hydroelectric development and public recreation. The friendly staff is knowledgable about the area, and you can pick up all sorts of information, including a booklet on Georgia Power's lakes and recreation areas. The campground charges a fee, average for the area, and offers 51 sites for tents and RV's with full hookups and hot showers. There is a trail and gorge overlook from the campground. Throughout the year some special events are held at the Visitor Center. Telephone 404/754-3276.

Tallulah Falls/Lakemont
Lakemont/Lake Rabun/Rabun Beach/Recreation Area

Except for the fortunate few who have summer homes (or friends with summer homes) in this serene, secluded lake area, Lake Rabun and Lakemont may be the Georgia Mountains' best kept secret. Tucked in the Chattahoochee National Forest about five miles from Tallulah Falls and 20 miles from Helen, it has changed little since it became a hideway for summer home owners back in the twenties. Even those who've driven the narrow winding road through Lakemont may not have known that a village—of sorts—existed. There are no shops, no service stations or motels, although there is a tiny post office. Edging the road are old rock walls, iron gate entranceways or densely wooded lawns behind which are hidden charming cottages or elegant estates. But there are limited accommodations here, and part of the fun of Lakemont is finding it. There is a marina (and boat rental) as you continue west through the village. Lake Rabun Recreation Area has camping facilities, boat dock, fishing pier, picnic area, trails, and a public beach. Call the National Forest Tallulah Ranger District; 404/782-3320. (Closed at the end of the summer season.) Take US 441 to the second bridge. Watch for the small Lakemont sign and road on the left. Keep left when the road forks. (From Helen, Take GA 356 or GA 255 to GA 197. Go north on GA 197 and turn at the Brooks Convenience Store.)

Tallulah Falls/Lakemont
The Barn Inn Bed & Breakfast

Converted, renovated, redefined; this 1920' stone and frame dairy barn must be one of the most unique bed and breakfast inns anywhere. It is also one of the most inviting and comfortable. There is a greatroom with a great stone fireplace, an antique baby grand, and a real oldtime chicken coop for a cocktail table. This room sets the tone for the luxury, whimsy and downright comfort throughout. There are private baths for all seven spacious guest rooms, and king or queen beds covered with pretty quilts or luxury comforters. Breakfast is available as early as you want it; a serve yourself affair of muffins, fruit, cereal, juice, tea and coffee. Enjoy it where you choose; in the kitchen, in your room or on the great deck overlooking Lake Rabun. A serene place for a quiet getaway for two, the inn is also available to small groups and family reunions, complete with full kitchen use for all meals when the entire inn is reserved. Open all year. For reservations, contact Innkeeper, Jerry Eppinga, The Barn Inn, P.O. Box 192, Lakemont, GA 30552; phone 404/782-5094.

Tallulah Falls/Lakemont
Lake Rabun Hotel

T his small, rustic inn retains all its 1922 charm. A stone fireplace in the lobby gathering room is surrounded with antiques and handmade furniture of rhododendron and mountain laurel branches, polished to a warm glow with years of wear. The 16 guest rooms are sunny, airy, cheerful and country-comfortable with quilts and ruffled curtains. Most have sinks in the room, and most share a bath. No air conditioning is needed, and no room phones or television intrude upon this escape into yesteryear's tranquility. Rates seem out of the past, too—they're quite moderate and include a complimentary breakfast of homemade muffins, juice and coffee or tea. Innkeepers Sandy and Pete Tsivoglou welcome guests (including children) from April 1 through Thanksgiving weekend. This is a long-time regional favorite and reservations should be made as early as possible for weekends and the peak season. Contact Lake Rabun Hotel, Route 1, Box 2090, Lakemont, GA 30552; phone 404/782-4946.

Clayton/Mountain City
Rabun County Welcome Center/Ranger Station

W atch for the sign, and a little log cabin on the east side of US 441/23, just north of the intersection with 76 West in downtown Clayton. This is a good place to stop for lots of information and maps, including directions to waterfalls. Some nice exhibits too, of local crafts and area history. Friendly and knowledgable staff. Telephone 404/782-4812.

For trail maps, camping and recreations areas, stop at the Tallulah District, US Forest Service Office on North Main; phone 404/782-3320.

Clayton/Mountain City
Black Rock Mountain State Park

T his is Georgia's highest park, stretching across almost three miles of the Eastern Continental divide. The park's central feature, Black Rock Mountain, is named for the huge outcrop of dark granite near the peak's 3,640-foot summit. On a clear day, mountain-top views extend more

Cowee Overlook, Black Rock Mountain State Park

Photo by Anthony Lampros

than 80 miles. Facilities on the 1,500 acres include 10 cottages; 53 RV sites with full hook-ups, 11 walk-in tent sites, hot showers, a group camping area, picnic area, a 17-acre fishing lake, and a ten-mile trail system. Activities include an overnight backpacking trip in autumn (call for information), and wildflower trips in the spring. The park remains open all year, and is especially lovely in the quiet of winter, and is a great spot for scenic vistas when snow blankets the mountain crests. The entrance is on US 441 three miles north of Clayton. For information and cottage reservations, telephone 404/746-2141.

Clayton/Mountain City
Chattooga River/Bartram Trail

F ighting the famous Chattooga rapids may not be everyone's cup of water, but everyone can enjoy the challenge vicariously, and experience the setting for the filming of the movie *Deliverance* in this remote section of Rabun County. From Clayton take US 76 east to reach a good viewing area of the Bull Sluice Rapids. Immediately after crossing the bridge into South Carolina, there is a parking lot from which a short trail leads to some rock outcroppings, offering the best views of the action. The Chattooga is one of the longest free-flowing rivers in the southeast, with over 50 miles included in the Wild and Scenic River system. If the activity looks like too much fun to just watch, go a bit farther east to the Wildwater Ltd. for a guided, safe trip.

The Bartram Trail is named for the Quaker naturalist who explored this area by foot over 200 years ago. There are 30-odd miles winding through the extreme northeast section of Rabun County, partially following the Chattooga River. The trail begins just *before* the bridge. Blaze colors may have been changed from yellow to white (check with ranger for extended walk). This section of the trail eventually leads to several waterfalls, through wildlife areas, and to the observation tower on Rabun Bald (4,696 feet). The trail can also be accessed from the following Warwoman Dell. For more information on the trails and recreation areas, contact the Tallulah Ranger District on Main Street in Clayton, phone 404/754-6221.

Clayton/Mountain City
Warwoman Dell Recreation Area/Trails/Waterfalls/Scenic Tour

T urn east on Warwoman Road at the Dairy Queen in Clayton for a 14-mile scenic drive through the fertile Warwoman Dell. It's about three miles to the recreation area parking lot. A short steep trail—about a half mile—leads to Becky Branch Falls. (The Bartram Trail also crosses here, near the entrance to the recreation area.) Continue driving east about 10 miles, and watch for a forest service road just after you cross the Chattooga River. It's about seven miles on the forest service road to the parking area, then about three miles round trip on the trail to Holcomb Creek Falls and Ammons Creek Falls. For an auto loop tour, continue east on Warwoman Road until it connects with Highway 28 to Highlands, North Carolina, taking NC 106 back into US 441 near Dillard, or continue on 28 north into the scenic Cullasaga River Gorge, to US 441 near Franklin, North Carolina.

Clayton/Mountain City
Wildwater Ltd. Rafting, Cabins and River House

A full kitchen with microwave, color television and a pink marble fireplace . . . is this the lifestyle of a river rat?! Well, it's available if your getaway includes a rafting trip with these licensed river outfit-

Georgia 49

ters. They offer their own moderately priced accommodations consisting of modern cabins (on a small lake near the Chattooga River) which sleep up to four each unit, and are complete with grill, full kitchens and color television.

Or there's the River House Bed & Breakfast, which has five guest rooms, four bathrooms, sleeps up to 15, offers a TV and game room, a pink marble fireplace and a Scandinavian breakfast of cereal, fruit, pastries, juice and coffee. Get a group of 10 or more together and have your own cookout catered by the professional resident chef. Go all the way with ribeye steaks accompanied by all the right stuff, or go for the budget Three Dog Night with franks, burgers and trimmings.

For your rafting experience you may choose the easy mini-trip—a half-day on the Chattooga rapids suitable for kids up to 99, families and first timers. Or take the seven-hour "Deliverance Trip" on Section III, or the ultimate challenge on Section IV. Or you may go for the gusto and take the overnight trip— two days of rafting and a camp night on the river bank, with all the comforts supplied (except sleeping bags), from tents to a steak dinner and hot mountain-sized breakfast.

It's best to get reservations, whether for lodging and rafting or just rafting. (You may call ahead and use your credit card). The Chattooga Rafting Center is located in the historic Long Creek Academy on US 76, about 12 miles east on Clayton, just over the South Carolina state line. Write or call; Wildwater Ltd., Box 100, Long Creek, SC 29658; phone 803/647-9587.

Clayton/Mountain City
The Stockton House Restaurant

L ocated on a hillside on scenic Warwoman Road, this restaurant is worthy of the view from its glass-fronted dining room and porch. From the pleasant dining room, set with fresh linens and flowers, or from the porch—weather permitting—all tables have a sweeping view of rolling pastureland where cattle graze below forested mountaintops. The Stockton House seems right at home here in this picture postcard setting. Relax and enjoy lunch or dinner.

From 11 a.m. until 2 the menu includes omelets for those who slept late. There is also a hot and delicious, small but complete, buffet and creative salad bar. From the menu there are hearty sandwiches and homemade soups. Dinner selections from 5 to 9 include the salad bar. There are pasta specialties such as fettucine or pasta primavera; several steak choices from the grill; roast prime rib of beef on Fridays and Saturdays; some gifts from the seas and the mountain streams, and what may be the best liver and onions served anywhere. But be prepared—the desserts are homemade and almost impossible to resist.

Open daily, all year. (Try this for a winter snow scene!) Handicap access, senior citizen discounts, major credit cards accepted. Located about one mile east of US 441/23—turn across from the Dairy Queen in Clayton. Reservations accepted, not required. Telephone 404/782-6175.

Clayton/Mountain City
A Small Motel

"T here's a small hotel,
    A wishing well,
    And I wish we were there together."

From the Rogers and Hart 1930's musical, *Pal Joey.* Here's a small *motel,* a wishing well, a not-so-small cottage-turned-lodge, and a complimentary continental breakfast in the office/sitting room of hosts Hank and Mad Dearborn.

This congenial couple enjoys visiting with guests as much as they enjoy expeditions on the Chattooga River, about seven miles down the road. Love of the river is what brought these Atlantans to the mountains and turned a former teacher, Mad, and a real estate entrepreneur, Hank, into innkeepers. Mad still does some tutoring in Clayton schools, and Hank says he is now a specialist in real estate restoration—the motel was a "boarded up mess" when they bought it. Motel closets were converted to fireplaces (who needs closets in motels!), and a wishing well was created out of some old barn wood and imagination.

Furnishings of flea market gleanings and garage sales are as reminiscent of the 1930's as the framed sheet music of *A Small Hotel* adorning each room. (Hank will sing the entire song with the slightest encouragement.) The lodge/cottage has a large living room with fireplace, a large, fully furnished kitchen, two baths, four good-sized bedrooms, more old comfortable clean furnishings, and enough beds in every size to sleep 8 to 10 comfortably . . . or up to 14 if they're all very friendly. The lodge has ceiling and wall fans; the motel rooms are air conditioned—all of them—but only a few have fireplaces. Open all year, a good winter getaway, and the rates leave you extra fun money. Take US 76 off 441/23 at Clayton. Contact A Small Motel, Route 3, Box 3025D, Clayton, GA 30525; phone 404/782-6488.

Clayton/Mountain City
The York House

B ed and breakfast is offered here in a white, two-story inn with double-decker porch, situated amidst towering century-old spruce and cedar trees. Now listed on the National Register of Historic Places, its history began in the 1870's when it was an overseer's one-story log cabin. In 1873, Hiram Gibson deeded a 40-acre parcel of land on which the cabin stood to his granddaughter Mollie. When Mollie married Civil War veteran William T. York, they enlarged the cabin into a two-story farmhouse. When surveyors for the Tallulah Falls Railroad came to the area, W.T. (Papa Bill) and Mollie

(Little Mama) took them in as guests, and the idea for an inn was born. The York family continued the tradition of innkeeping for almost 100 years until they sold the York House in 1979. The inn was renovated in the early 1980's.

Current owners, Phyllis and Jimmy Smith, now offer 13 guest rooms with private bath. Color cable television is available. A continental breakfast is brought to each room on a silver tray. All guest rooms are individually furnished with comfortable antiques, as is the spacious lobby where guests gather to relax, sit by the fireplace and swap stories about the day's activities. The York House has become a popular year round gathering place for those who enjoy four seasons of outdoor activities, ranging from skiing to whitewater rafting.

Look for the "Romantic Lodging" sign between Mountain City and Dillard on the east side of US 441/23. The inn is secluded a few hundred yards off the highway, on a pretty hillside with a nice view of the mountains. Well-behaved children are welcome. No pets. Credit cards accepted. The York House, P.O. Box 126, Mountain City, GA 30562; phone 404/746-2068.

Rabun Gap/Dillard
Rabun Gap-Nacoochee School

S ituated on a 1,200 acre campus along US 441, this school, established in 1903 and fully-accredited, is affiliated with the Presbyterian Church (USA). Bruce Dodd, Jr. is president. Serving students who are in the middle-to-upper range of academic achievement, the school offers a solid academic program, and over 90 percent of the graduates continue their education. The school enrolls approximately 250 boys and girls in grade 7–12. Some 40 are day students from the surrounding communities; the remainder are boarding students representing many states and foreign countries. The birthplace of the Foxfire folklore publications (which has since become a separate organization), the school's mountain location is ideal for its many outdoor activities. There is a full range of interscholastic sports.

The school's three-fold program of study/worship/work is unique. Every student must work eight or nine hours per week. Those needing financial assistance are given work scholarship-grants on the basis of need and the school's ability to provide. Visitors are welcome to tour the campus. For information and admission application, contact Rabun Gap-Nacoochee School, Rabun Gap, GA 30568; phone 404/746-5736.

Rabun Gap/Dillard
Rabun Gap Craft Shop

T his interesting shop is operated by, and is just across the highway from, Rabun Gap-Nacoochee School. Woven items are produced on the looms in the shop, and visitors are welcome to watch various stages of the process. Special items may be ordered if they are not in stock. In addition to the woven items, many other authentic Appalachian crafts are available. Among these are Nan's original corn shuck dolls, woodcarvings, enamel on copper, wooden toys, books for all ages, including the Foxfire series, and notepaper illustrated by local artists. Jams and jellies are available from several varieties of berries picked by the students at the school. The shop is an authorized outlet for the famous Bybee pottery created by the Cornelison family since 1845. Proceeds from sales at the craft shop help to support the student scholarship fund. The Rabun Gap Craft Shop is open Monday through Saturday from 9 until 5, and closes January and February. Phone 404/746-5343.

Rabun Gap/Dillard
The Dillard House

I t seems that everyone who has ever been through northeast Georgia has enjoyed the Dillard House family-style meals. Over a million travelers have been served since 1915 when a circuit riding minister became Authur and Carrie Dillard's first guest in their modest mountain valley home. In fact many mountain visitors are so inclined to "think food" when they think of the Dillard House, that they seldom think about what's beyond the dining rooms. And there's plenty more to see and do at the Dillards'.

There is the old Dillard Inn, restored and furnished in antiques for comfortable and interesting lodging. Nine guest rooms include three with private baths and six with connecting baths. The entire inn can be reserved for family reunions or small groups—or by anyone preferring country inn ambiance. For those who want phones, color television and private baths, there's the 53-unit modern motel lodge, and, more recently, cabins have been added to the lodging choices. All guests have use of the swimming pool and tennis courts. There's a farm petting zoo in back of the split-rail fence, and at the stables there are horses and trail rides for all. A short jog or stroll leads to trails beside the Little Tennessee River. This is all still owned and operated by three generations of Dillards, in the same fertile valley surrounded by the Blue Ridge Mountains. Breakfast, lunch and dinner still feature the famous Dillard Farm hams, in addition to bowls and platters filled with other mountain favorites. Open year round and located just off US 441/23 at Dillard. For lodging rates and reservations, contact the Dillard House, P.O. Box 10, Dillard, GA 30537; phone 404/746-5348.

Rabun Gap/Dillard
Gingerbread House Bed and Breakfast

H ansel and Gretel should've had it so good: A large hot tub and pool, a "gathering room" with VCR, movies, games, fireplace; guest rooms and suites, private baths, king, queen and rollaway beds for the little ones, all tucked into a small rhododendron forest a few hundred yards off Highway 441 at Dillard.

The three-level inn, built as a private residence in 1922, now fully modernized, has pre-wormy chestnut log railings to the upper level and hand-pegged, heart pine flooring, now polished to a honey glow and accented with area rugs. There are comfortable country and antique furnishings throughout the inn. Above the swimming pool is a large deck with a breathtaking view; a place to breakfast, snack or just enjoy the scenery. There's a "fattening up" room (call it a dining room if you wish) where guests are treated to gingerbread cake, cookies, pie and beverages in the evenings, and served a great country breakfast in the mornings. There's also a gift shop featuring edible gingerbread houses, a variety of antiques, collectibles and handcrafted items. Open all year long. Contact innkeepers, Syble & Terry Park, Gingerbread House Bed & Breakfast, P.O. Box 365, Dillard, GA 30537; phone 404/746-3234.

Hiawassee/Young Harris
Young Harris College

R ecreational facilities as well as a schedule of summer cultural events are all open to the public at this liberal arts junior college with an outstanding reputation for academic excellence for over 100 years. Campus recreation facilities, with regularly scheduled hours open for public use, include an olympic swimming pool, gym, tennis courts and billard room. Both the Rollins Planetarium and the Clegg Auditorium have regularly scheduled events open to the public. The campus is located on US 76. For additional information contact Young Harris College, Young Harris, GA 30582; phone out of state, 404/379-3111, in Georgia, 1-800-241-3754.

Hiawassee/Young Harris
Georgia Mountain Fair

T his is the big one, continuing for 12 days and nights at the Georgia Mountain Fairgrounds. Visitors by the thousands come every day for the demonstrations by over 60 craftspeople, for the country, bluegrass and gospel music, and for plenty of not-so-serious contests. There are carnival rides and other attractions for the youngsters. The fair always begins the first Wednesday in August. The Fairgrounds also hosts other activities throughout the year, including the Spring Festival the third weekend in May; the Fall Harvest Festival the third weekend in October, the Ole Time Fiddlers Convention the fourth weekend in October, and the following drama during mid-summer. Adjacent to the fairgrounds is the Fred Hamilton Rhododendron Garden. No admission is charged for an auto tour or walking tours through the garden which features over 2,000 rhododendron and azalea plants, one of the largest gardens of its kind in the southeast. For more information, contact Georgia Mountain Fair, Inc., P.O. Box 444, Hiawassee, GA 30546; phone 404/896-4191.

Hiawassee/Young Harris
Appalachian Drama: The Reach of Song

T he Reach of Song is a celebration of the history and culture of the people of Georgia's mountains. It is told in music and drama as seen through the life and works of North Georgia mountains' own writer/poet Byron Herbert Reece (1918–1958). It features the live music of award-winning Fiddlin' Howard Cunningham and his band, and its cast includes professional actors plus a large cast of superb local talent. The play was written by Tom Detitta and was developed over three years of interviews and research. It is a poignant and often humorous story about the passage of time—"the winds of change" — and its effect upon an Appalachian community: the customs, the culture and the people who've gone from being almost isolated even from the rest of their state to receiving the entire world on their satellite dish. The Reach of Song captures the essence of a changing way of life in a way that brings smiles, laughter, a touch of tears, some toe tapping (and perhaps an urge to join in the "church singing" lead so perfectly by Georgia mountains native, James Farist), and a heartfelt burst of applause at the end of performance. Decoration Day, dinner on the ground, box suppers, whittlers carving out tall tales, preachers with powerful voices to equal their unequivocal messages, dirt roads, kerosene lamps, well buckets, a distant war which claimed the lives of many mountain lads and changed the lives of others, a farmer/poet behind a plow . . . all gone except for the reach of song, longer even than the memories of the oldest mountainers in the audience. The play is performed indoors on the Anderson Music Hall stage at the Georgia Mountains Fairgrounds. The performances run from mid-June through July. For schedule, ticket informations and reservations, call 404/896-3388 or 1-800-262-SONG.

Hiawassee/Young Harris
Lake Chatuge/Camping

S et alongside the southern reaches of Lake Chatuge, a few miles from the Tennessee state line, this pretty little valley town is almost surrounded by lakes and forested mountains. The 7,500-acre TVA lake is a water playground for fishing, skiing, sailing, canoeing, swimming and lakeside camping in *two* beautiful public campgrounds; The Towns County Park (which also has tennis courts) and the Chattahoochee National Forest Lake Chatuge Recreation Area, located on a pine-covered, dogwood-decorated peninsula. Go to sleep with moonlight on the lake, wake to soft morning mists and the sounds of water fowl. (Unfortunately the recreation area is closed after Labor Day. Call 404/745-6928 for forest service information.) For more information on this enchanted valley area, contact the Towns County Chamber of Commerce, P.O. Box 290, Hiawassee, GA 30546; phone 404/896-4966.

Hiawassee/Young Harris
Fieldstone Inn, Restaurant and Marina

H ow naturally this new resort, opened in 1987, fits into the setting on a Lake Chatuge cove surrounded by the Blue Ridge Mountains. The low-level, two-story inn, constructed mostly of native fieldstone with many windows and a cedar shake roof, is designed in a "C" shape, offering lake or mountain views from every guest room. The view is continuous from the semi-circular sunken lobby which has a great stone fireplace to enhance winter getaways. The view and fireplace are repeated on the second level where morning coffee awaits each guest.

The 40 guest rooms, including two completely equipped handicap rooms, are luxuriously appointed with deep rich colors complimenting the fine traditional furnishings. All rooms have a kingsize or two double beds, satellite-dish television, clock radio and a deck with chairs for enjoying the view. There is a swimming pool, lighted tennis court and marina with boat slip, pontoon boat rentals and free docking privileges for guests. There is also a conference room which can accommodate up to 40 people.

The separate restaurant offers wonderous views from the almost floor-to-ceiling windows in the gray and mauve dining room, open 7 days a week from 6:30 a.m. until 10:00 p.m. The menu offers American favorites from prime to babyback ribs, chicken and seafood, and several Italian specialties. A private dining room is available for parties and wedding receptions. Reservations are not required but are accepted.

The Fieldstone Resort was developed, built and is operated by a Towns County native, Bob Cloer. The resort is located 3 miles west of Hiawassee near the Georgia Mountains Fairgrounds on US 76. For information, rates and reservations, contact Fieldstone Inn, P.O. Box 670, Hiawassee, GA 30546; telephone 404/896-2262.

Blairsville

T he county seat of Union County is surrounded by Georgia's tallest mountains and some of it's most scenic places. In addition to the following listings, some other nearby places to visit include Sosebee Cove, off GA 180, Helton Creek Falls, located about 5 miles down a forest service road off US 129/19 just south of Vogel State Park, Lake Nottely for boating and fishing, and the Track Rock Archaeological Area (off 19/129 south for 3 miles, left on Towns Creek Road) a 52-acre site of ancient Indian petroglyphs, still undeciphered, of carvings resembling animal and bird tracks, crosses, circles and human footprints. There's hiking from the state park, the forest recreations areas, and on the Appalachian Trail, crossing 19/129 just south at Neels Gap. The US Forest Service, Brasstown Ranger District number is 404/745-6928. The Blairsville/Union County Chamber of Commerce address is P.O. Box 727, Blairsville, GA 30512; phone 404/745-5789.

Blairsville
Brasstown Bald

Georgia's highest mountain has a national forest service visitor center and an observation tower atop the 4,784-foot summit, from where visitors have a 360-degree view across miles of mountain ridges into four states. There are also exhibits and slide programs, and at the parking area, a craft shop and picnic facilities. The craft shop, housed in a new log cabin, features some authentic Appalachian arts and crafts, and has a good selection of field guides, regional books and other information. From this area, which is as far as automobiles are allowed to travel, there are several steep hiking trails to the tower, and mini-buses departing every few minutes, for which a small fee is charged. Brasstown Bald opens weekends only in April, and seven days a week from May through the first week in November; 10 a.m. to 5:30 p.m. From south of Blairsville, go east on GA 180 to SR 66 to the parking area. The craft shop phone is 404/896-3471, the visitor center phone is 404/896-2556.

Blairsville
Vogel State Park

One of the state's most beautiful parks offers rental cottages, secluded and private sites for tent and camping, picnic areas and a small clear lake with bathhouse, beach and paddle boat rental. Its 240 acres contain nature trails, and trailheads to two longer trails: Bear Hair Gap, a four-mile moderate loop, and the Coosa Backcountry Trail, a tough 12 mile plus loop used for the park's two scheduled overnight backpacking trips in spring and fall. Several other annual activities are scheduled, including the wonderful Old Timer's Day in August. Call the park for more information and cottage reservations; 404/745-2628.

Blairsville
Sorghum Festival

It takes the first three weekends in October to see and do all there is to see and do at Union County's biggest festival. All the folks around here get involved, preparing for this event weeks, months, even an entire season ahead of time, making crafts, arts and putting up canned goods, planning parades, practicing their music and dancing, and of course, raising cane—which is converted to sweet sorghum syrup right before your eyes. Lots of free samples too. There is almost continuous entertainment, some of which you may provide yourself by joining in the square dancing, greased-pole climbing and other contests. A small admission is charged. Located in Fort Sorghum, near downtown. For more information, call 404/745-5789.

Blairsville
Mountain Crossing/Walasi-Yi Center

The 2,000-mile-long Appalachian Trail crosses US 19/129 here at Neels Gap a bit south of Vogel State Park. By auto or by trail, it's one of the most scenic tours in north Georgia. Blood Mountain, the highest point on the trail in Georgia, is a two-mile hike; a four to five hour round trip. Mountain tourists and mountain hikers cross paths and mingle here in the Walasi-Yi center, owned by State of Georgia, Parks and Historic Sites and privately operated by Jeff and Dorothy Hansen since 1983.

Built by the Conservation Corps in 1930, the great stone and chestnut log structure houses a unique craft shop. Many of the crafts are locally made and include baskets, pottery and traditional Appalachian toys, dulcimers and other mountain instruments. Craft and musical demonstrations are held periodically for the enjoyment of hikers and tourists. Weather permitting, these events are held on the ground's scenic overlook against a background of mountains, trees and rolling clouds. Also available in the shop is a wide selection of vacation information for roads, campgrounds, lodging and hiking, plus racks and racks of regional and outdoor maps, guidebooks, regional and historical books on the north Georgia outdoors, and a complete range of hiking and backpacking supplies—from camping gear to spare parts, sleeping bags and tents. Shuttle service for Appalachian Trail hikers is also available. For more information contact Mountain Crossing, Route 1, Box 1240, Blairsville, GA 30512; phone 404/745-6095.

Blairsville
Goose Creek

C abins, camping, meals and more than a touch of enchantment are located here, one-half mile north of Vogel State Park. Goose Creek is an idyllic setting, with a trout pond watched over by two geese, and a wooded hillside where secluded cabins and campsites nestle near a mountain stream. Keith and Retter Bailey call this home, and they've made it as homey for guests as for themselves. The cottages are contemporary rustic, with decks, fireplaces, modern baths, and completely equipped kitchens. (Catch your trout for supper at the trout pond.) There are no telephones or television, just the sounds of the stream, crickets and frogs to lull you to sleep after a day of hiking or sightseeing. The cabins and camping facilities are open all year.

The restaurant is open May through October and their specialty is trout—catch it yourself or they'll do it for you. There are daily specials and a variety of simple country meals. Goose Creek is a special place—simplicity without starkness, charm without cuteness—a place for kids and grandparents, bicyclists and motorists, backpackers and honeymooners, and lovers of all ages. Go for a night, a weekend, a long vacation, or go for a fresh trout dinner in a peaceful country place. Meal prices and lodging rates are very modest. Contact Goose Creek, P.O. Box 906, Blairsville, GA 30512; phone 404/745-5111.

Blairsville
Blood Mountain Cabins and Country Store

T he Appalachian Trail crosses US 19/129 a few yards from these cabins near the top of Blood Mountain. Each cabin is tucked in its own mountain garden of flame azalea, laurel and rhododendron. Each has a full bedroom plus sleeping loft, a living room with fireplace, central heat, air conditioning, ceiling fans, large deck with rockers and grill, a fully furnished kitchen and modern bath. Some are secluded in the woods near a small cascading stream, others sit high on a ridgeline with four-season views of the mountains. The cabins are open all year and there's an exceptional early week bargain—the MTW special. A two-night minimum is required on weekends only. Children are welcome. Pets are not allowed.

Proprietors Tom and Barbara Welden are available for helpful information on what's to see and do nearby. You'll find them in the country store where there is always fresh coffee, cold soda pop, hot dogs with the trimmings, and tables available on the deck. Among the wide variety of crafts, gifts and souvenirs are real handmade Appalachian toys and crafts like Gee Haw Whimmy

Diddles, wooden mountain whistles and maple twig flowers, and Gourdies, transformed from garden-variety gourds into "collectible friends" by Sharron Barron. Gourdies are delightfully imperfect individuals, handpainted, signed and dated, and come in all sizes and shapes. The store also has an excellent selection of rocks and gemstones at exceptionally reasonable prices. For cabin rates and reservations, contact Blood Mountain Cabins, US 19/129, Blairsville, GA 30512, phone 404/745-9454.

Blairsville
7 Creeks Cabins

O ff scenic highway, GA 180 a gravel road meanders around meadows and cornfield to the hideaway of Marvin and Bobbie Herndon—a 70-acre hideaway which these two early retirees from Miami share with several goats, ducks and chickens, one dog, one cat and one pony. They also share it with a few fortunate weekenders and vacationers—those who are looking for housekeeping cabins in a quiet country setting. It *is* quiet here, and peaceful, and pretty as a picture.

There's a spring-fed, one-acre lake with bream, bass and catfish. No license and no charge for your catch. (And there are fishing poles on the premises.) There's a picnic area, fire ring, tetherball and horseshoes. The gravel road and trails offer country walks and mountain loop hikes up to five miles. By car it's only a few minutes to several nearby attractions including Brasstown Bald.

Dogwood trees literally surround each of the five cabins. Four cabins can accommodate up to six people; one can accommodate up to four. Most have fireplaces, all have cordless phone, radio, color television, fully equipped kitchens, showers in modern, private baths, and simple furnishings. Cleaning supplies are provided and guests are on the honor system to leave the cabins as clean as they find them. Pillows and plenty of blankets are furnished. Bring your own towels, sheets and pillowcases for the lower "housekeeping" rates, or the Herndons will supply them for an additional charge. Laundry facilities are on the premises. The cabins are available year round on a weekly or nightly basis with a two-night minimum. For rates and reservations, contact 7 Creeks Cabins, Route 2, Box 2647, Blairsville, GA 30512; phone 404/745-4753.

Suches/Woody Gap/Woody Lake

T he remote little community of Suches and Woody's Lake sits right in the national forest, just south of where the Appalachian Trail crosses GA 60 at Woody Gap. Good view here, and a place to picnic, but be warned; it may possibly be the windiest spot in the mountains. From here it's about 8 miles up to Blood Mountain on the AT, or you can drive 5 miles to the following lake and take a shorter hike to the top.

Blairsville
Lake Winfield Scott Recreation Area/Blood Mountain Hike

A n absolute jewel, this clear and sparkling, mountain high, 18-acre lake sits in the forest recreation area which also offers camping, picnicking, swimming, fishing, boating (electric motors only), and some terrific hiking challenges. From here, the infamous Blood Mountain can be tackled via the one mile hike from the recreation area to Slaughter Gap on the AT, then another 1.1 miles to the top of the 4,458-foot mountain. It's a steep climb but the views at the top are worth the effort. (Be sure to follow the blue blazes.) A hardy dayhike roundtrip with a rewarding dip in that cool, clean lake on your return.

This area is only about five miles east of the community of Suches on GA

180, about 17 miles south/southwest of Blairsville on 19/129 to Vogel, then 180 west. It's in the Brasstown Ranger District, phone 404/745-6928 for information and maps.

Blue Ridge/Ellijay
Art in the Park/Harvest Sale/Blue Grass Festival

B lue Ridge, in Fannin County, is surrounded by farms and national forest land bordered by the Cohutta Wilderness on the west, and is just south of the Tennessee state line and the beginning of the next section in this book. Arts in the Park, is held in the town park on the fourth Saturday in May; phone 404/622-2144 for more information. The Harvest Sale is the real thing, involving farmers and homemakers from the area. It is held at the Farmers Market on the third and fourth weekends in October and has exhibits as well as fresh baked and canned goods, arts and crafts, and truckloads of locally grown produce. Blue Grass Music Festivals are held one weekend in June and July, twice in October at the Sugarcreek Music Park, rain or shine, under a pavillion; phone 404/632-2560. There's a welcome center in the caboose of the old depot downtown, call the Chamber of Commerce, 404/632-5680.

Ellijay, a few miles south/southwest and also adjacent to the national forest's Cohuttas, is the county seat of Gilmer County. Ellijay bills itself as the apple capital of Georgia, and holds an apple festival the second weekend in October. When the apples are ripe, you can buy 'em by the bushel along highway roadstands, along with gallon jugs of fresh apple cider. The little mountain town is built around a town square. The Ellijay Chamber of Commerce phone is 404/635-7400.

Blue Ridge/Ellijay
Lake Blue Ridge/Camping

T his stocked lake has 100 miles of shoreline, a boat launch, beach, picnic area and a campground within walking distance of the lake. There are cold showers and flush toilets, but no hookups for RV's— which may account for its nearly always available campsites, even on weekends. Whatever the reason, it's a beautifully peaceful place for tent campers and for day recreation, open only from Memorial Day through Labor Day. Several opportunities for hiking too, including the nearly eight-mile-long Rich Mountain Trail which crosses near this national forest recreation area. From Blue Ridge take US 76 east for two miles and follow the signs. For maps and information, contact the US Forest Service, Toccoa Ranger District (E. Main Street in Blue Ridge), 404/632-3031.

Blue Ridge/Ellijay
Cohutta Wilderness' East Cowpen Trail

T o sample the following Cohutta Wilderness from Blue Ridge on a relatively easy to follow trail, start your hike on Old Highway 2 where the pavement ends. Easy to follow, although not necessarily always easy hiking, but you can double back whenever you want—the next access point is seven miles. The old, deeply eroded, gutted and rocky roadbed continues on through the center of the wilderness, connecting with several other trails. Take Highway 5 north from Blue Ridge for just over four miles, and watch for Georgia Highway 2 on the left. Follow the road for nearly 19 miles to the wilderness boundary. See Forest Service Cohutta District under Chatsworth.

Blue Ridge/Ellijay
Forge Mill Crossing Restaurant & Shops

S ix miles east of Blue Ridge on the Appalachian Highway (US 76) at Forge Mill Road, watch for a hillside surrounded by a white rail fence and treat yourself to something special. This restaurant is owned and operated by Kay and Phil Kendall, who use the freshest food possible when preparing their fare. Vegetables are sauteed or steamed. Fresh Georgia trout is broiled or pan fried to order. The stroganoff is so good that it started as a special and ended up on the menu every day. There are special menu items added for each Friday and Saturday night. The homemade raisin bread, served with every meal, has become the Forge Mill Crossing calling card. Kay does the desserts, using only Granny Smith apples for her famous Sour Cream Apple Pie. There is a sinful fudge pie, and a chess pie to be savored slowly so each ingredient can have time to pop out and delight your taste buds. The main dining room is contemporary country rustic; there is also a front screened porch for dining with a view. (And speaking of view, try timing your evening meal, so you can head west as the sun bathes the ridges in blue light, or sinks behind them for a spectacular sunset, especially during the winter. The western view from here on US 76 is as beautiful as it gets!)

The surrounding complex of shops carries out the Forge Mill feeling of relaxed mountain hospitality. Windy Ridge Gallery & Gifts specializes in pottery, glass, fiberwork, jewelry and other crafts by regional artists. Under the same roof, the Mountaineer Times Book Shoppe features regional authors and subject matter in addition to a variety of current books. At Forge Mill Crossing Antiques & Gifts each room is filled with antiques, collectibles, crafts and wonderful gifts for yourself or someone special. Ask about their line of custom-built hand painted furniture. At a third shop, Loving Chocolates, you will find the "candy ladies" busily making an assortment of exquisite handmade chocolates. They sell both wholesale and retail, but every single piece is made lovingly by hand which accounts for the excellent flavor and freshness. They also do a large holiday mail order business. All shops remain open for holiday shopping but close for three weeks after New Year's. Usual hours for the restaurant are 11:30 a.m. until 9 p.m. The entire complex is closed on Mondays. For more information call 404/374-5771.

Blue Ridge/Ellijay
Creekside Farm Bed & Breakfast

T his farmhouse retreat makes a wonderful getaway for one, two or up to six friends or a small family. There's a major trout stream bordering the 8 1/2 acres of woods and gardens. Along the cool shady creek you can fish, wade or sit on the banks and daydream.

Host Pat Haynie is a prize-winning cook (14 blue ribbons in one year alone!) and your bountiful, full country breakfast will include some of her special breads and jams. For lunch or dinner there is a variety of restaurants in the Blue Ridge area, or you may take advantage of the refrigerator privileges and put together your own light meal. Weather permitting, breakfast can be enjoyed on the wide screened porch, which has a swing and rockers for just sitting, watching the fireflies in the evening and listening to the crickets. If you have a favorite TV program, you are welcome to watch television in the living room. During the day you can pick berries, take a walk around the gardens, grounds or down the country road, enjoy the birds and wildflowers, explore the creek, or just rest and relax in this quiet hideaway at the very end of a country lane, seven miles from Blue Ridge; less than two to three hours from

Atlanta, Chattanooga or Asheville.

The spotlessly clean farmhouse has three guest rooms with choice of twin or double beds, and one includes a Murphy bed. They're each beautifully and comfortably furnished in good country antiques and pretty accessories. The three guest rooms share two bath rooms. Pat welcomes guests all year and offers modest rates (which include the big breakfast). This is a lovely place in the real bed and breakfast tradition. Contact Creekside Farm Bed and Breakfast, P.O. Box 220, Blue Ridge, GA 30513; phone 404/632-3851 or 404/492-7815.

Blue Ridge/Chatsworth/Ellijay
Sunnybrook Bend Getaway Cabins

I magine relaxing in a luxurious hot tub surrounded by the sights and sounds of a nearby rippling creek flowing through a peaceful valley surrounded by Blue Ridge Mountains.

There's a large hot tub on the deck, and a fireplace or woodstove in these cabins. The location is very private—one mile from the national forest's Cohutta Wildlife Management Area surrounding the Cohutta Wilderness. Secluded in a 17-acre wooded valley cove bordered by trout-stocked Little Fighting Town Creek, Sunnybrook Bend's four different cabins are romantic enough for a honeymoon, large enough for a family, and combined, can accommodate a family reunion or other groups.

The contemporary rustic cabins have wraparound decks, fully equipped, wood panelled kitchens (three have washers and dryers), one or two bedrooms with king, queen, single or double beds, extra sofa bed sleeping space in the living rooms, and modern bathrooms with tub/showers. Firewood is provided. Guests bring their own linens. Moderate rates are discounted further for weekday getaways and during the off-season. Located on a private road off GA 2, about 8 miles northwest of Blue Ridge. Contact Rebecca of Sunnybrook Bend, 404/843-2626.

Blue Ridge/Ellijay
The Elderberry Inn

T his restored country Victorian home, circa 1897, is the *new* Elderberry Inn. Ellijay's premier bed and breakfast inn was actually established in a different location: above a shop in a section of a building on River Street. The shop was the June Bug, featuring antiques, collectibles, a tea room, and the interior design studio of June Handte. When innkeepers June and Charles Handte bought this large two-story home, they relocated the shop nearby, gave the inn a new address, and set about furnishing it with all the imagination you'd expect from a good interior designer who'd always been active in historic preservation. There is a Colonial room, a Victorian room, a Country French mini-suite with small kitchen, a delightful Art Deco room and a small garden room off the upstairs porch; seven guest rooms in all (with three and a half baths), each creatively furnished in period antiques. There is also a great country kitchen, two levels of porches, and a sunroom surrounding the original well, gourd dipper and well bucket. Guests are served wake-up coffee at 8:15 and a full gourmet breakfast here at 8:30. A continental breakfast is available for late sleepers. The entire inn may be reserved for weddings and other special occasions. Open all year; moderate rates. Contact Elderberry Inn, 75 Dalton St., Ellijay, Ga 30540; phone 404/635-2218 or 5738.

Chatsworth
Fort Mountain State Park

A t an elevation of over 2,800 feet this park, near the Cohutta Wilderness, is generally considered the western end of the Blue Ridge Mountains. The park area was never a fort. Its name is derived from the large stone formation, 855 feet long, which stands on the highest point of the mountain, and is believed to have been built by Woodland Indians over 1,000 years ago. Facilities include cottages, tent, trailer and group camping, fishing, swimming and hiking on nature trails and the newly completed backpacking trail. Two overnight backcountry trips are scheduled in the fall and spring. Located on Hwy 52, a few miles east of Chatsworth. Telephone for information and cottage reservations, 404/695-2621.

Chatsworth
The Cohutta Wilderness

B efore you hike here, take the scenic route, GA 52 from Ellijay across Fort Mountain and into Chatsworth for more complete information and maps at the ranger station listed below.

This 34,100 acre wilderness sits in the middle of the Chattahoochee Forest's Cohutta Wildlife Management Area near the southern end of the Blue Ridge Mountains. It's a favorite area for anglers; the Conasauga and Jacks River are widely known for trout fishing. Bear, wild hogs and whitetailed deer are a few of the wildlife species hikers might see here in the isolated mountain coves where access is only by trail. For hikers who appreciate rugged terrain, and don't mind frequent fording of streams, its 85 miles of hiking trails are among the most scenic and challenging in the state. The trails wander up and down and around elevations ranging from nearly 1000 to over 4000 feet, often following and (it seems) endlessly crossing Jack's River and other incredibly clear streams. Crossings are not always easy, or safe, especially during and following heavy rains. Hikers should be prepared with maps and information from the district ranger office. Being prepared might also include some old sneakers for fording streams—river rocks can be hard on the feet as well as slippery, and this isolated wilderness is no place for a bad fall. Information is available, and a map may be purchased for a small fee at the National Forest Service Cohutta Ranger District Office, 401 Old Ellijay Road, Chatsworth, GA 30705; phone 404/695-6736.

Chatsworth
Cohutta Lodge & Restaurant

T alk about rooms with a view! There are views from all guest rooms in this Old English-style lodge on the summit of Fort Mountain, and the view from the dining room and deck is probably the best from any lodge in Georgia. The restaurant is open to the public for three meals a day, serving favorite southern fare; steaks, trout, ribs, chicken and a Sunday buffet. On cooler days, enjoy a meal and that view in front of the largest fireplace in the Georgia mountains. Rooms, suites and effeciencies are available, all with private baths, air conditioning, phones and television. Facilities also include a convention center which can accommodate up to 360. Guest amenities include a heated pool, night lighted tennis courts, and various seasonal activities. And it's all next door to the Cohutta Wilderness! Contact Cohutta Lodge, 5000 Cochise Trail, Chatsworth, GA 30705; phone 404/695-9601.

Jasper
The Woodbridge Inn

Atlanta's pickiest food critics have praised the Woodbridge for over a decade. To quote one, "If there is a single best restaurant in North Georgia it's the Woodbridge Inn." Classic European and American specialties include veal oscar, rainbow trout and sweetbreads. Delicate sauces are prepared for individual orders. Bavarian-trained chef, Joe Ruffert, wife Brenda and their two children opened the restaurant in 1977 in what was originally an 1880's boarding-house-style hotel. It wasn't long before the rockers on the porches were filled every Sunday before lunch time and every evening before dinner time with Atlantans and others who'd heard of the rare combination of southern hospitality and exceptional continental cuisine.

The restaurant's success and the beautiful mountain setting made the 1982 addition of lodging accommodations almost inevitable. The contemporary three-level lodge, located a few yards away from the century-old restaurant building, is specially designed so that each of its 12 rooms, suites, patios and balconies has a view of the mountains. The upper level rooms feature a spiral staircase to an extra sitting area/bedroom loft. Both the restaurant and the lodge are open all year. For rates and reservations, contact The Woodbridge Inn, 411 Chamber Street, Jasper, GA 30143; phone 404/692-6293.

Tate
The Tate House Restaurant and Resort

The Tate family began mining pink and white marble in the foothills of Georgia's Blue Ridge Mountains in the late 1800's. In the 1920's Colonel Sam Tate used the rare Etowah pink marble for construction of the Pink Marble Mansion, a showplace for the Georgia Marble Company. Today, thanks to painstaking restoration by Ann and Joe Laird, the mansion is once again a showcase, and is listed on the National Register of Historic Places.

The 27-acre resort features lodging suites in the mansion, and in nine private mountain cabins. Traditional fine southern dining and special events catering is available in the mansion and the glass enclosed marble courtyard pub, added in the 70's.

Marble floors, magnificent furnishings and landscaped grounds add to the grandeur of this historic treasure. A sweeping stairway leads from the main floor to the upper level guest suites, each with a marble inlay bathroom. The modern mountain log cabins are luxurious with hot tub, wet bar, fireplace and extra sleeping loft. Weekend cabin and mansion guests are served champagne and a full country breakfast in the dining room. A continental breakfast is served for weekday lodging guests. Amenities on the estate include nature trails, tennis courts, a swimming pool, horseback riding, and a gift shop featuring small antiques and craft items.

The restaurant is open to the public for lunch, Wednesday through Saturday and for Sunday brunch, 11 a.m. until 3 p.m., and for dinner, Wednesday through Saturday, 6 p.m. until 9 p.m. All or part of the estate may be reserved for fully catered special occasions and corporate meetings. Open year round. Contact The Tate House Restaurant and Resort, Highway 53, Tate, GA 30177; phone 404/735-3122, or toll free in Georgia, 1-800-342-7515.

Gatlinburg, Tennessee nestled in the Great Smoky Mountains

Photo: Courtesy Ben Humphries

TENNESSEE

T *he following map generally indicates only those towns under which information is listed plus major highways, cities and towns, and should be used in conjunction with a state map. The towns covered are not organized alphabetically but as they appear along and off main travel routes, generally from the southwestern tip of the national forest to the northern tip of the Cumberland Plateau, back south to the Smokies area, then to the northeastern tip of the state, appearing as follows: Ocoee/Benton, Tellico Plains, Sweetwater, Watts Bar/Spring City, Crossville, Clarkrange, Allardt, Rugby, Jamestown/ Big South Fork Area/Oneida, Townsend/Wear Valley, Pigeon Forge/Sevierville, Gatlinburg, Erwin/Roan Mountain, Elizabethton/Laurel Bloomery, Kingsport/Rogersville, Greenville/Jonesborough.*

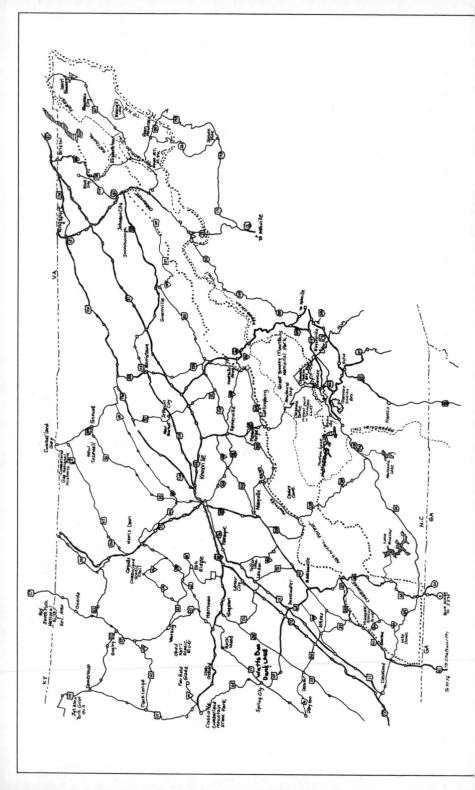

Tennessee
. . . .

North Arch of the Twin Arches in the Big South Fork National River and Recreation Area

Tennessee:
An Introduction and Sources for Additional Information

T his book covers three distinctly different mountain ranges in eastern Tennessee, from the rugged terrain of the Cherokee National Forest and the Great Smokies along the state's southern borders, through landscapes dotted with TVA lakes and dams, to the Cumberland Plateau and a new national park at its north central boundary to the gently rolling hills and farmlands along the Cumberlands in its fertile northeastern boundary.

This variety of terrain offers an almost endless variety of vacation experiences. Rivers, dams and lakes offer fishing and other water recreation, and also create a waterway to the Gulf of Mexico. Camping facilities include private campgrounds, national parks and forest lands, and a superb state park system which offers lodging and restaurant facilities in many of its parks. Other accommodations include a scattering of cabins, inns and bed and breakfast establishments, with a higher concentration in the Smokies area. The Smokies is the most visited park area in the east, and shopping competes with outdoor activities for visitor leisure time. For early American history lessons, go exploring the upper eastern tip of the state.

If you don't find the information you are looking for listed under the towns on the following pages good sources for further information include the following:

Tennessee Tourist Development, P.O. Box 23170, Nashville Tennessee, 37204-3170, phone 615/741-2158. (Toll free for state park cabin and inn reservations, 1-800-421-6683.) The Tennessee Valley Authority (TVA), 1-800-251-9242. Upper Cumberland Development District, 615/432-4111. Upper East Tennessee Tourism Council, 615/753-5961. The Cherokee National Forest Ranger District Offices as follows: the Nolichucky District at Greeneville, 615/638-4109; the Unaka District at Erwin, 615/743-4451; the Watauga Ranger District at Elizabethton, 615/451-2942; the Tellico District in Tellico Plains, 615/253-2520; Ocoee District at Benton, 615/338-5201 and the Hiwassee District at Etowah, 615/263-5486. Maps and trail guides are available.

Good hiking guides include *Hiking the Big South Fork* by Brenda Coleman and Jo Anna Smith, published by the University of Tennessee Press and *Tennessee Trails* by Evan Means, published by The East Woods Press.

Ocoee/Benton

If you take US 64 (The Old Copper Road) along the Ocoee River Gorge, through the Cherokee National Forest, between Ducktown and Ocoee you'll not only be traveling along an astonishingly scenic route, you will also have an unusual number of opportunities for outdoor recreation, from whitewater rafting to hiking, swimming, skiing and more, all within whistling distance. Take TN 30 north through the forest for more of the same, except you'll have the gentle Hiwassee River instead of the rapids of the Ocoee. For maps and more information stop at the US Forest Service, Ocoee District Rangers office located at the intersection of US 64 and Forest Service Road 77; phone 615/338-5201.

Ocoee/Benton
Ocoee River/Lake Ocoee

When the Toccoa River flows from Georgia into Tennessee it gets a new name, the Ocoee, and a new reputation as one of the most challenging whitewater rivers in the east.

Along this river where the water flow is dam-controlled there's a five-mile stretch with a 250-foot drop, where rapids have earned such names as Toothache Hole, Hell's Hole, Slice n'Dice and Broken Nose. There are good reasons for the names, and for a state law which prohibits anyone from rafting here that is not at least 12 years old. Reason too that all except expert paddlers ride this river only with experienced guides. The Ocoee can be dangerous as well as exciting. A number of rafting companies operate on the river, which is controlled for rafting at the following specified times: Saturdays, Sundays and holidays from April through October, plus Mondays, Thursdays and Fridays during June, July and August. Allow a half day for the activity including bus travel time from the outfitters and back. Making reservations is a good idea.

When the rapids end, the lakes begin; Lake Ocoee, Parksville Lake . . . whichever stretch you are on will offer opportunities for swimming, boating, (there's a marina for rentals) waterskiing, fishing and camping, all against a national forest scenic backdrop dominated by Sylco Ridge, Big Frog Mountain, and the unmistakeable peak of Sugarloaf Mountain.

Ocoee/Benton
Scenic Byway/Chilhowee Recreation Area/Benton Falls

America's first US Forest Service Scenic Byway includes segments of two roads: US 64 through the river gorge, and paved Forest Service 77 which turns north off 64 to climb Chilhowee mountain. There are several fantastic overlooks for photos, picnics and general "Oh's and Ah's," then the crest to a recreation area which includes a mountaintop lake with a beach and bath house, a picnic area, campground, and a three-mile round trip, super easy trail to what may be one of the world's most beautiful waterfalls, Benton Falls. Worth a drive and a hike anytime, extra beautiful in the late spring when it's bordered on both sides by rhododendron. Take your camera—you can safely walk on large stones directly in front of the base of the falls for some exceptional photo opportunities. You may continue on 77 (now unpaved) for another few miles to its junction with TN 30 for a loop along the Hiwassee River back to US 64.

Ocoee/Benton
Hiwassee State Scenic River/John Muir Trail

Flowing across the national forest between US 411 and TN 68, this 23-mile section of the Hiwassee River is the first designated State Scenic River in Tennessee. It's the place for those who seek quieter moments than the Ocoee offers; a chance to do some nature photography, trophy trout fishing, to float lazily down the stream on a raft, or paddle its gentle currents in a canoe or funyak, to hike, picnic and camp away from crowded, more developed areas.

The relatively easy John Muir Trail follows long stretches of the river on its 17 miles through this forest, part of John Muir's route on his 1,000-mile hike to the Gulf of Mexico. It connects with the Unicoi Mountain Trail and the Oswald Dome Trail, both moderate hikes of 5 to 6 miles. The John Muir trailhead is just east of TN 30 and Forest Service Road 108. There are also several access points to the trail along the river. Best get a map from the Hiwassee Ranger District at Etowah; phone 615/263-5486.

Ocoee/Benton
Ocoee Outdoors, Grumpy's Pub & Sugarloaf Campground

Take a guided, wild whitewater Ocoee trip, or an unguided leisurely canoe or raft float, or a guided float-fishing trip on the gentle, scenic, trout-filled Hiwassee, stop afterwards at Grumpy's for supplies and a little relaxation, and end the day around your campfire. It's all available here on US 64 at Tennessee 314. Watch for the Grumpy's Store sign. In back of the store is, for lack of a more colorful word, a pub. A pub which literally evolved, beginning with paddlers gathering around picnic tables for a little bluegrass music, pea gravel added when the grass stopped growing, then bleachers, all still part of the interior, which now has a wall and roof—of sorts. There's live music on weekends, and a lively mixture of patrons ranging from occassional paddlers to sunburned river rats, campers, curious tourists and a smattering of Polk County residents.

Adjacent to the store is Ocoee Outdoors, the headquarters for 12 years of the Ocoee Pros; about two dozen men and women who are fun-oriented, safety-conscious, skilled and experienced in the ways of the Ocoee rapids and Hiwassee trout. (Make arrangements here for canoe or raft rental and shuttle service for the unguided Hiwassee trips).

The campground is about a quarter mile down the road. No Silver RV Garden, but it does have some full hookups and wooded sites for humble tent campers, clean flush toilets, and bath houses with lots of shower stalls and real hot water. And you'll pay only about half the going rate for your campsite. For more information, contact Ocoee Outdoors, P.O. Box 72, Ocoee, TN 37361; phone 615/338-2438 or toll free out of state, 800-533-7767.

Tellico Plains

A tiny little fish called a snail darter made Tellico a household word back in the late 70's. Would the proposed dam on the Tellico River destroy the habitat (and was it the only habitat) of this suddenly beloved mini-fish? A court battle ensued. The snail darter lost—but is still in abundance in the area's many streams, according to local residents.

Tellico Plains' biggest attraction for mountain vacationers is that it is such a relatively unknown and uncongested area, yet is less than two hours from the Great Smoky Mountains National Park, and less than three hours to the new national park, the Big South Fork (see table of contents). Located at the very edge of the national forest on TN 68, about 30 miles between the Ocoee River area and Sweetwater, Tellico Plains is more a state of mind than a tiny town, said state of mind being primarily loafing—creatively perhaps, but definitely loafing. There's plenty of uncrowded room to loaf in the thousands of acres of national forest covering most of this mountainous area. It's a loafer's glory, all these woods and streams for fishing, hunting, canoeing, tubing (some say gold prospecting in Coker Creek) camping, hiking and photographing four water-falls within 10 miles of town. And taking a scenic side trip to Stratton Meadows, atop a mountain via the Cherohala Skyway (which will eventually connect the national forests of Tennessee and North Carolina at Robbinsville) to view the highest bridge in the southeast; 4,000 feet in elevation and over 700 feet in length.

The best place to get maps, information and directions to various rivers, waterfalls, forest service campgrounds and recreation areas (nine of these!) is to contact the District Ranger Office in Tellico Plains, 615/253-2520. Another good source of information is the booklet, *Appalachian Way* available from the Arrowhead Land Company which offers the following lodging.

Tellico Plains
Arrowhead River Lodges, Cabins & Chalets

T he lodges are new, rustic-designed log chalet efficiencies, clustered on the banks of the Tellico River, near the edge of the national forest. You could almost catch trout from the decks—and there's a fully furnished kitchenette for all meal preparations. Each unit will sleep up to five with queen, doubles and convertible bed/chairs. There is one modern bath, cable television, central heat and air, carpeting and clean comfortable furnishings. Other rentals, each in a secluded area, range from large, luxury log homes to mountaintop efficiencies. For more information, contact Dixie Witt, Arrowhead River Lodge, Inc., Highway 68, Tellico Plains, TN 37385; phone (in TN) 615/253-3670; out of state, toll free, 1-800-251-9658.

Sweetwater

From Sweetwater east it's only a short drive to the Great Smoky Mountains National Park. Going north and west, the dams and lakes of the Tennessee and Little Tennessee Rivers are less than 15 minutes away. Head north on TN 68 in the morning and you'll arrive in the Cumberland Plateau and the Big South Fork National River and Recreation Area in time for a hike before lunch. Or go south on 68 and you'll be in the Cherokee National Forest in minutes. The town is also surrounded by three major highways: I-75, US 11 and TN 68. Surprising that such a central location for mountain vacations should remain such a lovely, quiet and peaceful small town.

Sweetwater
The Lost Sea

Designated a Registered Natural Landmark by the US Department of the Interior, and listed by the Guinness Book of World Records as the "World's Largest Underground Lake," the Lost Sea is part of the vast Craighead Cavern system in East Tennessee. A moderate admission is charged for the guided hour-long cavern tour which includes a glass bottom boat ride on the 4 1/2 acre lake. Visitors should come prepared with flash cameras, and comfortable walking shoes. (There are no steps, but there are a few inclines.) Various rooms contain relics of past usage, from Cherokee Indian council rooms to pioneer food storage and Civil War saltpeter mining. Picnic grounds, nature trails and authentic log cabins housing an ice cream parlor, gift shop and a cafe offering real pit barbeque are located on the grounds off Highway 68, between Sweetwater and Madisonville, 7 miles from I-75, exit 60. Open rain or shine, from 9 a.m. until dusk, daily except Christmas. Lost Sea, Route 2, Box 657, Sweetwater, TN 37874; phone 615/377-6616.

Sweetwater
Fox Trot Inn

It's only about 20 miles to the Great Smoky Mountains National Park from the pleasant little town of Sweetwater. No congestion. No resort town rates. But in this grand Victorian bed and breakfast inn there's plenty of pampering, loads of luxury. You'll find terrycloth robes and fireplaces in the spacious, airy and beautifully furnished guest rooms. The common area includes an extensive library and a TV/VCR with over 100 tapes. There's a porch with swings and rockers, and a lawn and garden set off by an antique iron fence. A short stroll away is Duck Park, populated by a large and pampered flock.

Fox Trot guests are served afternoon tea and a hearty country breakfast. All this European ambience and southern hospitality are made possible by hosts, Lonnie and Merrill Jobe, retirees from Atlanta. Contact them at Fox Trot Inn, 402 May Street, Sweetwater, TN 37874; phone 615/337-4236.

Watts Bar/Spring City
Watts Bar Dam & Lake

W atts Bar, the site of TVA's first coal-fired stream plant, built in 1944, is the only site that now includes a hydroelectric dam, a coal-fired steam plant and a nuclear plant. Visitor facilities include exhibits and a scenic overlook with a panoramic view of the lake and surrounding countryside.

The lake has 39,000 acres of water surface and 783 miles of shoreline for swimming, fishing and boating. Its waters form a link in the nation's inland waterway system, providing a throughfare for water traffic between Knoxville and points downstream and also creates a channel for commercial navigation more then 20 miles up the Clinch River. The dam takes its name from a bar to navigation in the original river bend at Watt Island. The village of Spring City is located at the western tip of the lake, offering access to many of the lake's coves and recreation areas.

Watts Bar/Spring City
Watts Bar Resort

T he serenely beautiful shores of Watts Bar Lake provide the setting with a view for this garden-like 200-acre, family owned and operated resort. Originally built as a self-contained village for the workers constructing Watts Bar Dam, the resort is complete with its own tiny post office. Fifty neat, clean cottages, which sleep one to eight, are spaced for privacy and furnished for family comfort. Some have kitchens, all have color television and air conditioning. There is a large swimming pool with plenty of poolside lounge chairs, a playgound, tennis courts and a launch ramp plus canoe, pontoon and fishing boat rental, wooded trails for hiking and bird watching, and bird houses everywhere with a variety of residents. Bring your bird identification book and binoculars! Bring your flower identification book too. Carlos, the gardener at Watts Bar for many years, makes sure there is always a variety of flowers in bloom at any given time. You'll find them throughout the grounds—and their fresh cut blossoms adorning the dining room tables.

Tabletop-to-ceiling windows provide a view for every restaurant table, of lake, tree-shaded lawn, flowers, and probably the most protected birds in Tennessee. Meals are reasonably priced, from the country breakfasts through luncheon soups, sandwiches, salads and daily specials, to the steaks, chicken and catfish dinners. (The restaurant is open to the public, and offers a pleasant oasis if you are only traveling through to another destination.) The adjoining gift shop offers a variety of vacation related items from film to funwear, wish-you-were-here cards, nice gifts and inexpensive souvenirs. The dam is within walking distance, and within a few miles there are a number of attractions including golf and horseback riding. Hosts Ed and Joyce Probst, and Carl and Kay Hesselbach will be happy to give you more information and directions to exploring this beautiful area. Open April through October. Very moderate rates. Contact Watts Bar Resort, Box M, Watts Bar Dam, TN 37395; phone 1-800-365-9598.

Watts Bar/Spring City
Toestring Cottages & Campground

W aldo and Mary Boyce have turned these ten wooded acres on a pretty cove on Watts Bar Lake into a serene and peaceable place to retreat for a vacation or weekend. There are four roomy, fully and comfortably furnished, spotlessly clean cottages, set among shady trees a few feet from the water, each with its own boat dock. All have two bedrooms, (crib and rollaways available) modern bath, living/dining/kitchen area, A/C, and porches overlooking the lake (bring your binoculars to watch the fish jumping, the birds nesting and the moon shining on misty waters). All have electric heat and two have open woodstove fireplaces. There's a swimming pool plus tot pool for all guests.

In the camping area, sites are large, level and shady, some with pull-throughs and sewer connections, all with water and electric hookups. The bath house is exceptionally clean, the light is always on, and the showers (with private dressing areas) never seem to run out of hot water! The Boyces have thought of everything to help you settle in for your entire stay: laundry, gas dock, pedal boat, boat and motor rentals, bait, fishing licenses, bait, tackle and fish cleaning dock for all those bass, bream, bluegills, catfish and rockfish just waiting for your arrival. Mary and Waldo may even be willing to cook your catch for you and serve you in their little cafe, where you can always get a full breakfast, burgers, fries and other short orders, and even a special request dinner with enough notice. If you wish to explore the area, its only 2½ miles to Highways 68 and 27 at Spring City and nearby attractions in all directions. For rates and reservations, contact Toestring Cottages & Campground, Route 1, Box 395, Spring City, TN 37381; phone 615/365-5712.

Cumberland Plateau/Big South Fork Area

G oing north on 68 there's an abrupt climb to the Cumberland Plateau at the aptly named community of Grandview. (There are two time zones in towns covered here, so remember to ask "CT or ET" when checking opening and closing hours.) In addition to the new national park— The Big South Fork National River and Recreation Area (see contents pages), henceforth to be referred to as the BSFNRRA—the Cumberland Plateau includes beautiful state resort parks, spectacular geological formations and waterfalls, and many historic sites. Its cross-cultural history includes German settlers, an early experimental English community, the pioneering Scots-Irish and a Mennonite community. Its landscape is just as diverse. Well-tended farms are liberally sprinkled on gently rolling hills and in narrow valleys— almost ravines, surrounded by sandstone cliffs. For additional hiking and other information, maps and park information, contact the following: Upper Cumberland Development District at Cookeville, phone 615/432-4111; Tennessee Department of Tourist Development, Nashville, 615/741-2158; (state parks have a toll free reservation number for lodging reservations, 1-800-421-6683), and the BSRNRRA number is 615/879-4890.

Crossville

T he county seat of Cumberland County is a good place to stop for maps and information about the Cumberland Plateau area. The Welcome Center is located at the Chamber of Commerce on US 127 downtown. Contact P.O. Box 453, Crossville, TN 38555; phone 615/484-8444.

Crossville
Homesteads

T his historic community is a remnant of the New Deal Administration of Franklin D. Roosevelt and that adminstration's attempt to deal with the severe rural depression here in the 1930's. The government acquired 10,000 acres of land for a "homesteading" community for 250 local families. Many of the neat little stone cottages built by the "Steaders" can be seen along Highways 68 and 127 south. At the 68/127 junction, an 80-foot octagonal tower, housing a museum detailing the story of the Homesteads experiment, is open to visitors. Climb the tower steps for a view of many of the homesteads. Phone 1/615-484-2697.

Crossville
Cumberland Mountain State Park

O riginally acquired as a recreational area for the above Homesteaders, this 1,720-acre park now includes 37 modern rustic cabins with fully-equipped kitchens, a group lodge (with kitchen) for up to 16 people, a restaurant for reasonably priced buffet meals (breakfast, lunch and dinner) in an attractive dining room overlooking a 50-acre lake, 155 campsites, tennis courts, nature trails, an overnight backpacking trail, canoe and rowboat rental and other recreational opportunities. Located a few miles south of town off US 127. Reservations for cabins may be made by calling the park at 615/484-6138, or toll free out of state, 1-800-421-6683.

Crossville
The Cumberland General Store

A natural outgrowth of the surrounding Homestead community, this old back-to-basics-living mercantile and hardware store still offers hundreds of practical items, all new for home and farmstead. You can browse for hours, and if you can't get there, you can send for their 250-page illustrated catalog, the $3 *Want and Wish Book* and browse from your armchair.

The nearby Mennonite community supplies the store with some products such as harness and tack. Selected crafts from local artisans are also available, including signed, dated and numbered twig chairs, and exquisite handcarved, handpainted birds mounted on driftwood. But the focus is on the functional, from flat-irons to woodburning ranges or wood/electric ranges. Have you a need for nesting eggs? How about well buckets or whetstones? There are toys and toiletries, drygoods for the family and patent medicine for man and beast; tools, utensils and gadgets for the kitchen, barn and blacksmith shop, and you can finish your vacation in a buggy, buckboard or surrey with the fringe on top. You can also bring back some good things to eat, including horehound candy and Original Homestead Hams which are still dry cured and slowly smoked with real hickory (not liquid) smoke. The store is located on US 127 just south of town. For the catalog or information, contact Route 3, Crossville, TN 38555; phone 615/484-8481.

Crossville
Cumberland County Playhouse

"Tennessee's Family Theatre" has multiple meanings for one of the oldest theaters in rural America. "The family" can mean the hundreds of volunteers — cast and crew, from pre-schoolers to senior citizens—who join the resident professional company and staff each season. It can also mean that each season includes, along with classics and current hits, new works on Tennessee subjects, regional classics and works reflecting rural culture. Family would also include the corporate sponsors for the eight plays each season—sponsors like the developers of Fairfield Glade who have helped the Playhouse establish a Living History Series, new works based upon people and events in Tennessee history. The family would also mean the 50,000-plus patrons each season—an audience several times the size of the entire population of Crossville where the theater is located. Reflecting the region's family values a stated goal of this company, formed by a Tennessean, the late Paul Crabtree. His widow, Mary, and son, Jim, are consulting producer and production director, respectively. For the current season's schedule (mid-March to mid-December), ticket prices, group rates and special discounts, contact Cumberland County Playhouse, P.O. Box 484, Crossville, TN 38555; phone 615/484-5000.

Crossville
Fairfield Glade Resort

Whether you want a weekend getaway or an extended vacation, you'll find a warm welcome at this full service resort community. Accommodations range from guest rooms in the 100-room lodge to two-bedroom condominium or villa units. The resort is situated on 12,371 acres of rich forests, fresh water lakes, and outstanding resort facilities including four 18-hole championship golf courses. (Their Stonehenge Golf Course was designated by *Golf Digest* as the best new resort course in the nation in 1985.) A tennis club with four lighted outdoor courts and two indoor courts is also available. The resort has one indoor and two outdoor swimming pools, sauna, whirlpool, miniature golf, marina, boating, fishing, a beach, volleyball, basketball and miles of hiking and jogging trails. Located about 10 miles from town. (Exit 322 off I-40.) For reservations contact Fairfield Glade Resort, P.O. Box 1500, Fairfield Glade, TN 38555. Telephone in Tennessee 1-800-262-6702; out of state 1-800-251-6778.

Clarkrange
Cumberland Mountain General Store

Watch for this old store about 18 miles north of Crossville, 18 miles south of Jamestown on US 127. What's outside is as interesting,—indeed astonishing—as what's inside. Out back and all around are moonshine stills, molasses, grist, soap and cider mills, antique farm equipment, engines, wagons and buggies, what appears to be every iron bedstead ever abandoned, and other assorted junk or Junke, depending on your needs and knowledge. Inside, almost hiding the original 1923 store fixtures, are isles and shelves of merchandise, most of it old, a little of it new, some of it merely outdated, ranging from beautiful, rare and collectible to camp to tacky to downright ugly—keeping in mind that one browser's ugly is another's prize find—and ranging in price from 50 cents to several thousand dollars. There are dolls and dishes, quality crafts and cheap souvenirs, churns, jugs, jars, trunks, and hundreds of other items, some of which you may never have seen before and probably won't see again. The store's five-acre rural location is the site of an annual Homecoming-Harvestfest the first Saturday and Sunday in October. It's free and features demonstrations on the old mills and stills, blue grass, country and gospel music plus games your grandparents might have played. The store is open 9 to 5 weekdays and 12 to 5 on Sundays and is closed January and February. The address is Clarkrange, TN 38553; phone 615/863-3508.

Allardt
Colditz Cove Natural Area

Just south of Jamestown, take TN 52 east to Allardt, population about 700, a prosperous German farming community. Watch for the sign to Colditz Cove, and drive about one mile to the parking area. From there an easy 1.5 mile loop trail will take you to one of the most beautiful spots in the Cumberland Plateau. The focal point is the 60-foot Northrup Falls, named for the family which homesteaded the cove. Colditz Cove was donated to the state as a natural area in the early 1980's by its then current owners, Rudolph and Arnold Colditz. There is a small stream, hundred-year-old hemlock trees, lush flora including rhododendron and laurel, and great overhanging cliffs and "rockhouses," believed to have once been inhabited by cliff-dwelling Indians. The cove is an unusually quiet and peaceful spot, not to be missed while you are in the area. There are no bathroom or picnic facilities.

Rugby
Historic Rugby

This living historic village was founded in 1880 by English author and social reformer, Thomas Hughes, best known in America as author of *Tom Brown's School Days.*

The colony floundered and flourished for a decade; at its peak in 1884, it had 70 buildings and a population of 450. In the early 1900's most of the original colonists were gone, and Rugby had become a small farming community of 125 residents. In 1966 area residents formed Historic Rugby, Inc., a nonprofit organization, to preserve and restore the colony. Seventeen of the original buildings still stand and are on the National Register of Historic Places. A small admission is charged for guided tours. These begin with museum exhibits housed in the visitor center at the Rugby School House, built in 1907 to replace the original 1880 school destroyed by fire. The 1887 Christ Church

Episcopal is on the tour, as is the restored home of Rugby's founder and the Thomas Huges Free Public Library, opened in 1882. A guest register and library cards are from the 1880's and 90's. The thousands of volumes of old and rare books are protected from light and time by heavily shuttered windows, opened only during tours. The tour covers several blocks, so wear comfortable shoes. Tours are from March 1 through December 15, Monday through Saturday 10 to 4:30, Sunday 12 to 4:30.

There is no admission for the following facilities, open year round for lodging, dining and shopping.

Percy Cottage Bookshop

This cottage is a reconstruction of the original built in 1884 by Sir Henry Kimber, a wealthy railroad magnate and chief financial backer of the Rugby colony.

Rugby Craft Commissary

This is also a reconstruction of an original Rugby building which served as a cooperative general store. Now it houses a wide and beautiful selection of high quality, traditional crafts, all made by artisians and craftspeople in the Cumberland Plateau region.

Harrow Road Cafe

Near the site of an 1880's cafe, the Harrow Road Cafe building was constructed by Historic Rugby, Inc., to serve the hundreds of daily visitors. It's a pleasant, informal restaurant, open seven days a week during tour season, with breakfast and lunch daily, and dinner on Friday and Saturday only. The menu offers regional country cooking, some British Isle Specialties, and a super-duper homemade breakfast coffee cake.

Pioneer Cottage

Thomas Hughes slept here in the first frame house in Rugby, built in 1880, as did many of the other colonists, travelers and settlers, until other housing was built. Although its exterior looks pretty much as it did 100 years ago, the interior of the completely restored home offers today's lodgers plenty of comfort. Just the right size for a big family or small group, the cottage has a spacious parlor and three bedrooms with period furnishings, a modern bath-and-a-half, a fully-equipped kitchen and a screened back porch.

Newbury House

"Bed & Tea" is again offered in the colony's first boarding house. Sash and pulley cords on the windows reveal an 1879 date. During the early years, board and lodging was advertised at $4.50 to $6.50 per week, with meals costing 24 cents. No meals now; lodging is average for the area, and complimentary tea or coffee is served to house guests. The completely restored inn has five upstairs bedrooms and a downstairs guest parlor, all with Victorian period furnishings.

Historic Rubgy located on TN 52 between US 127 and US 27. For further information on tours, facilities, rates and reservations, contact Historic Rugby, P.O. Box 8, Rugby, TN 37733; phone 615/628-2441 or -2269.

Jamestown/Big South Fork Area/Oneida
Jamestown

T his little village, population 2,500, is the Fentress County seat. There is a welcome center on Central Avenue just off US 127 downtown on the courthouse square. Near the square is the small Mark Twain Park, containing the spring from where the parents of the writer carried water to their nearby home which now serves as the post office. The park also contains a larger-than-life oak tree sculpture of Twain by local artist, Robert Slaven. Actually Mark Twain never lived here—he was born after the Clemens family moved to Missouri.

The county's most famous resident was World War I hero, Alvin C. York. York helped raise funds to build the Agricultural Institute established in 1926 as a private school for disadvantaged rural youth, now operated by the state as a high school. The school is located on a 400-acre campus on the northern edge of town on US 127. Continue north for seven miles to the community of Pall Mall, in the Wolf River Valley, York's homeplace area and gristmill, a State Historic Site. There is a small museum located at the mill, a picnic area, restrooms, playground and good places for the children to wade in the mill stream.

Across from the York school in Jamestown is the Mountaineer Craft Center, housed in the old County Poorhouse. This is an exceptionally good place to buy handicrafts made by the 100 or so members of the Fentress County Arts and Crafts Association. Articles range from simple pot holders to very nice woodcarvings and are as reasonably priced as you'll find anywhere in the mountains. For more information on Fentress County, contact the Chamber of Commerce, P.O. Box 496, Jamestown, TN 38556; phone 615/879-9948.

Jamestown/Big South Fork Area/Oneida
Highland Manor Winery and Vineyard

Y ou'll need to get on a long waiting list if you want to buy this winery's international gold medal winning Muscadine wine, but you can sometimes sample it here. There are several other varieties for tasting and purchase, also international gold medal winners, including a Chardonnay, a Rosé and a delightfully fruity Riesling. Cumberland Plateau native Fay Wheeler, wife Kathy (originally from Scotland) and Tennessean Irving Martin, (the state's first university-trained enologist) are the principals at Highland Manor. You'll meet Kathy in the tasting room, and the "family" if you take a tour of the wine cellar. It's educational, fun and offers an opportunity to take home award-winning wines available only at this Cumberland Plateau winery. Tour buses are welcome, but an advance call for large groups is appreciated (and wise because the tasting room closes on special holidays). Hours are 10 am to 6 pm (Central Time), Monday through Saturday. Located on US 127, four miles south of town. P.O. Box 213, Jamestown, Tn 38556; phone 615/879-9519.

Jamestown/Big South Fork Area/Oneida
Pickett State Park

L ocated on Highway 154 north near the northwestern edge of the new Big South Fork National River and Recreation Area, this state park also offers vacation rental chalet cabins for those who prefer park lodging over camping when visiting either the state park or the national park. The park area includes interesting geological formations, natural bridges, interesting caves, beautiful timberlands, a variety of vegetation and abundant wildlife. Fishing, boating and a picnicking area are available and camping facilities include a year-round group camp. Hiking trails include a scenic trail to the Sgt. Alvin York's Gristmill and Park, designated a State Historic Area, located about seven miles north of Jamestown in the town of Pall Mall. For cabin reservations, phone 615/879-5821 in state; out of state toll free, 1-800-421-6683.

Jamestown/Big South Fork Area/Oneida
The Beggar's Castle

It's a long, long way from Saarbrucken, Germany to Jamestown, Tennessee. But it's only four miles from Jamestown to Germany. Just turn off TN 127 at the Mobile station in Jamestown and follow the signs. The winding, 13-degree downgrade ends in a verdant glen, a natural garden almost hidden by sandstone cliffs. Across a small stream spanned by a wooden foot bridge, a single-level stone and wood building seems to have grown among the trees. Seating is available in the garden or in the dining room cooled by air pumped from underground. There's a stone fireplace, a cathedral, oak-beamed ceiling, and sturdy tables and chairs all with views of this straight-out-of-a-storybook setting. Start with a fine dark or light German beer. And don't eat too many hunks of black walnut or crusty rye peasant bread with the freshly herbed vegetable soup. Coming up is a chicken Rouladen. Or maybe a meat pie filled with pork, chicken, goat cheese and mushrooms. Or a platter of cheeses and rolls of paper-thin slices of the restaurant's own hams, cured on the premises in the second-generation tradition of German-born chef/proprietor Roger Salomon. The menu includes schnitzels, bratens and wursts, side dishes of wine sauerkraut, hot potato salad, mushrooms in shallot butter sauce, whole sauteed green beans coated with a rich cream. The tempting dessert list includes lizen tortes, cheese cakes, and brandied apricots with whipped cream and shaved chocolate. On Saturday evening there are special musical programs. The restaurant is open from 11:30 Tuesday through Sunday, closing at 10 weeknights, at 11 on Saturday, and at 8 on Sunday. Reservations are advised but are not required. Telephone 615/879-9815 or -8993.

Jamestown/Big South Fork Area/Oneida
Angel Falls Overlook/(Hike in BSFNRRA)

The following hike is recommended by Brenda Coleman and JoAnna Smith, authors of *Hiking the Big South Fork*, published by the University of Tennessee Press. The book is available or can be ordered from most book stores and outfitter shops in the area, and from the Big South Fork National River and Recreation Area visitor center gift shop at the Bandy

Angel Falls Overlook

Creek Campground. Highway 297 between Jamestown and Oneida is the only auto access to the Tennessee portion of the Big South Fork and the Bandy

Creek Campground. (For more extensive information on the Big South Fork, see the table of contents.)

Angel Falls Overlook, one of the most scenic trails in the Big South Fork Area, gives you a spectacular view of the river and gorge. The 6-mile round trip hike, rated difficult, begins from the Leatherwood Ford Trail area where the highway crosses the river. Begin this hike by crossing the river on the old wooden bridge. The trail, a portion of the blue and white-blazed John Muir Trail, follows the river northward past several rapids. In about two miles, the trail turns to follow the rhododendron-filled valley of Fall Branch. At a wooden footbridge you can rest and watch the river swirl around large boulders below. The last mile is the most strenuous as you climb stone steps and begin the ascent to the ridgetop. Opposite a large overhang, a side trail gives a beautiful view of the Fall Branch watershed. When the trail seems to disappear, climb up to the rock shelf and carefully make your way around to the right. The trail, using a short ladder and several switchbacks, ascends the narrow gap in the bluff. At the intersection with the Grand Gap Loop, turn right and follow the trail a short distance to the Angel Falls Overlook.

The authors suggest a half day for this hike, and include several warnings about narrow sheer ledges and the unprotected overlook. Not recommended for inexperienced hikers or families with children.

Jamestown/Big South Fork Area/Oneida
The Big South Fork National River and Recreation Area

F or more extensive coverage of this new national park, see the table of contents where it is listed with other national lands covered in this book. The park has over 100,000 acres, offering opportunities for wilderness and developed camping, rafting, canoeing, fishing, hunting, hiking and horseback riding. For an especially scenic tour, desending into and out of the gorge of the Big South Fork of the Cumberland River, take the only road offering automobile access to the Tennessee section of the park, TN 297 between Jamestown and Oneida. The Visitor Center is located off the highway at the Bandy Creek Campground. Telephone 615/879-4890.

Jamestown/Big South Fork Area/Oneida
Charit Creek Lodge

L ocated deep in the Big South Fork National River and Recreation Area, this wilderness outpost is accessible only by foot or horseback and the shortest trail, just under one mile, begins from a remote parking area near Pickett State Park. Whether you hike or go in by horse, take the short trail or one of many others connecting to Charit Creek, getting there is half the fun.

When you arrive you'll find a creek to cool your feet, a rocking chair to rest your seat, and a cool glass of lemonade to tide you over 'til mealtime. As a lodge guest, you will be served a hearty dinner and ditto breakfast. Lunch is only by reservation for lodge guests and the general hiking and horseback riding public. (For horses there is hay at the stables or grazing in the pasture.) The creek is not the only running water here; there are complete restroom facilities, even showers, partially supplied by solar energy. But the only light at the lodge is supplied by sun, moon, stars, fireflies, kerosene lamps, and your own flashlight. Don't forget it. Private rooms or cabins are limited in number and can only be reserved for a minimum of six people. Two large bedrooms with many bunkbeds in the main lodge are the favored sleeping facilities.

Charit Creek is now managed by an authorized national park service concession, LeConte Lodge, Inc. If that name sounds familiar, it should—visitors to the Great Smoky Mountains make reservations as far as a year in advance to hike a minimum of 5.5 miles for a visit to their lodge on the summit of Mount LeConte (see Gatlinburg table of contents), so you know that this company knows how to create congenial surroundings in the wilderness and a warm glow at the end of the trail. For complete information, rates and reservations, contact Charit Creek Lodge, P.O. Box 350, Gatlinburg, TN 37738; phone 615/430-3333.

Jamestown/Big South Fork Area/Oneida
Oneida

Located on US 27 and TN 297, the eastern gateway to the Big South Fork National River and Recreation Area, this pleasant little city of about 3,000, the county seat of Scott County, offers motel lodging and reasonably priced good hot food and several places to replenish supplies before heading into the Big South Fork. There's a friendly welcome center at the Chamber of Commerce on US 27 at the northern edge of town; phone 615/569-6900.

Jamestown/Big South Fork Area/Oneida
Tobe's Motel & Restaurant

"Tobe's" is not only the restaurant and motel nearest the entrance to the Big South Fork, it has been *the* place to eat and lodge in Scott County since 1934. It has also been in the same family since then. (The third generation recently completed a large gazebo on the grounds, dedicated to Grandmother Tobe Phillips.) The family has always kept Tobe's up-to-date. A new swimming pool was installed a few years ago. Guest rooms, many with sofas and large enough for suites, are pleasantly decorated and offer modern tub/shower baths, color television, room phones, and individually controlled heat and air. Lodging units are on a shady hillside away from the street in a garden-like setting. The gazebo, large enough for 12 picnic tables, may be reserved without charge for family reunions and such, unless the Phillips' are planning a barbeque there and or entertainment for their motel guests.

The restaurant offers truly well prepared and hearty country fare, from breakfast through dinner. Noon features exceptionally bountiful lunch specials, and the dinner menu offers variety, from sandwiches to steaks to Creole style fish. Everything is Grade A and AAA recommended—and most reasonably priced. Located on US 27, north of the TN 297 turn-off to the Big South Fork. For reservations, contact Tobe's Motel, Oneida, TN 37841; phone 615/569-8581.

Towns Around the Tennessee Smokies

As you approach Tennessee's side of the Great Smoky Mountains (covered more extensively under National Lands—see contents), you'll have a number of choices for vacation essentials like food and lodging in the small towns and villages surrounding the park. There's also plenty of shopping, attractions and amusements to compete with the scenic beauty and outdoor activities of the most visited national park in America. Except for some congestion in the most visited towns during peak times, there are no traffic problems. Only one road crosses the entire park: the US 441 Parkway between Gatlinburg, Tennessee and Cherokee, North Carolina. The other main entrance into the park is on US 73 at Townsend which connects with the Parkway at the Sugarland Visitor Center just inside the park's Gatlinburg entrance. To explore all the small towns and communities around the park's boundary, take US 321 between the Townsend area and I-40. US 321 is also the main travel route to the historic Upper East Tennessee section, and to connecting roads into communities surrounded by the Cherokee National Forest.

Townsend/Wear Valley

Townsend is a pleasant little valley town on US 321 and Scenic Highway 73 which enters the Great Smokies National Park at the edge of town and connects with the US 441 Parkway at Sugarland Visitor Center near Gatlinburg. Townsend is the town nearest to the most visited section of the national park, Cades Cove. (See table of contents for information on the national park.) US 321 meanders through the lovely Wear Valley between Townsend and Pigeon Forge. Stop at the Visitor Center on 321/73 for more information and maps, including the *Foot of Ol' Smoky Bikeway* booklet with maps of bicycle trails along miles of scenic secondary roads through hills and valleys at the foot of the Smokies. In spite of being located at the entrance to the most visited national park in America, Townsend remains quiet, unspoiled and uncongested, and rightly bills itself as "The Peaceful Side of the Smokies." Contact the Chamber of Commerce for additional information, P.O. Box 66, Townsend, TN 37882; phone 615/448-6651.

Townsend/Wear Valley
Tuckaleechee Caverns

A trip through these caverns gives new meaning to the word "cavernous." Guided tours are conducted every thirty minutes along well-lighted, paved paths and steps, following a stream down and through large passageways connecting the several enormouns "rooms"—the largest in eastern America's caves. Stalactites and stalagmites grow from ceilings and floors, sometimes meeting to form large columns. A high, wide, double-tiered "waterfall" has been formed by millions of years of moisture dripping down cave walls. A real waterfall pours into the largest cavern, from where, no one knows, as exploring its source would be too dangerous, even for professional spelunkers. Open daily 9 to 6, April through October. For more information contact Tuckaleechee Caverns, Route 1, Townsend, TN 37882; phone 615/448-2274.

Townsend/Wear Valley
Little River Pottery & Country Store

This small white cottage is the studio and shop of Jim and Alice Nichols. Alice creates needlepoint art and minds the store. Jim is a folk potter, producing functional pottery that is simple in design, decoration, glazing, and is lead free, dishwasher and oven safe. Visitors may watch him at his wheel during evening hours and on weekends.

In addition to complete place settings, Jim produces candle lanterns, honey pots, mugs, vases and other unique gift items. The shop also features a selection of authentic mountain crafts—quilts, door harps, baskets, brooms, walking canes, and the handcarved and handpainted carousel horses from the High Country Collection. The store also has collectibles—old tools, pretty glassware and dishes. Located on 321/73 along the banks of the Little Tennessee River. Contact Box 143, Townsend, TN 37882; phone 615/448-6440.

Townsend/Wear Valley
Tremont Hills Campground

Bordered by the Great Smoky Mountains National Park and the Little River, this private campground has that basic amenity not available at park campgrounds—showers. And they have hot water too! It also has several little luxuries, some especially appreciated by families, such as a large swimming pool, wading pool, recreation room, playground, laundry and a store for replenishing food and supplies.

There are roomy and shady sites for tents and full hookups for RV's, many along the river's edge. Catch your dinner without leaving the premises—the river is stocked with trout. There are good wading, tubing and swimming areas a short walk up the road into the park. You can jog to the park, take a hike or bike ride, and a few minutes by car will take you to Cades Cove, Gatlinburg, and Dollywood in Pigeon Forge. This lovely campground is lovingly maintained and happily operated by new owners from Florida, Rob and Sherry Hill. Contact them if you want reservations, or just stop in. Located on Scenic Highway 73 near the park entrance. Tremont Hills Campground, Box 5, Townsend, TN 37882; phone 615/448-6363.

Townsend/Wear Valley
Davy Crockett Riding Stables and Bed & Breakfast Horse Barn

J. C. Morgan, who has operated stables since 1967, is the owner/operater of this lovely spot, adjacent to the following cabins and accessed through the following campground, all located next door to the national park. This is the fun place for 1 to 2 hours of guided rides where cantering is allowed for experienced riders, and for the overnight pack trips to J. C.'s private camp shelter. Bring your own food and drink for a moonlight cookout. Horses for all level of riders are available all day long with no appointment necessary except for the overnights, requiring a minimum of three people. You can also "bed and breakfast" your own horse overnight or for your entire vacation, in a new ten-stall barn. Open all year. Contact J. C. at Davy Crockett Stables, Hwy 73, Townsend, TN 37882; phone 615/448-6411.

Townsend/Wear Valley
Smoky Mountain Log Cabins

A lmost at the entrance to the Great Smoky Mountains National Park, across the driveway from the Davy Crockett Stables in the quiet cove on the banks of the Little River, these cabins are in an ideal location for a Smoky Mountains getaway. The cabins are equally ideal, with wood burning masonry fireplaces, decks and porches (some right over the river), color cable television, fully furnished kitchens, two to six bedrooms, with one to three baths. Furnished for comfort and convenience from living room sleeper sofas to porch swings and rockers, charcoal grills and picnic tables. Exceptionally moderate rates, from overnight to the season. Built, owned, beautifully maintained and operated by third generation residents of the area. Contact Jerry Grant, Smoky Mountain Log Cabins, Inc. P.O. Box 115, Townsend, TN 37882; phone 615/448-6016 or 579-0326 (evenings).

Townsend/Wear Valley
Laughing Horse Inn

T his small, quiet, one-level inn is located near the entrance to the national park on the banks of the Little River. It has the charm of a country inn, with some nice extras like television, air conditioning, electric heat, modern private baths with tub and shower, and two of its six deluxe units have kitchens. All the rooms are exceptionally large, with lots of windows that open to the fresh mountain air. Each is individually and pleasantly decorated, and each has access to the big rocker-lined front porch, or to back porches within a few feet of the river. It's a place that everyone loves and wants to return to, so reservations should be made as early as possible. You will occasionally find a vacancy on a spur-of-the-moment trip, but this is usually the first place filled in Townsend. Innkeepers Louis and Violeta Grief will make you feel right at home, all through the seasons, right up through the winter holidays. They are closed for a short time early in the year but re-open early enough for springtime in the Smokies. For rates and reservations contact Laughing Horse Inn, Route 1, Box 90, Townsend, TN 37882; phone 615/448-6316.

Townsend/Wear Valley
Strawberry Patch Inn & Antique Shop

C hoose a fireplace suite in an 1860's restored log inn, with a deck beside the Little River. Or a separate cabin high on a cliff over the river. Or a suite above the shop, large enough for up to 12 people, with sliding glass doors to a secluded riverview deck. Or several sizes in between, each offering a variety of features ranging from skylights to a kingsize waterbed and a mirrored ceiling. Most have fully equipped kitchens; all are air conditioned and have cable TV and HBO.

Hosts Ted and Linda Wright have supplied everything you'll need for convenience, and have added a few "no-charge" extras just for fun, like the tubes for river tubing (you may swim and fish too, right here in the inn's back yard). They even keep bikes handy so guests can explore the Townsend bike trails. There are shady riverside picnic tables and grills on the spacious lawn. The inn's lobby is an antique shop, featuring a variety of keepsakes and collectibles including some real finds in old and rare books. Reservations require a two-night minimum; one nights are on available basis. Family and group rates are available, and there's a 25% discount January through March. Pets are accepted. Contact Strawberry Patch Inn, US Highway 321, Townsend, TN 37882; phone 615/448-6303.

Townsend/Wear Valley
Von-Bryan Inn Bed & Breakfast & Guest House

S unrise. Sunset. A 360 degree view of a starry, starry sky and a moonlight bathed world. The view alone would make a visit to this mountaintop getaway worthwhile. But there are more than a few other enticements. There's a kidney shaped pool with private dressing area. And in the Garden Room, a 10 person hot tub. Inside the many-windowed, contemporary log inn, the views are still there from every room—of Wear Valley and the Smokies.

Five spacious guest rooms include a red and white sweetheart of a honeymoon suite with a private jacuzzi. There's a great room that's really great, and a stone fireplace to match. If you can tear yourself away from the views, there are lots of books and magazines, TV and games. You may have evening refreshments on the porch or deck, and a large sumptious breakfast is served in the antique furnished dining room. The separate log "guest house," on one corner of these six heavenly acres, has fireplace, decks and can accommodate up to six.

If you'd like even more extras—like not having to leave this place for your entire stay, your hosts, D.J. and Jo Ann Vaughn, will be happy to customize your visit, from helicopter taxi to special dinners to picnic baskets; from group gatherings to honeymoon packages; from corporate retreats to mountaintop weddings. Guests are welcome all year, and there is a 10% discount on stays of two or more nights. Von Bryan Inn, Route 7, Box 91A, Sevierville, TN 37862; phone 615/453-9832 or toll free out of state 1-800-633-1459.

Townsend/Wear Valley
Old Smoky Mountain Cabins, Duplexes & Inn

N estled on wooded mountain acreage in various Townsend locations, these private cabins, duplexes and the inn come in all sizes from the one-bedroom honeymoon hideaways with fireplace and jacuzzis to the inn with its 10-person jacuzzi and five complete units which can accommodate individuals, couples or groups of up to 20 people.

Built by local builders, native to the area, James Webb, Sr. and James Webb Jr., all are finished beautifully down to the last decorating and furnishing details. All units have cable TV, phones, full modern baths and completely equipped kitchens. There are many large windows for expansive views, decks and porches, hot tubs or jacuzzis, barbeque grills and comfortable to luxurious furnishings from linens to deck chairs. Everything is within 10 minutes of the national park. The Webbs are always available to make sure everything is just right. For further information, rates and reservations, contact Bobbi Webb, Old Smoky Mountain Cabins, Highway 321. Box 437, Townsend, TN 37882; phone 615/448-2388.

Pigeon Forge/Sevierville

P igeon Forge is to the Smokies what Panama City Beach is to the Florida Gulf Coast; a "miracle strip" of amusements, entertainment, shops, motels, and restaurants. Although it's only eight miles from the national park, this is where the action really is for youngsters—of any age. From the southern end of town where the highway leads to Gatlinburg or the national park to the Sevierville/Pigeon Forge city boundary line, US 441 is a maze of helicopter rides, indoor skydiving, miniature golf, magic worlds, thrill rides, musical entertainment featuring country and gospel, and the biggest attraction in the Smokies next to the park itself: the Dollywood theme park.

It's all family-style fun in Pigeon Forge (no bars or cocktail lounges) but that favorite of all adult entertainment is here by the acre: shopping. Outlet stores —entire outlet mall/cities seem to spring up overnight like mushrooms after a rain. Shoppers come by the busloads looking for bargains in everything from cookware to underwear. There is an abundance of restaurants, from fine dining to fast food and 40-odd motels offer accommodations with a lot of emphasis on family rates. Bed and Breakfast inns are starting to catch on here. And there are campgrounds along the Little Pigeon in and around the town.

Traffic moves relatively well along the divided parkway with right and left turn lanes. For trips into Gatlinburg, there's a park-and-ride trolley stop between the towns, and you can drive the bypass into the national park. For a free 16-page color brochure with maps and directory, contact Veta Wilson, Pigeon Forge Department of Tourism, PO Box 209, Pigeon Forge, TN 37863; phone 615/453-8574 in state or toll free out of state, 1-800-251-9100.

Pigeon Forge/Sevierville
The Apple Barn and Cider Mill

A few yards off US 441 where Pigeon Forge and Sevierville meet, visitors may stroll along the park-like banks of the Little Pigeon River and look up at an entire hillside planted in neat rows of apple trees. This is Riverbend Farm, a place to enjoy the fragrance of the apple blossoms in spring, and sample all the fruit at harvest time. There's a large parking lot (people come by the busloads to this lovely place), benches on the grounds and plenty to see, do, smell and taste; so give yourself lots of time.

Adjacent to the big white apple barn is the modern apple kitchen, with a viewing window. Fried pies, baked pies, apple dumplings, candied apples, apple donuts and apple muffins are prepared here. The Cider Bar in the apple barn serves these treats still warm from the kitchen, or you can order them packed in boxes-to-go. They also serve ham biscuits from an adjacent smokehouse where ham and bacon are smoked slowly with hickory and applewood. Aromatic yes, but nothing like stepping into the apple barn during harvest season! Hundreds of bags, boxes and bushels fill the barn with a tantalizing, tempting aromatic mixture of Jonathans, Rome Beauties, Winesaps, Red and Golden Delicious, Granny Smiths, Stayman, Criterion, Empire, Paula Reds and Mutsu—a cross between a Golden Delicious and a Japanese apple.

The 1910 barn, which has been scoured and scrubbed, painted white and floored with white planks, also houses stalls of gifts, crafts, and other food items such as the hams and bacon, Tennessee chedder cheese, jams, jellies, molasses, honey and relishes. For further information contact Riverbend Farm Apple Barn, 230 Lonesome Valley Road, Sevierville, TN 37862; phone 615-453-9319.

Pigeon Forge/Sevierville
Applewood Farmhouse Restaurant

T his country-good restaurant is located a few yards up Lonesome Valley road from the Apple Barn. The classic farmhouse is framed by almost 4000 apple trees, and the Little Pigeon continues its route near the front door. Whether you breakfast, lunch or dine, on the sunporch, in the parlor or the country kitchen, the decor is enticing and so are the menu choices. Dinners can be as uptown as poisson de coquille or as downhome as barbeque ribs. The trout is smoked with (guess what?) applewood, and served with dill sauce. Desserts are just as sensational and if you can't decide whether to have pie or cake, you can have both here: the apple pie cake. Just about everything is touched with the magic of apples at this really special restaurant. Open every day of the year—8 am to 9 pm, ('til 10 on Friday and Saturday). Just off 441 where Sevierville and Pigeon Forge meet. Phone 615/428-1222.

Pigeon Forge/Sevierville
Old Mill & Craft Village Area

T urn at traffic light #2, to an old mill on the banks of the Little Pigeon River. This is where Pigeon Forge began—and where the town got its name. The forge is gone and so are the thousands of pigeons that flocked to feed on the grain spilled around the mill. But the mill is still working and is listed on the National Register of Historic Places. Grinding is still done on the original two-ton French Buhrs. The river turns the 24-foot wheel to produce products for sale in the mill store: white and yellow cornmeal, grits, cracked wheat, wheat bran, wholewheat, rye, barley, buckwheat and unbleached white flour. Tours of the mill are conducted repeatedly throughout the day for which a small admission is charged. Phone 615/453-4628. (Several quality shops in the Old Mill Area include the following.)

Ward Brothers Primitive Country Furniture

Across from the old mill, this shop carries pine furniture by the Ward family who has been building these sturdy pieces by hand for five generations. The selection includes hutches, dry sinks and pie safes, some handcarved with traditional designs, all finished with an oil base and rubbed to a warm glow. There are special pieces for children—doll cradles, chairs, trunks and wooden toys. Open Monday through Saturday, 9 to 7 during the season. If the showroom is closed, the mailing address is Route 3, Box 539, Seaton Spring Road, Sevierville, TN 37862; phone 615/453-7762; at the Old Mill Area shop, phone 615/428-1872.

Pigeon River String Instrument

The Appalachian dulcimer and other handcrafted string instruments, including banjos and lovely celtic harps, are available here. The word "dulcimer" means "sweet sound," and you can often catch the sound accompanied by the voices of Bob and Anne Lazenby performing a spontaneous concert at their shop. The Lazenbys have been making these instruments by hand since 1974, some with overlays or inlays of mother-of-pearl or rosewood. All are made of select walnut, cherry, maple, spruce or mahogany. The shop also has kits for making your own instruments and a selection of music, song and instruction books of traditional and folk music. Phone 615/453-3789.

Broken Anvil Forge

Charlie Fuller is a real blacksmith and this is a real blacksmith shop. Don't expect a "show" here but do expect to enjoy your visit. No matter how busy Charlie is, he will welcome you and answer your questions. You can watch him at work and browse among works he has created; fireplace andirons and grates, iron and copper candlesticks and chandeliers, hinges and door pulls, clocks and pot hangers. Charlie has studied his craft under the masters and it shows. If you have a special project in mind, bring a sketch or just an idea, whether for railings, fences, or perhaps an elegant iron screen for your fireplace. Open 9 to 5 daily "except Sundays during the winters and once in a while for vacation." Phone 615/453-1933.

Waynehouse Artcrafts

Tiny handcrafted and handpainted bird pins by Wilray, stained glass and woodcrafts by Taylor are featured in this shop owned by the two artists. The perfect little replicas of exquisite hummingbirds, cardinals, jays, robins and other species are ideal gifts for birdwatchers. Taylor's replicas of pink and white dogwood blossoms are used in his woodcrafts and his stained glass art.

The shop also carries the work of other craftspeople and a selection of cook-books. This is a good place to shop for little unusual gifts with modest prices. Open 9 to 5 daily during the season, weekends only in the off-season, closed during January and February. Phone 615/453-6798.

Pigeon Forge Pottery

This may be one of the largest, most beautiful pottery shops you'll ever visit —certainly the largest where you can "see it made." Douglas Ferguson is the master potter here (fourth generation), working with dozens of other crafts-people, carefully trained to produce all the different items attractively displayed in the spacious gallery. Also on display and on sale is the pottery of Jane Ferguson, a fifth generation potter whose origins are from the potters of Stoke-on-Trent, England. A graduate of California Arts and Crafts at Berkley, Jane's creations are primarily one of a kind, formed both at the potter's wheel and by hand-building techniques. Every item in the shop is made from local clay, and glazes are made from minerals gathered in the Smokies. Each is hand decorated and signed with the Pigeon Forge Potter's mark. Phone 615/453-3883.

Pigeon Forge/Sevierville
Blue Mountain Mist Country Inn

There are unexpected luxuries in this bed and breakfast inn, set on a hillside meadow framed by the Great Smokies. You can enjoy the view from the backyard hot tub as well as from the wraparound porch. Two of the 12 spacious guest rooms have in-room jacuzzis, one behind a beautiful stained-glass dividing wall, the other located in the corner turret. Two other rooms feature a deep, old-fashioned claw-foot bathtub in a tiled corner; all rooms have a private bath, individually controlled heat and air conditioning, and comfortable antique furnishings. Each level of the Victorian-style inn has a living room with a fireplace, always lighted for gatherings on cool evenings, or guests may gather in the TV and game room. Smoking is allowed on the rocking chair porches. There's a full country breakfast or, for early or late risers, a deluxe continental breakfast. In spite of the quiet country location, the inn is less than 4 miles from the heart of Pigeon Forge. Contact innkeepers Norman and Sarah Ball, Blue Mountain Mist Country Inn, Route 3, Box 490, Sevierville, TN 37862; phone 615/428-2335.

Pigeon Forge/Sevierville
Hidden Mountain Log Cabins & Chalets

This is luxury in the middle of a forest. Hot tubs, fireplaces and waterbeds are some of the choice amenities in these 120 handhewn log cabins and chalets, secluded in thickets of trees and wildflowers along Smoky Mountain coves and ridges on several acres of Hidden Mountain woodlands. (The mountain really is named Hidden Mountain.)

The decorating is outstanding and everything is spotlessly clean. Each chalet and cabin comes equipped with everything—modern kitchens and baths, color TV, heat and air conditioning, large decks, chairs, grills and tables . . . even maid service. If you are thinking this might cost a fortune, think again and figure the cost of a four-course dinner for four in downtown Gatlinburg—that's about the cost of a cottage for four. There are more amenities, including a big swimming pool and small stocked pond for fishing with no license needed. Open all winter. Hidden away just off the country road leading to Wear Valley, Townsend, Cades Cove and the Great Smoky Mountains National Park. It's only a few minutes into Pigeon Forge and Gatlinburg. For free brochure, rates and reservations contact Hidden Mountain Resort, Route 5, Box 338A, Sevierville, TN 37862; phone 616/453-9850.

Gatlinburg

This famous little mountain resort is located on US 441 at the main entrance to the Great Smoky Mountains National Park. In 1935, US 441 was still a gravel road and tourism here was only a gleam in the eyes of a few of early settlers. Unfortunately the road, now paved, is not much wider, although Gatlinburg now hosts many of the eight-million-plus annual visitors to the national park. Traffic congestion is the big complaint here, but it needn't be; little trolleys travel the streets constantly, taking you anywhere you want to go for only 25 cents, even to outlying communities. And you have to *stroll* the town in order to really discover and appreciate it. Gatlinburg is built alongside, and on the islands of the boulder-filled Little Pigeon River and several other mountain streams. Native tree and shrubs along walkways, the sounds of rushing waters, little shop-filled cobble-stone backstreet areas, or wooden foot bridges to island restaurants or lodging facilities, crowds of honeymooners, families, old and young vacationers, all mingle together to create the unique sights, sounds and experiences of Gatlinburg. So park your car in your lodging parking lot or in one of the several private lots and go explore. Stop at the visitor center on the parkway (public parking here, too) for all sorts of information. Phone 615/436-4178; out of state, call toll free 1-800-822-1998.

Gatlinburg
Sweet Fanny Adams Theatre

The two-hour show here is alone worth a trip to Gatlinburg. Each season this madcap troup of thespians produces and presents two different original musical comedies which alternate nightly. Nothing is ever quite as you expect it to be at Sweet Fanny Adams where the evening's fun ends with an exceedingly unusual sing-along. You'd better sing. Big talent, tiny theatre, reserved seats only for nightly shows at 8, closed Sunday. Phone 615/436-4038.

Gatlinburg
John Cody Gallery

Paintings of some of the most exquisitely colored moths in the world are on display at this unique gallery. This is the exclusive showcase for the work of Dr. John Cody, who has been honored with a one man show in the Museum of Natural History in New York, and had eleven of his moth paintings featured in the May, 1986 issue of Audubon Magazine. Dr. Cody, of Hays, Kansas, who has been a practicing psychiatrist for over two

decades, painted his first moth at age five. He is also the author of the widely acclaimed book, *After Great Pain: The Inner Life of Emily Dickinson,* and a recent large work on Wagner.

Dr. Cody has completed paintings of more than 30 of these colorful silk moths—large, magnificent saturniids from all across the globe. They are for sale exclusively in Gatlinburg where he and Barbara Huff-Beville formed a partnership and opened the John Cody Gallery. The gallery is housed in the distinctive gift shop, Barbara's Elegants in Riverbend Mall at the intersection of US 441 and US 321. For more information contact the John Cody Gallery, 45 Parkway, Gatlinburg, TN 37738; phone 615/436-6492.

Gatlinburg
The Arrowcraft Shop

O ne of Gatlinburg's oldest and finest shops, Arrowcraft was established in 1926 by the women of Pi Beta Phi. Sales from the shop benefit regional craftspeople and Arrowmont, the adjacent accredited School of Arts and Crafts. The gallery-like setting offers all kinds of moderately priced arts and crafts. Wall hangings, linens, afghans, and clothing items are all handwoven exclusively for Arrowcraft. There's pottery, traditional and contemporary basketry, crafts of wood, metal, fibers, paper, glass and more. There is also free parking at the shop located near the Welcome Center on US 441 Parkway. Phone 615/436-4604.

Gatlinburg
Burning Bush Restaurant

T his is one of Gatlinburg's favorite restaurants for breakfast, brunch, and dinner. Its parking lot seldom has an empty space, but you can walk or take the trolley to the door where you'll receive a warm welcome and a meal to remember. For breakfast there are specialties like eggs Florentine, French toast, and a list of "bountifuls" which *include* eggs, grits, gravy, stewed apples, sliced tomatoes, buttermilk biscuits and *eleven* choices of meat ranging from country sausage to quail, trout and filet mignon. Oversleep and you can still enjoy the breakfast until 2 or the brunch beginning at 11: filet burgers, grilled chicken breasts, exquisite salads or country ham with red-eye gravy. There's a wine list, plus beer and cocktails, too.

Thirty-two dinner entrees range from continental to mountain delicacies and include brace of quail, shrimp scampi, lobster tail, mountain trout and crabmeat jambalaya. The restaurant has a wonderful way with vegetables including a cream of cauliflower soup and a marinated broccoli salad. For youngsters a special menu includes dessert. Prices are a bit above average for the mountains, but so is the food, service and atmosphere, and there's a 20% Sunset Discount from 5 to 6 for dinner. Reservations are not required but are suggested. Located on the parkway a few feet from the entrance to the park, and open 365 days a year. Phone 615/436-4669.

Gatlinburg
Pioneer Inn Restaurant

The Pioneer Inn has been a Gatlinburg tradition since 1933 when this town was little more than a logging camp. Logs were used to build this haven for travelers, a warm place with a hot meal by a crackling fire. The tradition is still the same, but now there's a few more choices on the menu. For breakfast there are hotcakes, waffles, Tennessee country ham with redeye gravy, biscuits, eggs, grits and more plus a never empty mug of real good coffee. For lunch you can choose pot pies, casseroles, fried chicken, chops, trout, roast beef sandwiches, salads, soups with cornbread sticks and big burgers with fancy trimmings. Dinner offers a Pioneer Game Pie combining quail, pheasant, duckling, onions and potatoes topped with a pastry crust. There's also prime rib, steaks, lamb chops and seafood entrees including a shellfish casserole combining lobster, shrimp and crabmeat with celery, onions and a wonderful sauce. The pioneers may have had elderberry, plum or dandelion wine, but you'll have to settle for Paul Masson, Bolla Soave . . . or maybe a California Cooler. Watch for the log house (to which awnings have been added) near the northern end of the US 441 Parkway. You can take the trolley or park across the street. Reservations are not necessary but are accepted for dinner. Phone 615/436-7592.

Gatlinburg
Teague Mill Restaurant

This place down in Webb's Creek Hollow used to be the best kept secret in the Smokies, but it got to be so good and word kept spreading and now nearly everyone seems to be going to see what all the fuss is about—and then coming back for more. It's about dining on the edge of a mountain stream lined with laurel, rhododendron and magnificent mountain magnolia; dining on trout you have just caught, or had caught for you, served with cole slaw and hush puppies—or chicken peglegs (sounds scrawny but they're good) or country ham. There's iced tea too, and homemade biscuits and desserts. Terry Arterburn and David Bailey invite you and your family (kids love to fish for the trout) to come join their families at this unique mountain place, 13 miles north of town on US 321. Look for the smokehouse beside the road—the restaurant is really down in the hollow and so is the Teague Mill. Take a creekside stroll on brick terraces and pathways to this old working mill where you can purchase cornmeal, grits, wholewheat flour, sourwood honey, sorghum molasses, peanut brittle, jams, jellies and country cured ham and bacon. Open every day from 5 to 9. For a mail order list of the Teague Mill store items, contact The Teague Mill, Webb's Creek Hollow, Route 3, Box 666, Gatlinburg, TN 37738; phone 615/436-8869.

Gatlinburg
The Buckhorn Inn

A small country inn built in 1938, the Buckhorn is nicely secluded on 40 acres, located 1½ miles from the Greenbrier entrance to the Great Smoky Mountains National Park. The inn's 6 guest rooms and 4 cottages all have separate baths and are comfortably furnished with antiques. The beauty of the large elegant living/dining room with its mountain stone fireplace is topped only by spectacular views of Mount LeConte, visible from the many windows. Enjoy the view with the full breakfast included in the lodging. A gourmet dinner is optional and is by reservation only. Open all year. Contact John and Connie Burns, Route 3, Box 393, Gatlinburg, TN 37738; phone 615-436-4668.

Gatlinburg
Copeland Creek Log Cabins

S tone fireplaces, large jacuzzis, queensize beds, a "courtin' swing" on the porch and a honeymoon special will appeal to the romantic. For the practical, there's a choice of one or two bedrooms in these new hand-hewn log cabins, free firewood in winter months, fully furnished kitchens, modern baths, comfortable, contemporary furnishings, a choice of settings on either a wooded mountaintop or in a country meadow. Both locations are quiet and convenient; a few hundred yards from the Little Pigeon River, three miles from horseback riding facilities (and stables if you bring your own horse), hiking trails close enough to walk to, one-half mile from the Greenbrier entrance to the Great Smoky Mountains National Park, three miles from an 18-hole golf course, seven miles from downtown Gatlinburg, and two miles to the trolley to take you there and bring you back so you can avoid parking hassles. Good rates and helpful, pleasant owners/managers Austin Green and family will be your neighbors and storekeepers. The Greens have been here for three generations—you want to know anything about the area, just ask. For rates and reservations, contact them at Copeland Creek Log Cabins, Route 3, Box 951, Gatlinburg, TN 37738; phone 615/436-6143.

Gatlinburg
Huff's Motel & Cottages

W hen Jim Huff chose the site for Gatlinburg's first resort cottages back in the mid-thirties, he did it right. Bordered by LeConte Creek just before it flows into the Little Pigeon River; near enough to the national park for a brisk walk; on spacious grounds shaded by large maples; set well back from what was then a little used road through a sleepy mountain village. He also suggested to city officials that the new highway, built in 1939–40, ought to be a six-lane. But at the time that seemed absurd to all except Mr. Huff. So he built the cottages way back at the end of the site, away from what is now the Parkway through the busiest resort city in the Smoky Mountains. He built them right, of native stone, some with woodburning fireplaces. A large swimming pool was added later, and still the grounds are spacious, garden-like with dogwood and thickets of rhododendron planted by Mr. and Mrs. Huff; nurtured by their daughter, Barbara, the current keeper of these historic accommodations. Historic, but with modern amenities: color TV, air conditioning in each. Modern, complete kitchens in some. (Catch your trout and cook it too, without leaving the grounds.) Rates are ridiculously low for Gatlinburg—Barbara hates to raise them because many guests remember when they were much lower. For a four-night minimum, the cottages may be the best value. For overnight or weekending, the motel rooms are priced right, and are homey and roomy. Twin beds, doubles and rollaways are available. Open April 1 to November 1. For reservations, contact Barbara Huff-Beville, Huff's Motel & Cottages, 965 Parkway, Gatlinburg, TN 37738; phone 615/436-4878.

Gatlinburg
Marge's Yellow Ribbon Log Cabins & Cottages

You want real seclusion for your honeymoon, romantic retreat or getaway? And authentic, rustic, historic charm? But also modern life's little necessities? Maybe a decadent luxury or two? No problem. Just follow the yellow ribbons tied to the old oak trees (we're talking major seclusion here) to the cabin or cottage of your choice—and your dreams. The one-of-a-kind old log cabins and frame cottages each has its own acreage, private locked gate, and winding driveway. All have a fireplace, telephone, stereo, VCR, electric heat and air conditioning, modern kitchens and baths. Individual features range from hot tubs and sweetheart jacuzzis to antiques, including a fireplace with swing away cooking rack and pot for real fireplace cooking. Some have a second bedroom or loft. There's a waterbed or two, sunrooms, porches and decks. . . . and views, views, views! That's Mount Le Conte and the Greenbrier Pinnacle towering above this section of the Great Smoky Mountains. These cabins are very special to owner, Marge Struzel, who keeps them available all year at the same moderate rates for those who want real seclusion. If you prefer privacy with less seclusion, she also offers the following chalets. For more information, contact her at the chalet address below.

Gatlinburg
Marge's Mountain Chalets

Close to the ski lodge, five minutes from downtown, 10 minutes to the national park, yet each of these two to eight bedroom chalets offers wooded mountainside seclusion. And all the amenities you'd expect in privately owned second homes; full clubhouse privileges such as swimming pool and tennis courts. Furnishings are for luxury as well as comfort, from hot tubs, to fireplaces, waterbeds to color cable TV, decks with views, outfitted kitchens and lovely modern bathrooms. Contact Marge Struzl for the place of your choice, rates and reservations; Box 288, Gatlinburg, TN 37738. Phone 615/436-9475.

Gatlinburg
Mountain Laurel Chalets

Way up in the ski area, with good access to the slopes and to downtown, these 1 to 11 bedroom, 1 to 5 bathroom chalets and log homes all have fireplaces and just about anything else needed for a mountain getaway. They're fully furnished and equipped, from cable TV to kitchen toaster to extra blankets. Amenities differ, and range from game tables to hot tubs. All offer privacy, some are completely secluded, others have grand unobstructed views. Use of tennis courts, pools (seasonal) and game rooms is included in the moderate rates that are not increased for busy seasons or weekends. Leave your car at the office and take the trolley into town (two minutes away) to avoid congestion and parking problems. To find the right size with the desired amenities, contact Mountain Laurel Chalets, Inc., Route 2, Box 648, Gatlinburg, TN 37738; phone 615/436-5277.

Gatlinburg
LeConte Lodge (In the Great Smoky Mountains National Park)

T his is the place to get away from it all—and above it all. Near the 6,593-foot summit of Mount LeConte, high above the parkway traffic, sets LeConte Lodge, the highest overnight accommodations in the eastern United States. It is, however, a uniquely exclusive getaway accessible only to those with the zest for a long hike and a willingness to literally leave it all behind—there are five trails and no roads to LeConte Lodge. There is also no electricity, no phone, no bathtubs or showers. Tapped, icey-cold spring water, flush toilets, the lodge's two-way radio and bottled gas and kerosene for heat and refrigeration are the only ties to the 20th century, unless one counts the helicopter that brings in supplies at the beginning of the season. Replacements arrive via trail, carried up the mountain on pack llamas.

The shortest (and steepest) of the trails is 5.5 miles one way, about a four-hour hike. The longest is 8.2 miles and takes only about five hours. If you start early, hike at a comfortable pace, and don't stop too long and too often to admire the scenery, you can reach the lodge by mid-afternoon in plenty of time to rest (!) before dinner. Served at 6, the simple hot, hearty meal may be the most memorable of your life, totally satisfying an appetite sharpened by the hike and pure freshness of high mountain air. After dinner, if the weather is clear, it's "showtime at the Clifftops," watching the sun sink slowly, filtering through clouds to cast moving shadows across an immense expanse of cove and ridge, and finally creating a magnificent color show in the sky. Almost by the time the light fades you'll be ready to snuggle down in a cuddlesome bed under virgin wool blankets in one of the seven snug cabins or three group lodges. A big country breakfast is served at 8 am but don't wait for the aroma or the sunlight to awake you. If you do, you'll miss the unforgetable sunrise from Myrtle Point—and before that the dawn, breaking in a rosy glow over distant peaks. Should Mount LeConte be shrouded in clouds, you can snuggle back under the blankets 'til breakfast time, or take a stroll surrounded by morning mist.

You won't need to pack much for your getaway to LeConte Lodge, but what you do take is important so check your list: a poncho, flashlight and warm sweater or jacket—the temperature up here will be 30–40 degrees lower at night than when you left the base of the mountain that morning. Take only the barest minimum of personal articles, some trail snacks and a little pocket money for lodge employee tips. Wear loose comfortable clothing (layered if the weather is cool), and well-broken-in, flat-heeled shoes. If you want to carry them that far, take a camera and binoculars. That's all you'll need except reservations, and you'll need to make those early; many hikers return annually, booking a year in advance. You can leave your car at your trail parking lot. The lodge is open from late March until mid-November. For a brochure with trail choices and map, rates and reservations, contact LeConte Lodge, PO Box 350, Gatlinburg, TN 37738; phone 615/436-4473.

Gatlinburg
The Wonderland Hotel (In the Great Smoky Mountains National Park)

L ocated about seven miles from Gatlinburg in the park's Elkmont area, this rambling rustic hotel offers the only lodging which can be reached by car within the Great Smoky Mountains National Park. Opened in 1912 and operated as a private club until the park was established in 1934, the Wonderland is still privately owned and operated on a long-term land-lease arrangement with the National Park Service. Innkeepers Brenda and Darrell Huskey are Smoky Mountain natives—Brenda actually grew up in and around the hotel and Darrell grew up in Wear Valley.

The Wonderland still retains its rustic atmosphere, although it has undergone considerable changes and improvements including heat and smoke detection systems and a new water system. Amenities are not luxurious but are far from primitive unless you consider in-room television and phones essential. All guest rooms are carpeted and comfortably furnished with queensize or twin beds. Most have a private bath or share a connecting bath, mainly with showers. The dining room has an old-fashioned atmosphere as wholesome as the mountain cooking. Meals are open to the public with the menu posted daily at the front desk. Serving hours are sometimes adjusted to fit the needs of the guests, so it may be best to call ahead to see what's being served at breakfast, lunch and dinner.

The exceptional setting is probably the best reason for staying at the Wonderland. Away from the park traffic, serene on its deeply wooded hillside at 2,400 feet, its rocker-lined porch is ideal for resting body and soul. The only sounds are the rustle of the forest, the song of birds and the rushing waters of the Little River which lies just beyond the doorstep. Innertubes are supplied by the hotel; there's a real old swimming hole nearby, and you can fish or hike or go wildflower hunting without getting into your car. Saturday nights are social events—usually a square dance where everyone joins in the fun, regardless of age or talent.

For those who want to get away from commercialism, regimentation, economic and social barriers, this hotel is about as far away as you can get without going totally primitive. Reservations should be made as far ahead as possible, especially for the peak seasons and holidays. Contact Wonderland Hotel, Route 2, Box 205, Gatlinburg, TN 37338; phone 615/436-5490.

Upper East Tennessee

T he Cherokee National Forest ends at the western boundary of the national park, and begins again at the eastern boundary. This rugged area has more of Tennessee's wonderful state parks including one near the base of beautiful Roan Mountain. Leave the mountainous national forest and you're in lovely rolling hills dotted with family farms and hundreds of historical markers and sites.

Sources for additional information include Cherokee National Forest, Nolichucky Ranger District at Greeneville, 615/638-4109; Unaka Ranger District at Erwin, 615/743-4451; Watauga Ranger District at Elizabethton, 615/541-2942; the Upper East Tennessee Tourism Council at Jonesbourough, 615/753-5961.

Erwin/Roan Mountain
National Fish Hatchery

T he nation's first fish hatchery began operation here in 1897. Visitors may tour the 42 acre complex which includes outdoor raceways and indoor tanks showing the development of thousands of rainbow trout. The visitor center and picnic area are open seven days a week. Adjoining the hatchery is the Unicoi County Heritage Museum, nature trails and a city park with swimming pool and tennis courts. Phone 615/743-4712.

Erwin/Roan Mountain
Roan Mountain State Park/Rhododendron Gardens

Rhododendrons in bloom atop Roan Mountain's 600-acre Rhododendron Garden
Photo Courtesy: Cherokee National Forest

A t the little town of Roan Mountain, take TN 143 to the State Park near the foot of the 6,313-foot Roan Mountain. Park facilities include vacation rental cabins, restaurant, full service camping and miles of trails, some of which are used for cross-country skiing during winter months. The park number is 615/772-3303; for cabin reservations call toll free, 1-800-421-6683.

Continue to the summit of the mountain for a scenic drive and a trip to the natural heath bald straddling the Tennessee/North Carolina border where a natual rhododendron garden covers 600 acres. Peak blooming season is usually late May through early July. Stop at the visitor center for trail maps and do some walking on the garden trails or take a scenic hike on the Appalachian Trail which crosses the summit.

Elizabethton/Laurel Bloomery
Sycamore Shoals/Carter Mansion/Doe River Covered Bridge/Watauga Lake

T here's almost as much early American history sites in and around Elizabethton as there are trails in the nearby national forest or campgrounds convenient to Lake Watauga shores. This beautiful lake is the place to go for a refreshing swim after a day on the trails (the Appalachain Trail passes near its western shores) or for fishing and water recreation. Camping opportunities abound. For maps and further information contact the US Forest Service, Watauga Ranger District at Elizabethton 615/451-2942.

Take Riverside drive to the Doe River covered bridge, built in 1882, one of the oldest and most used covered bridges in America. Listed on the National Register of Historic Sites. For more information on the town's other attractions and special events, contact the Elizabethton Chamber of Commerce; 615/543-2122.

This is the area where the first permanent American settlement outside the original 13 colonies was established in 1712—the Watauga Association which had the first majority rule system of government in what became the United States of America. It is also the area of the "Overmountain Men," a small group of frontiersmen who assembled at Sycamore Shoals and marched over the mountains and all the way to Kings Mountain in South Carolina to give the Red Coats a real thrashing—casualties; 1,018 British, only 28 Overmountain Men.

A remaining link to the Watauga Association is the Carter Mansion, home of a prominant citizen at the time, for whom Carter County is named. The mansion is located near the Sycamore Shoals State Historic areas on US 321 north, where there is a museum and reconstruction of Fort Watauga, and where an outdoor drama, *The Wataugans* is presented in mid-July. For more information call 615/543-5808.

Elizabethton/Laurel Bloomery
Iron Mountain Stoneware

Laurel Bloomery sets right in the national forest in the most remote section of upper east Tennessee, near Virginia and North Carolina. It can hardly be called a village, much less a town; it's post office is located in a "general store" and it has one industry—Iron mountain Stoneware. It's quite a prestigious industry however; Iron Mountain Stoneware has been compared to the fine porcelain dinnerware of Spode of England for its beauty and durability.

About 40 fulltime local residents, a dozen or so moonlighting farmers, designers Sally Patterson and Jim Kaneko and president/designer Nancy Patterson Lamb, along with marketing director Joe Lamb, make up the Iron Mountain "family." Machinery is used to mix and hand-jigger the clay in plaster molds. All other steps in the production process are done by hand: forming, decorating, dipping, glazing, trimming and "pulling" of handles. Pieces require about two weeks to complete, from mixing, to firing at up to 2550 degrees (at such high firing, the stoneware and its glazing has no porisity and is exceedingly resistant to chips and breaks) to preparation for shipping to over 600 exclusive shops in all 50 states.

A showroom displays all the pieces in the nearly two dozen patterns. Seconds, never shipped to stores, are on sale in the showroom. There are twice yearly four-day sales; one in spring, another near Thanksgiving. Hours are 8:30 to 5:30, Monday through Saturday; 11 to 6 on Sunday. Telephone 615/727-8888.

Kingsport/Rogersville
Bay's Mountain Park/Warrior's Path State Park

Bay's Mountain Park, owned and operated by the city of Kingsport, is worth a visit from anywhere in the upper east Tennessee area. The 3,000-acre nature preserve has a planetarium with daily programs, a 44-acre lake with naturalist-guided barge trips, 25 miles of nature trails and a large museum housing outstanding natural science and cultural history exhibits. Except for Christmas day, it is open to the public year round, seven days a week. There is no admission charge, only a minimal per-car parking fee. There is also a token charge for the barge trip, and a small admission for the planetarium shows. It's a great place for the family to spend an entire day without spending more than a bit of change, and chances are they'll want to return again and again. Phone 615/245-4192.

Warrior's Path State Park is the area's most popular recreation area. Located off I-81 on TN 36 on the shores of Fort Patrick Henry Lake, it offers everything you'd expect in a state park and more; an 18-hole golf course, miniature golf, driving range, tennis courts, bike and hiking trails, picnic area, swimming pool, waterslide, fishing, marina, boat rental and a 160-unit campground. Phone 615/239-8531.

Kingsport/Rogersville
Hale Springs Inn

Located on the square in one of Tennessee's oldest towns, this is the oldest inn in the state. The Hale Springs has been in continuous operation since it opened in 1825, except for a period during the Civil War when it served as Union Army headquarters. It has hosted many famous persons including Presidents Andrew Johnson, Andrew Jackson and James Polk. A complete restoration in the 1980's has brought back the inn's original grandeur. A gracious, open stairway in the lobby leads to wide hallways on the second and third floors of the brick structure. Most of the 10 large guest rooms and suites feature original fireplaces and have sitting areas, canopied poster beds, antique furnishings and deep antique bathtubs.

The inn's restaurant features Colonial decor, great warm fireplaces, candlelight dining, and food that brings rave reviews. Open to the public for lunch and dinner, with reservations required. Both the inn and restaurant are open all year. For rates and reservations, contact Hale Springs Inn, Rogersville, TN 37857; phone 272-5171.

Jonesborough/Greeneville

Enjoying the National Story Telling Festival at Historic Jonesborough

Jonesborough/Greeneville
Historic Jonesborough

This is the oldest town in Tennessee and the first entire town to be placed on the National Register as an historic district. Don't miss it, whatever the season. Most of the preserved and restored buildings contain interesting shops of all sorts. Arts, handicrafts and antique shops are abundant. There are ice cream parlors, snack shops, a couple of good restaurants, one bed and breakfast limited-lodging facility, and dozens of historical buildings to visit. Touring the town's days-gone-by variety of architectural styles of stores, city buildings and great old homes will keep you on your feet, so wear comfortable shoes—some cobblestone areas can hardly be managed on any other kind. Special events go on every month here. Two of the most interesting are the National Story Telling Festival in October and Historic Jonesborough Days, a three-day celebration around the Fourth of July. For more information and a schedule of events contact Jonesborough Information, P.O. Box 375, Jonesborough, TN 37650; phone 615/753-5961.

Jonesborough/Greeneville
Greeneville

This small city, over 200 years old, home of the 17th US President, has one of the prettiest Main Streets anywhere. Many grand old homes are included in the downtown historic district, on the National Register of Historic Places. The Andrew Johnson National Historic site is composed of two residences, the tailor shop and the burial place of Johnson who was an indentured servant here in Greene County in his youth. The Big Spring, source of Greeneville's water supply for 150 years, and the old Greene County jail, with original leg irons and dungeons dating from 1804, are among the town's other points of interest. The welcome center in the Chamber of Commerce is located at 207 North Main, telephone 615/638-4111.

Jonesborough/Greeneville
Big Spring Inn

Innkeepers Jeanne Driese and Cheryle Van Dyck welcome you to this grand three-story Victorian home in Greeneville's historic district. Located on Main Street near the Big Spring, the inn features leaded glass windows, early 1900's handpainted French wallpaper in the dining room, and five spacious guest rooms; two of which connect and can accommodate up to eight. Three of the rooms have private baths. All are individually decorated and furnished in a cheerful and charming mixture of antiques and reproductions. They offer privacy, comfort and no small amount of pampering: fresh flowers, small snacks, courtesy packages with information on the area and thick terrycloth robes. There is a downstairs parlor with a cozy fireplace, and a quiet upstairs library. Great porches are surrounded by a tree-filled yard large enough for a stroll. A full country breakfast is served in the dining room on a 1780's Hepplewhite table. For early or late risers, there is hot coffee, homemade muffins and assorted cold cereals. The inn is open all year. For rates and reservations, contact Big Spring Inn, 315 North Main, Greeneville, TN 37743; phone 615/638-2917.

Biltmore House in Asheville, NC

NORTH CAROLINA
PART I

*T*he North Carolina mountains section of this book is in two parts, with the following map covering Part I. The map generally indicates only those towns under which information is listed in the book and should be used in conjunction with a state map. The towns covered are not listed alphabetically, but as they appear along and off main travel routes. In Part I of the North Carolina mountains section, the route followed begins in the westernmost tip of the state, goes north as far as Mars Hill, south as far as Tryon, southwest to Scaly, back northward to Franklin as follows; Brasstown/Hayesville/Murphy/Andrews, Robbinsville/Fontana, Bryson City, Cherokee, Maggie Valley, Waynesville, Asheville, Mars Hill/Hot Springs/Trust, Bat Cave/Chimney Rock/Lake Lure, Tryon/Saluda, Flat Rock/Hendersonville, Brevard/Cedar Mountain/Lake Toxaway, Cashiers, Highlands, Scaly Mountain, Franklin, Dillsboro/Sylva/Cullowhee.

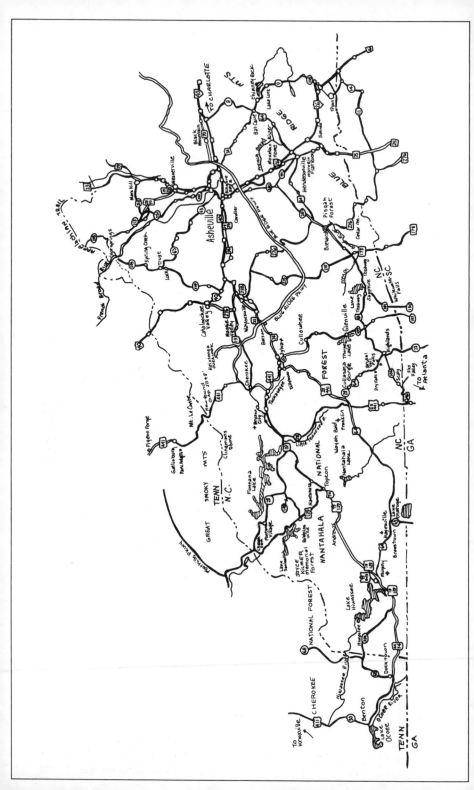

North Carolina: Part 1

Photo: Courtesy Nantahala Outdoor Center

Rafting the Nantahala

North Carolina, Part 1: An Introduction and Sources for Additional Information

T here are sections of two national forests, a national park, a national parkway, and a national trail all within this westernmost corner of North Carolina mountains. Add several major lakes and rivers, cultural centers, historic and natural attractions, a number of excellent restaurants, some secluded cabins and lodges, dozens of bed and breakfast and

One of North Carolina's many beautiful waterfalls

country inns, and if you decide you could spend all your getaways and vacations here and still not see and do it all, you would probably be right. You can go gem mining, castle touring, hike the Appalachian Trail, camp in the Great Smoky Mountains, attend summer stock theatre and a summer-long music festival, visit a Cherokee Indian village and discover that nearly every road you find yourself on is more scenic than the last.

Scenic touring at its very best would include not only the Blue Ridge Parkway (see table of contents), it would include nearly all of US 64, with the sections between Franklin and Highlands, and around Whiteside Mountain between Highlands and Cashiers a must. NC 215 between US 64 and US 276 is especially wonderful when summer's covering is gone. US 276 from the Parkway through the Pisgah Forest offers a number of reasons to stop plus some beautiful scenery. NC 209 between Waynesville and Hot Springs is banked with blue wild asters from late summer until winter.

Hiking in North Carolina is for everyone who walks (there are even handicapped trails) and can be enjoyed on nature walks which take little effort or time and on the long trails, including over 300 miles of the Appalachian Trail and North Carolina's own Mountains-to-the-Sea-Trail. A good trail map/brochure with directions and descriptions, published by the North Carolina Mountain Club and available at most outdoor recreation shops for $1.50 is 100 Favorite Trails of the Great Smokies and Carolina Blue Ridge.

If you don't find the information you are looking for in the following pages, good sources for additional information include the following:

The National Forests in North Carolina, 100 Otis Street, Asheville, NC 28802. The Nantahala National Forest has four district offices in the areas covered in the following pages. They are the Cheoah Ranger District in Robbinsville, 704/479-6431; The Highlands Ranger District in Highlands, 704/526-3,765; the Tusquitee Ranger District in Murphy; 704/837-5152 and the Wayah Ranger District in Franklin, 704/524-6441. The Pisgah Forest has two rangers districts in this (Part I) section. One is at the Pisgah Forest Visitor Center at Pisgah Forest (near Brevard), phone 704/877-3265 and the others is the French Broad Ranger District at Hot Springs, phone 704/622-3202. Recreation area and hiking maps plus other information can be obtained at any of the district offices.

Murphy/Brasstown/Hayesville/Andrews
Scenic Tour, Museums, Railway & Theatre

Highway US 19/129 between Murphy and Andrews will take you through one of the world's most beautiful, broad, clean and green valleys. It has an Indian name which no one in the area seems to be sure how to spell or pronounce, referring to it only as the Valley River Valley—the river which the highway crosses often is simply named the Valley River. No need to gild the lily—or to give such a lovely valley a fancy name.

You can catch the Great Smoky Mountains Railway for a mountain tour (see Bryson City for more details), and you can visit two museums in the area—both free. The Cherokee County Museum in Murphy features artifacts from DeSota's expedition, from the Cherokee Indians and from early settlers. In Hayesville there's the Clay County Museum in the old county jail featuring historical exhibits. Hayesville also has a good community theater featuring the Lick Log Players.

Chamber of Commerce telephone numbers are Murphy, 704/837-2242; Andrews, 704/321-3584 and Hayesville 704/389-3704.

Murphy/Brasstown/Hayesville/Andrews
Hiwassee Lake/Hanging Dog Recreation Area

The 22-mile-long Hiwassee Lake is part of the TVA dam system along the Hiwassee River, surrounded by the Nantahala National Forest in this westernmost tip of North Carolina. The Hanging Dog Recreation area is located four miles northwest of town. Its name is derived from Hanging Dog Creek, site of the last Civil War battle. The recreation area offers 66 camping sites with tent platforms and parking spurs large enough for campers and trailers up to 20 feet long. Sites have picnic table and fireplace but no hookups. Drinking water, toilet facilities, and a picnic area are also available and a launch ramp provides access to the lake which has 180 miles of shoreline and is fine for boating and waterskiing. Two nearby streams are designated as public trout waters, and there are plenty of hiking trails in the area. Contact the US Forest Service, Tusquitee Ranger District in Murphy for maps and additional information; phone 704/837-5152.

Murphy/Brasstown/Hayesville/Andrews
John C. Campbell Folk School

H undreds of people each year are discovering that they can learn a new skill by spending a getaway or vacation at this folk school founded in 1925. This sort of "learning vacation" features quality instruction, a totally restful environment deep in the mountains, sumptuous family-style meals, clean guest houses and good company—all at a cost which is comparable to standard motel rates alone.

The Folk School, as its name and course offerings reflect, is rooted in the traditions of the area. Weaving, wood-carving, blacksmithing and pottery are the school's "staple" courses although courses in various other art media are also scheduled, as well as sessions in music and dance. Workshops and courses are designed for weekends, one week and longer sessions extending for several weeks. A school for youngsters is held in June, and folks over 60 come for the Elderhostel programs.

The beautiful 365-acre campus, located about five miles east of Murphy in the unincorporated community of Brasstown, is included on the National Register of Historic Places. For further information and a schedule of courses, contact John C. Campbell Folk School, Route 1, Brasstown, NC 28902; phone 704/837-2775.

Murphy/Brasstown/Hayesville/Andrews
The Oak Barrel Restaurant

T ony and Ann Hopkins chose one of the most sparsely populated counties in the North Carolina mountains to open their dream restaurant. Would the shrewd small-town residents support a restaurant that served smoked salmon with caviar and offered a wine list, albeit small and carefully chosen? Would southern tourists beat a path to the door of a restaurant that sauteed chicken, smoked trout and served English afternoon teas? Would city dwellers from Atlanta, Chattanooga and Asheville drive two hours over mountains to dine in a rustic, attractive but actual former county home at dining tables with blue checkered bistro-style linens? Would anyone come to Ann's teas for scones with cream-and-cucumber sandwiches? Yes. Yes. Yes. Yes! For over seven years they've been coming. And coming back for more. More of Tony's dill sauce. More country duck and pork paté. More veal, boeuf a la mode, duckling bigarde. More fresh-baked breads and beautiful assortments of steamed and sauteed vegetables with every entree. Vegetables good enough for a gourmet vegetarian. Portions so generous that more than one diner has been heard to say, "That's far, far too much," then proceed to relish every morsel and accept dessert. The latter are accomplishments of both Tony and Ann—English sherry trifle, treacle tart with custard, Bavarian creams . . . As you may have guessed from the teas and small import gift shop, Ann herself is a British import.

Enjoy your selection with some English tea, French wine, café au lait or espresso. And the check will be very reasonable (remember all those shrewd local mountain residents). Go! Tea is 3–5, dinner 5 to 9:30. Closed Sunday and Monday. Reservations are suggested for Friday and Saturday dining. Located in a many windowed big blue house on a hillside above US 19/129 Business, off the four-lane bypass at the high school in Murphy. Address is 104 County Home Road, Murphy, NC 28906; phone 704/837-7803.

Murphy/Brasstown/Hayesville/Andrews
Huntington Hall Bed & Breakfast

There are five spacious, air-conditioned rooms with private bath and cable television in this home, circa 1881. There is also a houseful of downhome hospitality—via the British Isles—provided by innkeeper DeAnne Manchester. Call it an English Country garden home—southern style. Dogwood tress and low stone walls. One-hundred-year-old maple trees and an arbor—the perfect spot for complimentary wine before going out to dinner. A pretty dining room for enjoying a big country breakfast—crepes with fresh strawberries, or eggs Benedict, or maybe a big fancy omelet. Cozy corners and crannies are filled with books, magazines and Anglo memorabilia. English and American antiques and other comfortable, pleasant furnishings throughout. It's all quite elegantly homey, cheerful and sunshine bright. There's also a glassed-in plant-filled porch for DeAnne's Shoppe stocked with old-fashioned potpourri, small antiques, Victorian hats, eucalyptus wreaths and lots of *et ceteras*. Open all year. Located on a quiet residential corner a few blocks from the heart of Murphy. For rates and reservations contact Huntington Hall, 500 Valley River Avenue, Murphy, NC 28906; phone 704/837-9567.

Murphy/Brasstown/Hayesville/Andrews
The Walker Inn

Listed on the National Register of Historic Places, the Walker Inn was a stagecoach stop and the old Valleytown Post Office in the mid-1860's. Opened as a bed and breakfast in 1986, it is being restored to its original character and purpose. Within the walls of this peaceful inn, there is more than nostalgia; there's real history here. This is as close as you can get to the real thing and still have modern plumbing, heating and electricity. The original 1840's two-room log structure was expanded in 1850 to its present 11 rooms. The outside kitchen was connected to the rest of the house, making a dining room that is 30 feet long. Among other original features still intact are wrought iron door hinges, antique door latches, ceiling beams and bubble-glass windows.

There are six guest rooms (some with private bath) including one with the original post office boxes and another which once slept up to 12 men during the stagecoach era. Many of the furnishings and accessories are Walker Inn heirlooms including a grand piano in the parlor, photos and documents. The old slave house and the stagecoach stepping stone are still on the grounds. The lawn is shaded by an oak tree believed to be over 400 years old, clusters of giant hemlock trees and a rare ginkgo tree transplanted from Charleston in 1850.

The continuing labor of preserving and restoring the inn is a commitment made by Patricia and Peter Cook. They and their four children have built a log home for themselves on the grounds of the inn, which is located at the edge of Andrews. There's hiking and whitewater rafting nearby in the Nantahala Forest and Nantahala River. The moderate rates include a full country breakfast. Open April to December. The Walker Inn, 39 Junaluska Rd., Andrews, NC 28901; phone 704/321-5019.

Murphy/Brasstown/Hayesville/Andrews
Lakeview Cottages and Marina

 # 6

Lake Chatuge has been called the "crowning jewel" of the TVA lakes, and this lovely place could be called the most shining gem in the crown. Everything here sparkles with freshness and cleanliness. The lake, with more miles of shoreline than any of the Hiwassee Lakes, is framed by peaks of the Blue Ridge Mountains. In this picturesque setting, on eight acres of shaded grounds, nestles Lakeview Cottages, with docks, marina, rental boats, even a group cookout area for sharing catches of the day and swapping stories on the ones that got away.

The spotlessly clean cottages will accommodate two to eight. They're comfortably furnished, have modern appliances, air conditioners, electric heat and porches with rockers. There are picnic tables and grills and a small sloping beach area. Cottages are modified chalet-style except for the largest which is actually an older farmhouse to which a chalet-style deck has been added. Although there is plenty of lawn space between each, this largest cottage is even more secluded and private—ideal for large families or small groups. And when the lake is "up" you can fish from the deck!

Your catch may include trout, perch, blue gill, bass—*big* bass or catfish. In addition to the lake for all sorts of boating, fishing, and swimming, there are two nearby national forest recreation areas: JackRabbit Mountain Area on a lake peninsula is a heaven of serenity, set with lovely flowering trees, pines and hardwood; Fires Creek Area offers trout streams, small wildlife and miles of hiking trails including a handicap trail. Your hosts at Lakeview, proprietors Chuck and Ellie Saelinger, have trail maps and information at the office and will be pleased to make suggestions and offer directions to other points of interest. They keep the cottages open for a lengthy season, with possibly a few open all winter (call first). Rates are comparable to the area. No pets; that's a state law. Located on NC 175 (GA 75/17) south of US 64, six miles from Hayesville. Lakeview Cottages, Route 3, Box 101-A, Hayesville, NC 28904; phone 704/389-6314.

Robbinsville/Fontana

$ 70.00 *Bef. Hwy 64 on left*

Surrounded by the Nanathala National Forest, edged with miles of coves and shorelines of Lakes Fontanta, Sateetlah and Cheoah and bordered on the north by the Great Smoky Mountains and Tennessee's Cherokee National Forest, lightly populated, uncongested with those vacationers seeking the attractions and action in resort towns, this is a lovely unspoiled area for those who prefer nature's solitary gifts. Call the Robbinsville Chamber of Commerce: 704/479-3790 or the Cheoah Ranger District Office in Robbinsville, 704/479-6431.

Robbinsville/Fontana
The Joyce Kilmer Memorial Forest/Slickrock Wilderness

This 3,800-acre forest was dedicated in 1936 to the memory of Joyce Kilmer, poet and soldier killed in action in France in 1918. "I think that I shall never see/A poem lovely as a tree." is the opening line of

Kilmer's most well known poem, and this forest is an appropriate living monument to his memory.

Many of the trees in this virgin wilderness are hundreds of years old, over a hundred feet high and as much as twenty feet around the base. Yellow poplar, several species of oak, sycamore, basswood, beech, hemlock, dogwood and more still stand, undisturbed by man. Remnants and sprouts of the massive American chestnut trees which composed a large part of the timberland prior to 1925 can still be found, although the mature trees have all died as a result of the chestnut blight.

There is a picnic area and an easy two-mile loop trail, plus 60 more miles of trails following shimmering mountain streams, climbing high ridges, meandering around the giant trees, patches of ferns and thickets of laurel and rhododendron that bloom in late spring and early summer. Several smaller species of wildflowers can be found on the forest floor seeking out the sunlight filtering through the leaves of the hardwood trees. Bring your camera and binoculars for glimpses of deer, fox, mink, racoon, ruffled grouse, wild turkey, owls, hawks and the many species of songbird that inhabit the forest. Bear, bobcat and the pesky wild boar also inhabit the deepest wilderness: the 14,000-acre Joyce Kilmer-Slickrock Wilderness Area which extends into the northernmost section of the Nantahala National Forest and on into Tennessee's Cherokee National Forest.

For those who do not wish to camp on the hiking trails overnight, there are several "dispersed" (no facilities—no fee) camping areas along forest service roads, plus the nearby Rattler Ford and Horse Cove Campgrounds where there are restrooms, water and picnic tables for campers. To reach the Memorial Forest follow 129 through Robbinsville to paved State Road 1127 into the forest and follow signs. For a trail map and additional information, contact the Forest Service Cheoah Ranger Distrit, Massey Branch Road, Robbinsville, NC 28771; phone 704-479-6431.

Robbinsville/Fontana
Slickrock Expeditions

Venturing deep into the ruggedly beautiful and remote Joyce Kilmer Slickrock Wilderness requires proper equipment and at least some survival skills. Or it requires making a reservation with Burt Kornegay—writer, lecturer, president of the North Carolina Bartram Trail Society, ex-marine and veteran wilderness guide. Burt led his first expeditions in the Adirondacks in 1971, spent a year camping across Africa when he was 21, and has been leading backpacking and canoeing trips into the Slickrock Wilderness since 1985.

His expeditions may be for father-son, father-daughter pairs, all youngsters, all women, families or individuals with all levels of experience. Burt supplies the equipment and food—all participants need to bring are personal items, eagerness to learn camping skills and a lot of appreciation for the wilderness. He keeps the pace easy and enjoyable, affording time for flora and fauna identification, photography, natural history of the wilderness, cooling dips in mountain streams, and campfire camaraderie.

Hearty, hot meals such as chicken and dumplings with fresh biscuits, and campfire pancakes offer tasty variety, even on the longest of expeditions.

Participants learn by doing, from reading topo maps and paddling canoes to setting up and breaking camp—with the emphasis on low-impact camping. To join one of the scheduled trips or to arrange a family or group expedition, contact Burt Kornegay, Slickrock Expeditions, P.O. Box 1214, Cullowhee, NC; phone 704/293-3999.

Robbinsville/Fontana
Blue Boar Lodge

T his small retreat, operated by Roy and Kathy Wilson, is located about 10 miles from Robbinsville on 15 private acres surrounded by the Nanatahala National Forest and bordering one of Lake Santeetlah's many coves. The one-level ranch-style lodge has seven guest rooms. A stone fireplace fills one end of the living room, and is always lighted during the evening. The focus in the dining room is one very large lazy-Susan table where guests gather to enjoy made-from-scratch-everything. Meals include trout fresh from the lodge's own trout pond, vegetables from the garden, jams, jellies and cobblers from forest berries and daily-baked bread. Moderate rates include breakfast and dinner.

For some the favorite activity here is hiking and exploring the Joyce Kilmer Memorial Forest, or swimming, fishing and boating in the area lakes, and trout streams. Fishing licenses, boats and motors are available from the lodge. For those who put fishing first, a package is available April through September, which includes guide, bait and boat, along with food and lodging. The lodge is open only to hunters—individuals and groups—during hunting season, mid-October until January. The hunts for black bear and wild boar are led by Roy, a native of the area. For further information contact the Blue Boar Lodge, Route 1, Box 48-C, Robbinsville, NC 28771; phone 704/479-8126.

Robbinsville/Fontana
Snowbird Mountain Lodge

S *outhern Living, Country Inns & Backroads, The Chicago Tribune* and other national publications have described this hideaway as magical, awesome, majestic, spectacular and a wilderness Shangri-la. But the experience of being here defies description. Fortunately. Because only 46 guests can be accommodated in this Shangri-la.

The lodge is constructed of chestnut logs and native stone and sits on a mountainside at an elevation of 2,880 feet, at the edge of the Joyce Kilmer Forest about an eighth of a mile off the paved forest service road. A great terrace overlooks glimpses of Lake Santeetlah below and vistas of the surrounding ridges of the Snowbird Mountains. This gorgeous view is also the focal point of the lobby, with its floor-to-roofline windows and cathedral ceiling. Tables and shelves of books, comfortable chairs and sofas invite relaxing in front of the massive fireplace on cool evenings.

The 23 guest rooms are paneled in a variety of native woods with custom-made matching furniture. Comfortable beds and night sounds of the forest lull you into sound sleep, and you'll awaken to a hearty breakfast, served at 7:45. (The coffee pot is always ready.) All three meals are included with lodging. Lunches always include soup or juice and dessert with entree, or you may have a picnic lunch prepared for a day of outside activities. Dinner entrees change each day and range from New York strip to trout to Cornish hen to a chicken specialty and prime rib. Homebaked rolls, cakes and pies round out the dinners served at 6:15 to 7. Favorite activities include swimming in a nearby spring-fed swimming hole, fishing, boating (boat rental is available nearby), and exploring the virgin forest almost adjacent to the lodge, identifying trees, mosses and wildflowers, catching glimpses of birds and other small wildlife. For "days in" there's table tennis, card games, pool, skittles, darts, horseshoes and shuffleboard.

Innkeeper is Eleanor Burbank. Contact her for rates and reservations at Snowbird Mountain Lodge, Joyce Kilmer Forest Road, Robbinsville, NC 28771; phone 704/479-3443. 3433

Robbinsville/Fontana
Peppertree Fontana Village

A bout the only thing that hasn't been or isn't being renovated at this four-decades-old family resort is the pace and the atmosphere. It's still a sort of slow moving summer camp for kids of all ages—and all interests, from bass and trout fishing, to horseback riding, from miniature and par three golf to tennis, boating and water skiing, from nature hikes to hay-rides, horse shoes to water slides. Bordered on one side by the Great Smoky Mountains National Park, on another by the Nantahala National Forest, on another by 30-mile-long Lake Fontana, (with two more lakes in the immediate area) this self-contained resort is complete with its own post office, churches, fire and police department, stores and restaurants. The village was created in the early 40's to serve one purpose: to house and serve the engineers, officials, construction workers and their families who had come to construct the TVA's Fontana Dam.

When the Asheville headquartered Peppertree Resorts took over the operation in 1987, it immediately began long-needed renovations—about 10 million dollars' worth. Many of the 250 rustic cottages have been gutted, stripped, restored and redecorated. You can still go without the amenities, as many of the fishermen prefer, but there are now cottages with updated kitchens and baths, decorator furnishings and fireplaces. Even the 94-room modern inn with pool, saunas dining and banquet has been spruced up. And down at the new marina, there's a fleet of brand shiny new Wave Runners, bass, pontoon and ski boats for rent. There's also an "instant reward" kind of fly fishing school, an old log building housing a growing museum of the area (open free to all mountain visitors—go see), new activities such as a new indoor swimming pool, and all the old favorites like square dancing, clogging, and arts and crafts instruction for all ages. There's also new and old in the staff. Hikers will be happy to know that resident naturalist Tina Holland is still leading the hikes. There's a new food manager and it's rumored he only gets paid if he gets good food reviews, and that he seems to be living high on the hog. One other thing hasn't changed — this is absolutely arrid country, so if you want a cocktail, you can brown bag in the dining room but you'll have to bring your own, or drive 35 miles to the nearest package store in Bryson City. The resort is open all year. Contact Fontana Village, Fontana Dam, NC 28733; phone 704/498-2211 or toll free for reservations, 1-800-438-8080.

Bryson City/Cherokee
Great Smoky Mountains Railway

T here's an old romantic route to miles of new, close up views of mountain scenery in westernmost North Carolina: 67 miles of a 100-year-old railroad, offering passenger service again after 40-odd years. All aboard for a morning or afternoon excursion. Best make reservations too, especially on busy weekends.

Whether you've seen the mountains by auto, cycle, boat, on foot or by horseback, you'll get a different, oft'times closer and slower look at some places visitors have never seen. You'll go through tunnels of solid rock, and gorges so deep and narrow you can smell the wildflowers clinging to the cliffsides. You'll rumble over high trestles above mountain lakes, meander alongside rivers, cross broad valleys, and have time to savor it all. The average speed along this mountain track is about 15 miles per hour, slower on sharp curves and inclines. Seating is comfortable and visibility is fine on both the closed or open excursion cars. Light snacks, soft drinks and hot coffee are offered. Luncheon and early dinner excursions are also available.

The train operates March through New Year's, with private party excursions available all year. The round trip excursions depart Bryson City, Dillsboro, Andrews and Murphy. Fares are moderate, with discounts for children 12 and under. Call for departure times and locations. In North Carolina, telephone 704/586-8811; out of state, toll free, 1-800-872-4681.

Bryson City
Deep Creek (Great Smokies Campground & Recreation Area)

P eople who visit this section of the national park (by car, accessible only from Bryson City) seem to be having more fun or watching more fun than any place in the park. The most obvious reason is the tubing. (But there are lots of quieter pleasures here too.) There's a big tube rental barn just outside the entrance to the park boundary. The park service is not involved in renting tubes or encouraging the activity, so you are on your own— you and several dozen others of all ages, on any day that cold Deep Creek isn't absolutely freezing. Tubers tote big heavy duty tubes several hundred yards up the mountain, then come shrieking and splashing down the shoals. And with teeth chattering between blue lips, they haul themselves up again.

For those who like quieter (and dryer) activities, take all or at least part of the easy 4-mile loop trail. You'll pass a couple of really beautiful cascade areas, and a perfectly exquisite waterfall—it couldn't have been done better had it been planned by a Japanese landscape architect. There are a number of other trails including the terminus of the 20-mile Deep Creek Trail. Since it goes *up* the Smokies from here—all the way up to Clingman's Dome Road—it seems wiser to consider it the terminus instead of the beginning. You can stop at the campground office for maps. If you want to camp in the Smokies, this is a good place to do it. RV and tent sites are available April through October. See the Great Smoky Mountains National Park listing for specific information on camping facilities, address and phone numbers. To reach Deep Creek, take US 19 into Bryson City and follow the signs.

Bryson City
Nantahala Outdoor Center

About 12 miles south of Bryson City on US 19, down in the Nantahala River Gorge is the Nantahala Outdoor Center. You'll know when you get there. There are usually crowds along the river bank, watching and waiting for the rafters to finish their whitewater experience here, doing final battle with the last few hundred yards of rapids. When you tire of watching—go do. If you are over seven and under 97, even if you've never seen a raft before, you can join others in an NOC guided raft trip for a whitewater adventure which will leave you cold, wet—and absolutely exhilarated. The eight-mile trip takes about three hours. Open trips are scheduled twice daily and you can schedule a trip just for your own group—make reservations through the office located at the NOC complex. NOC has two restaurants, a variety of lodging accommodations usually reserved early by rafting groups, a gas station and a well-stocked outfitters store. (This is a good place to look for some maps and books on the area.) For more information and reservations, phone 704/488-6900.

Bryson City
Nantahala Village

The complete resort for family vacations in this area has lodge rooms, kitchenettes, secluded cottages (many with fireplaces) that sleep two to six, and a 100-year-old house that sleeps eleven. The latter has a fireplace, wrap-around porch, two baths and five bedrooms—great for family reunions.

Located on US 19, a few miles south of Bryson City, the resort's 215 acres of mountain woodlands is convenient to lakes, rivers, national forests, family attractions and the Great Smoky Mountains National Park. There is plenty to do on the premises: tennis, swimming, horseback riding, shuffleboard, game room, recreation hall, and a recreation director to plan daily activities during the summer months.

Great Smoky Rafting, just across the road, offers guided rafting trips, canoeing and kayaking clinics (and rentals) and a shop to outfit backpackers, rock climbers, and water enthusiasts. They also stock a good supply of maps and books on the area.

There's an excellent restaurant in the inn that serves country style meals morning, noon and night, and is open to those just passing through as well as to guests. The resort is open April through October, and a few of the cottages are open all winter for fireplace-cozy, secluded winter getaways, at about 20 percent less than the always reasonable rates, which are also discounted for extended stays and during April and September. For a brochure with descriptions of the different accommodations, contact Nantahala Village, P.O. Drawer J, Bryson City, NC 28713; phone 704/448-2826 in state, or toll free out of state, 1-800-438-1507.

Bryson City
Hemlock Inn

Before the bell rings for breakfast at 8:30 and dinner at 6, a stranger might mistake this for a private club instead of a 25-room inn. Except there are no strangers here. Guests begin to assemble on the rocking chair porches several minutes before mealtimes, as much, it seems, to get acquainted with each other, share adventures of the day, lend each other maps, give tips, directions and make suggestions for the coming day's activities as to wait for meals shared around large lazy-Susan tables.

Talking and sharing continues as the lazy-Susans turn. "This sure beats the boarding house reach," someone remarks and the conversation turns to swapping experiences in other country inns from Canada to Florida, Maine to California. Plates are filled and refilled with such downhome delights as roast turkey and dressing, country fried steak and gravy, corn on the cob, squash

casserole (light as a souffle), Southern seasoned string beans, relishes and homemade breads—followed (always) by homemade pies or cakes.

After dinner there's still time for the outdoor drama in Cherokee or a companionable game of bridge, more porch talk or just rocking and watching as the evening settles over the mountains. For most it's early to bed. The cool mountain air, a day of outdoor activities, the sing-song sounds of night creatures and the pervasive tranquility are powerful sleep inducers. No television is needed (or available) to coax one into relaxation. Guest rooms, fresh and clean, have big comfortable beds, private baths, ceiling fans—and a clock on the dressing table so you won't oversleep and miss the big country breakfast. Actually you'll probably awake early and refreshed with plenty of time for a short hike along an easy loop trail on the inn's 65 wooded acres. Coffee will be ready on the patio when you return. For week or longer stays you may prefer one of the three cottages complete with kitchen—your meals will still be included with rates.

The inn is open late April through early November. All seasons offer special reasons for visiting here, and during spring there's an additional reason;

naturalist-in-residence, Arthur Stupka arrives for his annual three-week visit. Hike with Arthur and enjoy his slide presentation; you'll be able to remember at least some of the names of the wildflowers. Whatever the season, you will appreciate the graciousness of hosts Ella Jo and John Shell and their staff. The inn is located near US 19 three miles north of Bryson City, seven miles south of Cherokee. Hemlock Inn, Bryson City, NC 28713; phone 704/488-2885.

Bryson City
Folkstone Inn

T his once-upon-a-time farmhouse sets on three acres of rolling meadows, one quarter mile from The Great Smoky Mountains National Park Deep Creek Recreation Area. Above the stone foundation, a wide front porch suggests soft summer evenings with wine or iced tea and the song of katydids. Inside are nine guest rooms, all with private baths, some with stone walls and cool flagstone floors, several with sitting areas, balconies and mountain views, plus a romantic room with a private deck popular with honeymooners.

Authentic country antique furnishings, comfortable common rooms, lots of good books, and a sunny, open-door welcome from innkeepers Norma and Peter Joyce all combine to make this bed and breakfast inn as idyllic as the scene suggests. Breakfast varies daily but is always hearty country fare—maybe a full English breakfast reflecting Peter's British background, or Norma's southern hospitality—Tennessee style—with homemade muffins and grits to go with the bacon and eggs.

The Folkstone Inn is one of the few in the area that is open all year. It is within walking distance of hiking trails and three waterfalls in the Smokies. All this adds up to an excellent getaway or hideaway particularly during the out of season winter and early spring weekends. Folkstone Inn, 767 W. Deep Creek Rd, Bryson City, NC 28713; 704/488-2730.

Bryson City
West Oak (and more) Bed & Breakfast

T he "and more" means a choice among four special places: a 100-year-old Queen Anne Victorian on a great expanse of lawn, garden and orchard, with a close-up view of the Smokies; an adjacent guesthouse for two, with a kitchen and porch; a spacious home of hand hewn logs with floor-to-ceiling living room view of the Smokies, plus a screened porch and large open deck with still more view; and a splendid contemporary with a hint of the Orient, completely enclosed and secluded in a lush 4-acre garden of native trees, shrubs and vines. (And, yes, there is another view of the Smokies from this in-town hideaway.)

The latter is the residence of Dr. Harold and Mercedith Bacon. The Queen Anne is an old family home where Mercedith's mother, Mrs. Virgie Shook, is the gracious innkeeper. The guesthouse was built in 1950, and the log home, though luxurious inside, is encased in logs salvaged from five pioneer structures from Swain County, and is on the site of the old frame house which Dr. Bacon rented when he came to practice medicine in Bryson City in 1935.

Guest room furnishings and amenities vary. There are singles, doubles, suites, private balconies, mostly private baths, color television, and always a full country breakfast. This is usually served for all guests by Mercedith at the log house, although it is sometimes served for the Queen Anne guests by Mrs. Shook herself in the original family dining room. To help you make the perfect choice from these perfectly delightful choices, contact Mercedith for more details. West Oak Bed & Breakfast, Fryemont Road, Bryson City, NC 28713; phone 704/488-2438.

Cherokee
Cherokee Indians' Qualla Boundary

An artist demonstrates pottery techniques to Cherokee Indian Village visitors.

With the North Carolina entrance to the Great Smoky Mountains National Park (opened in 1934) right on their boundary line, the Eastern Band of Cherokee Indians seem to have become as successful at pleasing millions of annual tourists as about a thousand of their ancestors were at escaping the roundup and forced removal of the Cherokees back in the 1830's. The story of that tragic removal and forced march to Oklahoma which became known as "The Trail of Tears," dramatized and presented here nightly, has been playing to visitors since 1950. Hundreds of shops, restaurants, motels, campgrounds, and amusements are crowded onto three short strips: US 19 (where you will find the Welcome Center), US 441 and just across the Oconoluftee River in the Sanookee Village area. The authenticity of some of the souvenirs, and the dress and teepees involved in what might be called photo ops, may be questionable, but there is no question about this being one of the most popular destinations in the North Carolina mountains, or about the many other reasons for its popularity.

The fishin's fine. No license required, just a permit to fish on any of the reservation's rivers and streams, stocked regularly. If bingo is your game, check the jackpots here. It'll cost you a good night's lodging rates just to get in on the action, but the stakes are high enough to attract up to 2500 people for twice-monthly games. (It is said that some actually drive from northern states just to play bingo here, never knowing, or caring, that they've crossed the Great Smoky Mountains.) People are friendly and helpful. The setting is beautiful. Frequent festivals range from fishing tournaments to Intertribal gatherings for stickball games and dance demonstrations. The following are among the most historically authentic and popular reasons to visit Cherokee, and are all located on US 441 near the entrance to the park.

For further information including a special events calendar, contact Cherokee Tribal Travel and Promotion, P.O. Box 465, Cherokee, NC 28719; phone (in state) 704/497-9195, toll free out of state 1-800-438-1601.

Outdoor Drama

Unto These Hills portrays the history of the Eastern Band of Cherokees and events leading up to and following their forced removal and march on the infamous "Trail of Tears." The cast includes local Cherokees, with professional actors and dancers. Music is by Dr. Jack Kilpatrick, a Cherokee. The play was written by Dr. Kermit Hunter, author of more than thirty other outdoor dramas including *Horn in the West* which is performed in Boone during the summer. The Cherokee drama, which has been running here since 1950, is performed Monday through Saturday, mid-June through mid-August. Until July 29 performances begin at 8:45; from then until the end of the season they begin at 8:30. But get there at least 30 minutes early for the pre-show entertainment of mountain folk songs and music. On US 441 toward the park's entrance; ticket office phone, 704/497-2111.

Museum of the Cherokee Indian/Oconaluftee Indian Village

For more authentic Cherokee history, visit this modern museum. Cherokee artifacts and several audio-visual exhibitions guide visitors through centuries of Cherokee myths, history and culture, including a chance to listen to the native language on special "hearphones." Open year round, 9 to 5:30 daily in the off-season, 9 to 8 daily and until 5:30 on Sunday from mid-June through August. Admission is charged. Phone 704/497-3481.

The Village is a re-creation of Cherokee village life during the 1700's. Guides are available, but visitors are free to stop, look, ask questions and wander about the village on their own, watching craftpeople at work creating baskets, pottery, even dugout canoes. The village includes a replica of the seven-sided council house used for social and religious gatherings. Adjacent to the village is a small botanical garden. An admission is charged for Oconaluftee Indian Village which is open daily from mid-May to mid-October 9–5:30. Phone 704/497-2315.

Qualla Arts and Crafts Mutual

Authentic Cherokee Indian Crafts are featured at the largest Indian-owned and operated arts and crafts cooperative in the United States, the Qualla Arts and Crafts Mutual

Photo: Courtesy Qualla Arts and Crafts Mutual

The beautifully designed free-standing building on US 441 near the park's entrance houses the largest Indian-owned and operated arts and crafts co-op in the United States. With over 300 members supplying the shop with items ranging from beadwork to baskets, ranging in price from under $5 to over $5,000, you'll probably find something to suit your taste and wallet. Handmade dolls, stunning woodcarvings, all kinds of pottery, rugs and other smaller woven items, and other arts and crafts, are all authentic, handmade by members of the Cherokee co-op. A one-room gallery in the spacious shop is dedicated to the showing of special exhibitions of today's outstanding Cherokee artists. The shop is open all year daily 9 to 5:30 and until 8 during the vacation season. No admission. Free parking. Telephone 704/497-3103.

The Newfound Lodge & Restaurant

Both new (relatively) and a real find, this attractive two-level lodge has 75 rooms along the banks of the Oconaluftee River. There's an additional 30 units just across US 441 at the foot of the mountain. It's a good location, near the above points of interest, and within walking distance to the national park entrance. All rooms have large picture windows facing the river, and management had the good taste not to draw attention away from this lovely scene with any sort of art on the walls. Indeed the decor is above average, understated and quietly pleasant. Both levels of rooms have private decks adjacent to or overlooking the river. Take a stroll along the river path, or you can watch from the deck or window while the children go wading or fishing. Air conditioning, phone, color TV cablevision, kingsize or two queensize beds make these rooms especially comfortable and convenient. A large pool surrounded by outdoor shade and sun deck completes the amenities.

Adjacent to the lodge on the river side is their Peter's Pancakes & Waffles. Enjoy these treats on the riverbank room from 6:30 until 2. They also serve deli-type sandwiches to eat there or to go—nice for a picnic/walk in the park. On the mountain side is the full service Newfound Restaurant, serving from 11 am til 10 pm daily during the summer, closing at 9 in the spring and fall. The menu offers wholesome and inexpensive complete meals including lots of nice vegetables.

The Newfound Lodge is open April through October. Address is 34 US Highway 441 North. Cherokee, NC 28719; phone 704/497-2746.

Maggie Valley

A bout 40 minutes between Asheville and The Great Smoky Mountains National Park, sunlit Maggie Valley, surrounded by mountains up to 6,000 feet in elevation, is the vacation hub of Haywood County. During the summer months its 500 or so population climbs into the thousands as summer residents return. Visitors from Asheville, from the National Park, and from Cherokee add to the resort-like atmosphere along it's three-mile long Main Street (US 19). In spite of all the visitors, there are no parking problems and seldom anything resembling traffic congestion. From early spring into the winter ski season, the village offers festivals, attractions and entertainment for the entire family. North Carolina's oldest ski area, a 140-acre golf and country club, a guest ranch, a mile-high theme park, nightly clogging, square dancing and bluegrass music are a few of the most popular reasons that vacationers love Maggie. It is also a friendly place—most of its businesses are family owned and operated; small, well-maintained motels, cottages, campgrounds, and a variety of shops and restaurants. For more information and a calendar of the many regularly scheduled events, contact the Maggie Valley Chamber of Commerce, P.O. Box 87, Maggie Valley, NC 28751; phone 704/926-1686.

Maggie Valley
Folkmoot USA

M aggie Valley hosts the opening night of this two-week-long event featuring folkdance groups from around the world. Beginning the last week-end in July and continuing through the first weekend in August, three or more groups perform nightly in a number of western North Carolina towns. On opening night, all the groups perform before a packed house at the Stompin' Ground in Maggie Valley. Four other all-group programs are also held at nearby Lake Junaluska and Asheville.

Folkmoot USA is one of the largest folkdance events in the US in terms of partici-pants and countries represented. Each dance group is accompanied by the traditional folk music instruments of its respective country. For a preview of the dance, music and beauti-ful, authentic costumes, don't miss the parade down Waynesville's Main Street. For exact performance dates and tickets, contact Folkmoot USA, P.O. Box 523, Waynesville, NC 28786; phone 704/452-2997 or the Waynesville, Haywood County Chamber of Commerce, toll free at 1-800-334-9036.

Maggie Valley
Cataloochee Valley (Great Smoky Mountains National Park Area)

T his section along the eastern border of the Great Smoky Mountains is the least-visited area of the most-visited national park in America. Yet it's 29-square-miles of valley and forest contain a campground (and ranger station), historical structures, split-rail fenced meadows, trout streams, hiking trails, abundant wildlife—and lovely solitude. The reason there are so few visitors here is the valley's relative inaccessibility. By auto it can only be reached by a winding dirt road, and although it is less than 10 miles each way from US 276 near Maggie Valley, the round trip on the serpentine road takes a beautiful 2.5 hours, (There is a short paved section into the ranger station and camping area.) The road is believed to have begun as a buffalo path and later used by Indians. In the mid-1800's it was named the Cataloochee Turnpike, and a toll was sometimes charged to maintain this linkage of the Tennessee and North Carolina mountains.

The road continues on through the edge of the park, past the Big Creek Campground into Tennessee where (still narrow) it becomes paved, (more or less) and continues on as TN 32 into the Cosby Campground, connecting with TN 73 into Gatlinburg. The entire drive from US 276 and Cove Creek Road to Cosby is 29 miles, and one could make a daylong loop—back through the park on 441, connecting with the Blue Ridge Parkway, exiting at US 19 to Maggie Valley. To reach the Cataloochee Valley, Take US 276 north to the final turn on the left before it deadends at I-40. You should be on Cove Creek Road. Turns can be confusing here and it's easy to take the wrong road while you are still in this community, so follow the Cove Creek Missionary Baptist Church signs. For more information on the Great Smoky Mountains National Park, see the table of contents for the listing.

Maggie Valley
Cataloochee Ranch

N ot to be confused with the above Cataloochee Valley, this mile-high resort spreads across a thousand acres atop the Great Smokies, bordering the national park. Though it was established in its present location in 1939, the ranch as an institution dates back to 1934, and was originally located in the valley before the establishment of the park. It is still owned and operated, as it always has been, by the Alexander clan, off-spring and in-laws.

The Ranch accommodates up to 70 guests at a time in seven family-sized cottages, ten bedrooms in the main ranch house, and more in the new luxury Silverbell Lodge, opened in 1986 and excellent for small meetings, family reunions as well as individuals. The cottages all have three bedrooms, one or two baths and a large fireplace. Two were original pioneer log homes and are over a hundred years old. The accommodations are used for skiers after the ranch season—offering the only on-mountain accommodations in the ski area.

The ranch is operated on the modified American plan with lunches optional. Hearty and varied meals are served daily and include seasonal garden vegetables, fresh-baked breads, homemade jams and preserves. Open to non-ranch guests by reservations, and one of the better places to eat in Maggie Valley. Outdoor meals are planned frequently, and lunches are packed for day-long horseback rides and hikes.

In addition to riding, the ranch has a tennis court and a spring-fed trout pond for fishing and swimming. (A heated enclosed swimming pool is included in plans for near-future expansion of facilities for year-round use.) Table tennis, horseshoes, croquet, bridge and other games, and a well-stocked library are available when you prefer to "stay in." For plant lovers and wild-flower hunters, miles of trails, both open and wooded, interlace the property and the adjoining national park. But horseback riding is what it's mostly about here. Half-day rides lead to nearby peaks with glorious views, or into deep woods and along tumbling streams. All-day rides go farther into the moun-

tains, as do pack trips of two or three days. The ranch's own horses are all trained for mountain trails. Novice riders will find gentle mounts; experienced riders will appreciate the more spirited ones. The spring back-country trips lead into the heart of the Smokies—high country well over 6,000 feet—and deep into virgin forests.

Rides are included in the rates, which are quite moderate, especially so for the "packages" during the off-season months of May and September. For more information, rates and reservations contact the ranch at Route 1, Box 500, Maggie Valley, NC 28751; phone 704/926-1401.

Maggie Valley
Cataloochee Ski Area

T he first ski area in the southern Appalachians was built near the above ranch complex in 1969. It quickly outgrew its original facilities and was rebuilt on the big side of the mountain. It's a regional favorite—a colorful complex highlighted by the awesome 2,200 feet of Omigosh slope. There are full facilities for all levels of ability, state-of-the-art snowmaking and slope grooming, ski school, rental equipment, and use of the excellent Cataloochee Ranch lodging facilities for skiers. Contact at above address; phone 704/926-0285.

Maggie Valley
Continuity

A delightful place to collect gifts—or just to collect—this celebrated multi-media gallery is a "must do" adventure in fine crafts while you are in the mountains. There's something for everyone here—a wonderful selection of handcrafted jewelry in a variety of media, fine decorative porcelains and functional clay works, handblown glass paperweights and perfume bottles, handcarved mirrors and jewel boxes, handwoven throws and rugs, fine wooden toys, kaleidoscopes—plus handmade paper prints and original drawings, watercolors and photography. This quality gallery represents over 50 artists and designer craftspeople from North Carolina and across the U.S.

Owners Shy and Elizabeth Lurie are knowledgeable and helpful in a friendly, unobtrusive way; and the gallery is warm, inviting and informal.

Continuity accepts major credit cards and offers full shipping and gift wrapping services. April through December hours are Tuesday through Saturday from 10 am to 6 pm, and Sunday from 11 am to 5 pm. The gallery is open on weekends from January through March. Located on Maggie's Main Street (US 19), in the Market Square plaza. Telephone 704/926-0333.

Maggie Valley
Twin Brook Resort Cottages

I f you're looking for seclusion and all the amenities right in the heart of Maggie Valley's three-mile stretch of activities and amusements, this is it. Set on 12 wooded acres, bordered on both sides by rushing mountain streams, surrounded by thickets of rhododendron and other wildflowers, these one-to-four-bedroom cottages are the answer. All have fireplaces (with free firewood), color TV, completely equipped kitchens, attractive, comfortable furnishings, electric heat, decks, porches and picnic areas with tables and grills. There's a big indoor heated swimming pool (although the children seem to enjoy spashing about in those streams as much as the pool). There is also a jacuzzi and a recreation room—everything you need to stay put and enjoy your hideaway. But take the private winding driveway out and you are on Maggie's Main Street, just half a mile from Cataloochee Ranch and Ski, a mile to the Blue Ridge Parkway and about half an hour from Cherokee and the Great Smoky Mountains National Park.

Twin Brook is an excellent base for exploring beautiful Haywood County and beyond . . . And you can get information, suggestions, directions, and all sorts of friendly advice on what to see and do all over these mountains from your hosts Carl, Viola and Dale Henry. The Henry family practically *started* Maggie's reputation as a great little vacation and getaway destination. Open all year. Twin Brook Resort Cottages, Route 1, Box 683, Maggie Valley, NC 28751; phone 704/926-1388.

Maggie Valley
Leatherwood Cottages

I f you enjoy good stories (and good story tellers) get Ruby Leatherwood to tell you how she managed to build Maggie Valley's first vacation cottages instead of a motel. And about her design feature which assures maximum privacy for porch sitters. The cottages are nestled under rows of shade trees that line both sides of a garden-like U-shaped private boulevard. At the top of the "U" sits a large and beautiful old log home with wide porch and rockers for guest/host visiting. Hosts are Jim and Diane, the 5th generation of the family to live in the log home, built by Ruby's great, great grandfather. The hillside was once the pasture, and the family still has cattle (and a charming two bedroom rental cottage) further up on the mountainside. There's a 1.5 mile loop trail from the premises, crossing the stream and meandering around the pasture.

But back to the cottages . . . Ruby knew what she wanted. She got it. You'll appreciate it. Private porches. Big windows placed for perfect cross ventilation. A good-sized bedroom in each with one or two double beds and a closet large enough for a summer's worth of clothing and sports gear. Modernized baths. Sofa bed in the living room. Television. A kitchen area outfitted complete to the dish towels. Pleasant furnishings for comfort and relaxation, and everything so clean it could pass army inspection, inside and out. Stroll down the gentle hillside setting (on US 19/Main/Soco Road) and you are in the heart of Maggie Valley. Reasonable rates for all visitors, overnight to seasonal. Leatherwood Cottages, 460 Soco Road, Maggie Valley, NC 28751; phone 704/926-1807.

Maggie Valley
Smokey Shadows Lodge

T his rustic, rambling lodge, with two adjacent log cabins, is perched upon a mountainside at 4,500 feet, about halfway between Maggie Valley and the ski area. It's old and quaint enough for the most wildly romantic. Constructed of native stone and handhewn logs salvaged from an old Cataloochee Valley gristmill before the valley became part of the national park, its primitive exterior belies the charm and comfort of the interior. There's an inviting greatroom with a massive stone fireplace. The long dining room has a continuous row of tables covered in old crocheted table clothes and lighted with kerosene lamps and candles. There are two levels and 12 cozy guest rooms, with private baths with showers.

Country and antique furnishings, cheerful quilts, curtains and coverlets, seasonal touches—wildflowers or bowls of fresh apples—and well-worn log railings blend warmly with the interior log and stone walls and unpeeled log-beamed ceilings. There's an old time swing on a long, long deep porch running the full length of the lodge from where there's an almost close-up view of the mountains framing Maggie Valley. And there's a hammock on a shady lawn for dozing, reading, bird and squirrel watching.

But mostly what makes this place so warm and comforting is Ginger Shinn (with a lot of help from husband, Bud and Girl Friday, Pat). Ginger vacationed here as a child, dreamed of someday making it her home, and although she had to wait until her own children were almost grown, is now the warm heart and cheerful spirit at the center of this very downhome lodge.

Ginger likes to cook too, and although meals are not included with lodging (except for the continental breakfast) she will put on a good country spread for you and your group with a bit of notice (even if you're lodging elsewhere), or fancy up the menu—even the entire lodge, for weddings, anniversaries, church groups, business meetings or other special gatherings. She'll plan a party—even get musicians and mountain cloggers in to entertain you and your group and arrange total packages for ski clubs.

The entire facilities can be reserved and can accommodate up to 50; the lodge sleeps over thirty, the adjacent "stable dorm" sleeps up to 10 (very popular with the youngsters), and the adjacent 100-year-old cabin with fireplace, the Shindig, sleeps up to six. For rates and reservations contact Smokey Shadows Lodge, P.O. Box 444, Maggie Valley, NC 28751; phone 704/926-0001.

Maggie Valley
Abbey Inn Motor Lodge

T his quiet little country motor lodge sets 4,000 feet above sea level, overlooking Maggie Valley. It's the first place off the Blue Ridge Parkway, north about two miles on US 19 toward Maggie Valley. The Cherokee Indian Reservation and the Great Smoky Mountains National Park are less than half an hour away. The view is outstanding, and the grounds include lovely little flower beds, swings for both big and little folks and a picnic area. Cozy rooms, including some with full kitchens, are mountain-air clean and sunshine bright. Each has one or two double beds, extra blankets for cool mountain nights, ceiling fans, quiet electric heat, and satellite color television. Small refrigerators are available. Mary Jo and Jim Shipe own this little motel and live right on the premises, so they can offer extra personal care and share lots of ideas on area tours and activities. Rates are reasonable throughout the season, May through October. Contact Abbey Inn Motor Lodge, US 19, Route 1, Box 545, Maggie Valley, NC 28751; phone 704/926-1188.

Waynesville
Waynesville's Main Street USA

Waynesville, the Haywood county seat, is 10 minutes north of Maggie Valley off the US 23/74 bypass, the Great Smoky Mountains Expressway. The four main blocks of Waynesville's Main Street run along the high ridge of Prospect Hill, surrounded by even higher ridges in every direction. As you drive down Main, you have the feeling of being on a high plateau, with mountains in your rear-view mirror, up ahead of you and to the horizon on either side.

But it's more than a panoramic view that makes this main street special. It's also the interesting mixture of service facilities, shops and businesses, many housed in turn-of-the-century buildings. There's a barber shop, pharmacies with soda fountains, a sprinkling of quality gifts, decorating and craft shops, an open air curb-side market that specializes in out-of-state newspapers and local produce, a gourmet wine and cheese shop, a thrift shop, offices of the 112-year-old *Mountaineer* newspaper, small local department stores and speciality clothing shops, a bank, the stately Haywood County Courthouse, a bakery, sandwich shop and the old Strand Theatre, restored after fire damage and used for live theater featuring performances by local thespians. It's an authentic, surviving, thriving Main Street USA, where local residents and farmers still come to do business—and where visitors can experience the genuine friendliness of a small city that has always welcomed vacationers and weekend visitors without becoming a tourists' town.

There's some pretty nice things off Main Street too; the beautifully designed, light-filled Haywood County Library sets a block away on Haywood Street, on a hillside landscaped to make the most of the mountain view. It's filled with all the books, materials and programs you expect to find in a large city library, plus a friendly staff that is eager to help visitors enjoy the library's services while they are in the area.

Waynesville hosts several special events during the year and will be happy to send you their events calendar and other visitor information. Contact the Haywood County Chamber of Commerce, P.O. Box 125, Waynesville, 28786; phone 704/456-3021 or 1-800-334-9063.

Waynesville
The Shelton House

This 1878 home, on the National Register of Historic Places, houses the Museum of North Carolina Handicrafts. Included in the collection are handmade toys, fishing lures, cradles, coverlets, spinning wheels, a copper still, a collection of Haywood County Indian artifacts and much more. The house itself has features almost as interesting as the collection. Windows are made of hand-pressed glass, stairways have dustcatchers, and the house has jib doors — a combination window and door supposedly invented by Thomas Jefferson. The big white frame house is located at the corner of Pigeon and South Welch, a short walk from Main Street. Open Wednesday through Saturday, 10 to 5 and Sunday 2 until 5. No admission.

Waynesville
Waynesville Country Club Inn

Of course, one doesn't *have* to be a golfer to enjoy a visit to the Waynesville Country Club Inn. Never mind if lush fairways, perfect bent grass greens, streams, ponds and spectacular mountain scenery are blended into 27 picturesque holes of golf. You don't have to lift a club to enjoy the view while participating in an equally popular mountain sport—porch rocking.

Only here, the porch is 270 feet long, overlooking all those green acres framed by blue ridges of mountains. Other on-premises activities range from tennis and swimming through hiking and jogging to browsing in the club's complete pro shop to a relaxing rubber of bridge. Lodging accommodations—which are on the modified American plan from April 22 to October 31 and European plan from November 1 to April 21—offer plenty of luxury, including the luxury of choice, from spacious rooms and suites to cottages and villas. A hearty country breakfast including fresh fruits and pastries, and dinner with a different menu each night, from elaborate buffet to charcoal broiled steaks, is served in the house guests' dining room. Lunch, including a complete buffet and a daily pasta special, can be enjoyed in the Tap Room. The American Heritage Restaurant is open to the general public for dinner with a menu ranging from duckling with wild rice to Delmonico steak. The inn offers daily golf packages and seasonal getaway packages, including Easter, Mother's Day, Thanksgiving, Christmas and New Year's Eve celebrations. For a complete package of information, rates and reservations, contact Waynesville Country Club Inn, P.O. Box 390, Waynesville, NC 28786; phone 1-800-627-6250.

Waynesville
Antipasto's

T his small restaurant on the stream in the Waynesville Plaza has been a local favorite for years and is equally popular with summer people, vacationers and weekenders who have been in or around the area before. Reservations are not accepted except for large groups, so go early or you may have to wait a bit. But it's a wait no one regrets.

All dinners start with their famous antipasto—a salad of fresh vegetables, imported cheeses and meats, and an Italian dressing which probably cannot be duplicated. Entree choices are all served heaping on a sizzling platter; delicate, deliciously seasoned rainbow trout, ribeye steak and steamed shrimp, both ordered by the ounce, hickory-smoked ribs (again from a secret recipe which probably cannot be duplicated) and a wonderful eggplant parmigiana . . . all these and more at moderate prices. They also offer pizza and charbroiled sandwiches at dinner as well as at lunch. The desserts are homemade, and there are domestic and imported beers and wines from the Vineyard Lounge. Lunch is served 11 to 2:30 weekdays (closed for lunch during winter) and dinner is served 4 to 10 or when everyone waiting is served. Closed Sundays. The Waynesville Plaza is located just off the US 23/74 bypass, exit US 276 south. Phone 704/452-0218.

Waynesville
Balsam Lodge Bed & Breakfast

T here's an especially homey atmosphere here in the Balsam Lodge main guest house, an old two-story yellow clapboard farmhouse built in 1904. It's as fresh and comfortably inviting as it might have been as the new home of a prosperous farmer. Behind the country home, just up the hillside are more accommodations in a real pure Americana train depot, built in 1908. The depot was moved to its present location in 1960 and transformed into a four-bedroom, four bathroom lodging facility, each unit with a private entrance and efficiency kitchen. There's a large deck with lounge chairs, picnic facilities on the lawn, and breakfast, which always includes fresh baked goods, in the parlor. Gather back in the parlor later for more homemade "treats" and beverages, for talk and games, or choose a rocking chair on the porch to enjoy the country sights and sounds as twilight comes over the mountains.

The lodge can accommodate 20 guests, which makes it an excellent place for family reunions and other small gatherings. Located almost adjacent to the

Blue Ridge Parkway at the Great Smoky Mountain Expressway Exit (US 23/74) just south of Waynesville in the Balsam community area. Balsam Lodge, Box 279, Balsam, NC 28707; phone 704/456-6528.

Waynesville
Belle Meade Inn Bed & Breakfast

T he developer of the Waynesville Country Club had this elegant home built for his private residence in 1908. In 1988 the current owners/ innkeepers restored many of its original charms, and renovated it to include contemporary comforts and modern, light, airy colors. The result is a welcome blend of the best of the old and new: four guest rooms with private baths/showers, chestnut woodwork in the common rooms, a splendid field-stone fireplace in the living room, and rocking chairs on verandas where you'll be served afternoon refreshments. There'll be "early bird" coffee outside your door in the mornings and a full country breakfast later. Belle Meade is French for beautiful meadow, like the one which once may have surrounded this home. But as Waynesville grew, the meadows gave way to other homes, quiet streets and a neighborhood only two blocks from the Waynesville Country Club and a five-minute drive to the town's pretty Main Street. Open all year. Belle Meade Inn, 804 Balsam Road, P.O. Box 1319, Waynesville, NC 28786; 704/456-3234.

Waynesville
Grandview Lodge and Restaurant

T he view *is* lovely. Very country, even though Waynesville has grown out and around the original home in the past 100 years. And guest rooms *do* offer some amenities many country inns don't—color TV, private bath and even a few private entrances. But the biggest attraction here is the food. Breakfast at 8. Dinner at 6. Except on Sunday at 1. House guests (and others with dining reservations) gather at large tables set with Sunday-best china for family-style, four-course classic Southern meals with all the trimmings. Meals are planned to utilize the freshest locally grown produce, and might include a light cream of lettuce soup, spinach salad, braised ham (yes, braised—indescribably delicious), fresh asparagus, corn pudding, cranberry conserve, spiced pears, homemade yeast rolls and homemade strawberry ice cream served in freshly baked tulip cookie shells.

The chef, Linda Arnold, is one-half the innkeeping team, a home economist, Culinary Institute graduate and author of her own cookbook. The other half is husband, Stan, chief dishwasher, all-around associate in house and grounds keeping, food serving and multilingual host. (Stan is originally from Poland and speaks several languages.) A few of the guest rooms are in the original section of the home. An addition includes private-entrance guest rooms with a common porch looking over rolling land to the nearby Balsam Mountain range. All rooms are comfortably furnished and have private baths. The lodge sits on its own 2 1/2 acres of lawn, apple orchard, grape arbor and rhubarb patch. Open all year. For rates and reservations contact Grandview Lodge, 809 Valley View Circle Road, Waynesville, NC 28786-5350; phone 704/456-5212.

Waynesville
Hallcrest Inn

T his 1880's farmhouse-turned-inn has a real tin roof and real working fireplaces in four of its eight guest rooms. That for the romantic. The "Side Porch" modular annex has four more rooms with sliding glass doors to private balconies. That for the more reserved. The dining room has three lazy-Susan tables laden family-style with country cooking, morning and evening, including made-from-scratch biscuits and yeast rolls. That for all the hungry guests—it's all included in the lodging rates. And for the nostalgic, there are hooked rugs, quilts, ancestors' photographs and furnishings, nooks and crannies for reading (and plenty of books), more fireplaces, porches for rocking (on both buildings), an oak-shaded lawn big enough for hide 'n seek and touch football (children are welcome here!), and a "visit at relatives" atmosphere where the coffee is ready when you are and you can go serve yourself in your bathrobe. Only private baths added to every guest room make this farmhouse much different than it might have been at the turn of the century. And it's all about a mile from the US 74/23 bypass, on top of 3,200-foot Hall Mountain, overlooking Waynesville.

Hosts, cooks, bakers and providers of this home away from home are innkeepers Russell and Margaret Burson. Russell does the baking and assists Margaret with the full country breakfast, served at 8:30, and the dinners served at 6. If there is room at the lazy-Susan tables, the public is invited to reserve space for the evening meal or Sunday dinner at 1 o'clock. These meals always include several vegetables, Russell's fresh breads, desserts and a southern style entree with all the trimmings. A "trade-recipes-by-mail" system between the Bursons and house guests attests to the goodness of these meals, and keeps a continuing supply of new recipes coming in.

The Burson's regular season is June through October, but they will take private groups in winter (except in January and February), and if they are home, may take a few of those romantic souls seeking a warm, cheery fireplace in their bedroom and a tin roof overhead. Reservations are required. Contact Hallcrest Inn, 299 Halltop Circle, Waynesville, NC 28786; phone 704/456-6457.

Waynesville
Haywood Street House Bed & Breakfast

Watching the sun set behind the mountains should not be missed from the veranda of this fine old home, perched on Prospect Hill just off Main Street. Enjoy the view with a beverage and the home baked cookies of innkeepers (and former Chicagoans) Jackie Stephens and daughter, Karen Kosec.

Complimentary treats are always available. There'll be more freshly baked biscuits, muffins, breads and fresh fruit at the continental breakfast, which you may take on the veranda or enjoy in the dining room. Your first cup of freshly ground hot coffee can be enjoyed in your room—it will be just outside your door when you awaken. Each of the five spacious guest rooms (with private and shared baths) has one of Karen's hand crocheted afghans and fresh cut flowers from the inn's garden. There's TV in the parlor, games, puzzles and a real variety of books in the library. Among the many antiques is a table made entirely of wooden sewing spools—made by a Wisconsin farmer one long cold winter (or did it take longer than one?) back in the mid-1800's. Original features in the 1906 home include chestnut wainscoating and a jib door.

Just across the street is the Haywood County Library; Main street is in back of the home, Shelton House is within a goodly stroll, as are several good places for lunch and dinner. If anyone could want more, it can be found close enough to be back for the sunset. Contact Haywood Street House, 409 S. Haywood Street, Waynesville, NC 28786; phone 704/456-9831.

Waynesville
Heath Lodge

This rustic 23-room log, stone and frame lodge is nestled at the end of a winding driveway on six and a half wooded acres less than a mile from Main Street. In spite of its air of seclusion, it is not the proverbial "best kept secret" as one quickly learns just about dinner time. Local residents and area vacationers join registered guests for the kind of southern cooking that required publication of a Heath Lodge cookbook, after innkeepers David and Bonnie Probst realized there was no longer enough time to fill all the requests for recipes. Meals are served family style from large, lazy-Susan tables. Dinners and traditional country breakfasts are included in the modified American plan rates.

Guest rooms are in several one-level units surrounding the dining lodge. Each has a private modern bath, ceiling fan, cable television and most have double beds. The wormy chestnut paneling, beamed ceilings, exposed stone walls, handmade basket lamps and window curtains combine with comfortable country furnishings to create a warm and inviting, homey atmosphere. Handmade, cane-bottomed chairs and rockers line the decks and porches. There's a hillside hot tub deck, and a common room with library, card tables and player piano—a popular gathering place for guests, especially in the evening hours. Open May through October. Reservations are required for nonregistered guests for the evening meals at 6 and 7:30 seatings weekdays, 12:30 and 1:45 Sundays. For rates and reservations contact Heath Lodge, 900 Dolan Road, Waynesville, NC 28786; phone 704/456-3333.

Waynesville
The Palmer House

This bed and breakfast inn was built in the 1880's—one of Waynesville's once-numerous tourist homes and old-fashioned hotels. Rockers invite guests to relax on the wide front porch. A common living room with piano and a game table is a warm and friendly gathering place on cool evenings. Each guest room has its own charm; braided rugs, white ruffled curtains, country furniture. Each room also has its own private bath with clawfoot tub. Chocolate mints and complimentary wine or jucie provide an extra touch of hospitality. A large continental breakfast is served in the dining room. The inn is located one block from Waynesville's pretty Main Street. For reservations contact The Palmer House, 108 Pigeon Street, Waynesville, NC 28786; phone 704/456-7521.

Waynesville
The Swag

A dip on a mountain ridge is called a swag. This is *some* ridge and some swag . . . 2,000 feet above the valley and 5,000 feet above sea level. This Swag is also *some* country inn. On a mountaintop meadow and its own 260 woodland acres, the Swag has only one close neighbor; at it's back door a split-rail fence built by the Civilian Conservation Corps in the 1930's opens into the wilderness of the Great Smoky Mountains National Park.

Designed and built by owners Dan and Deener Matthews, the native stone and log buildings are a recycling of history. The handhewn logs, cut in 1700, were salvaged from a church, a school, a post office and homes in North Carolina, Tennessee and Virginia. Arriving at the Swag is like walking back in history 200 years—not so much to a log cabin in the mountains as to a log castle on top of the world. There's a panoramic view of a great deal of the world (well . . . a great deal of Western North Carolina) from the cathedral-

ceilinged great room. There is also a great stone fireplace, a good library, a player piano, and room to gather for sing-alongs, board games and sharing of mountain adventures with other guests. The view and the warmth of the fireplace extend into the dining room where guests sit at long handmade walnut tables partaking of the inn's fit-for-royalty fare served onto pewter plates from handcrafted serving dishes made by local potters.

Dinner may feature rainbow trout, beef tenderloin or chicken breast teriyaki — the inn makes sure there are tasty cholesterol-free meal items. The lunch buffet is especially popular and includes hot soups, casseroles, burritos and a taco bar. Outside reservations are accepted for luncheons and the evening meal. Breakfast is hearty enough for hikers, some of which may bring back blueberries for next morning's pancakes. Picnic lunches are prepared on request for guests who leave for the day on hiking, fishing or sightseeing expeditions. For those who stay in, there's plenty to do besides look at the view: racquet ball, croquet, archery, even a sauna.

Guest rooms in the two-level inn and Chestnut Lodge annex all have private baths, some with steam showers, some have great stone fireplaces or wood-burning stoves. Furnishings in guest rooms and throughout the entire inn cheerfully combine the past and present in each unique room through the use of period furnishings, antiques, handmade quilts and native mountain artifacts. To reserve your place at this ultimate hideaway during their season, late May through October, contact The Swag, Route 2, Box 280-A, Waynesville, NC 28786; phone 704/926-0430, -3119 or -9978. (Out of season call the Matthews in New York City at 212/570-2086.)

Asheville

A sheville offers much to see and do, much of it free. Under the Parks and Recreation Department there are family activities, festivals, theatre and music performances throughout the year. Places to visit with little or no admission include Western Carolina Heritage Center, located in a restored 1840's home; the Asheville Art Museum and the Colburn Mineral Museum both in the downtown Civic Center; University of North Carolina Botanical Gardens; the Biltmore Homespun Shops and Antique Car Museum where you can watch craftspeople at work, buy fine woolen products and take a look at several elegant old automobiles. Walking tours are fine here, especially in the Downtown Historic District, much of which continues to be restored.

Frequent fairs and festivals include Belle Chere, the biggest—about a week-long event around the end of July which fills downtown Asheville with musicians, dancers, runners, bikers, jugglers, mimes, exhibits, international food, and various festivities continuing late into the evening, and apparently attracting all Asheville residents and all visitors in Western North Carolina.

The Mountain Dance and Folk Festival is in early August, the longest running festival of its kind in the nation, nearing it's 55th anniversary.

Catch free performances of Shakespeare in the Park by the Montfort Park Players or watch the Gee Haw Whimmy Diddle contests at the Folk Art Center.

There are two editions of the 40-something-year-old Guild Fair, for which a small admission is charged. Held at the Civic Center in late July and October, the Southern Highland Handicraft Guild show displays and sells the works of over 150 artisans. For information on all this and more plus a complete calendar of events, stop at the visitor center, just off I-240 downtown; phone toll free in state, 1-800-548-1300; out of state 1-800-257-1300.

Asheville
Shindig-on-the-Green

T here's a happening every Saturday night in downtown Asheville during the summer months. Beginning at 7:30 on the grassy green of the Buncombe Court House and ending whenever it ends, although the schedule says 9:30. First the audience gathers, with folding chairs, blankets and some with picnic baskets, trying to get the best locations in front of the Shindig stage. Then impromptu performances begin occurring away from the stage, under trees and other locations around the courthouse green—musicians who have not been scheduled to perform that particular evening but who still want to be part of the happening. Finally the shindig show begins, usually kicked of by a good oldtime hoedown. For the next two or more hours there'll be gospel music, blue grass, plain old country, lots of singing and even more clogging. There is audience participation too, with singing and "chair dancing" for those who don't care to join the youngsters, oldsters and everyone in between for square and round dancing or maybe a bit of buck dancing on the "dance floor" in front of the stage. It's all a great deal of fun, all free and everyone seems to attend—local residents and visitors. Shindig begins the first Saturday in July and continues each Saturday until the Saturday before Labor day except for the Saturday of the Dance and Folk Festival in early August. Call the Asheville Visitor Center above for more information.

Asheville
Thomas Wolfe Memorial

P robably every American, even those who've never read or even heard of Thomas Wolfe, have used or have heard used what has now become a cliche: the title of Wolfe's last novel, *You can't Go Home Again*, published posthumously in 1940. This boardinghouse at 48 Spruce Street which was operated by Wolfe's mother, was Wolfe's home as a young man, and was probably the setting for his first novel, *Look Homeward, Angel*. The house contains many of the original furnishings. One room is set aside for family photographs and the works of this gifted and prolific writer who produced five major novels and several less known works before his death at age 38. He and another famous American writer from Asheville, O. Henry, are buried in the Riverside Cemetery on Birch Street. There is only a minimal admission for guided tours of this famous homeplace, conducted daily except Monday. Call the visitor center, above.

Asheville
The Folk Art Center

On the Blue Ridge Parkway at the eastern edge of Asheville is the Folk Art Center—not to be missed, and to be visited often when you are in the area. The 30,000-square-foot-plus Appalachian folk art and craft center includes a retail shop—Allanstand—offering the finest in traditional and contemporary crafts from the southern highlands. The galleries have outstanding exhibits, demonstrations and special programs throughout the year featuring crafts, music, films and workshops reflecting mountain folklife. One of the most popular is the annual Gee Haw Whimmy Diddle World Competition, the first weekend in August, which includes storytelling, music and puppet shows.

The Folk Art Center serves as the base of operations for the Southern Highland Handicraft Guild, which also presents the region's oldest arts and crafts fair twice yearly at the downtown Asheville Civic Center, during the weekends of the third Thursday in July and the third Friday in October. The opening of this center in 1980 marked the 50th anniversary of the Guild, founded for the preservation, improvement and marketing of the best in southern mountain crafts . . . "bringing together the crafts and craftsmen of the southern highlands for the benefit of shared resources, education, market-

ing and conservation." The Center was constructed as a result of the cooperative effort between the Appalachian Regional Commission, the National Park Service and the Guild, and operational expenses are covered entirely by tax deductible grants and gifts from individuals, foundations and corporations. Admission is free, but contributions from visitors are always welcome and are tax deductible.

In addition to the galleries and the retail shop, the Center contains a 300-seat auditorium, a conference classroom, one of the southeast's most extensive craft libraries, and a Blue Ridge Parkway information center, operated by the National Park Service. Park personnel can provide visitors with tips on getting the maximum enjoyment from the parkway and with up-to-date information on parkway travel conditions.

The Folk Art Center is open every day except Thanksgiving, Christmas and New Year's from 9 am to 5 pm, with extended summer hours. It's a wonderful place to shop for distinctive Christmas gifts, especially during "Christmas with the Guild," a series of festivities including concerts and a Christmas tree exhibit during the month of December. For further information and the complete annual schedule of events and exhibits, contact The Folk Art Center, P.O. Box 9545, Asheville, NC 28815. The Center is located on the Blue Ridge Parkway at Milepost 382, about one half mile north of US 70, just east of Asheville.

Asheville
Biltmore Estate

The admission charged for a tour of this estate covers the entire day, and you'll need at least half a day to see it all. Established by George Vanderbilt in the late 1800's (still owned by the Vanderbilt heirs), the estate consists of 8,000 acres, including a vineyard and 17 acres of formal gardens surrounding the 255-room French Renaissance-style mansion. The tour takes visitors through over 50 rooms including the formal living areas with original furnishings and art treasures, the working and servants quarters, the recreation areas complete with a bowling alley, the formal garderns and the winery for a slide presentation and trip to the tasting and sales room. Visitors are free to move about the grounds and public areas on their own. Add a visit to the gift shop and a restaurant on the grounds and you've spent the greater part of a day. The Biltmore Estate is open daily year round, except for Thanksgiving, Christmas and New Year's, 9 to 6. The entrance to the estate is located on US 25, just north of I-40. Phone 704/274-1776.

Asheville
Biltmore Village Historic District and Craft Fair

On US 25, just before the entrance to the Biltmore Estate is the village constructed as a housing and service facility for the Vanderbilt estate workers and servants. It was declared an historic district in 1979. Two dozen of the original buildings include the All Souls Episcopal Church and several cottages now housing shops, galleries and restaurants. This is a nice place for a walking tour along tree-shaded old cobblestone streets. If you can arrange your visit to this area during the first weekend in August, you'll have the added attraction of the annual Biltmore Village Craft Fair, held on the church grounds and featuring fine arts and crafts from all over the southeast. (Their annual posters are collector items!) No admission. Call the New Morning Gallery, below, for more information on the fair.

Asheville
New Morning Gallery

Give yourself plenty of time for a visit to this exceptional gallery—a bright and airy showplace for the diversity of form and design in fine American crafts. The extensive collection of pottery, jewelry, art glass, sculpture, fiber art, painting, prints and much more ranges from the purely practical to the joyously whimsical, from the daringly innovative to the time-tested traditional. There's an array of kaleidoscopes in wood, copper and brass, many with interchangeable parts. There's a "made in North Carolina" section, another devoted to creative food preparation and presentation. The jewelry section has masterfully crafted original designs in silver, gold, copper and bronze, including a selection of stunning wedding bands in 14-carat gold. Throughout the year the New Morning schedules special exhibitions and also sponsors the annual Biltmore Village Arts and Crafts Show (above), always the first weekend in August. (Write them for information on the show and/or a full color gallery brochure.) The New Morning Gallery is located in the above historic Biltmore Village, a few minutes south of downtown Asheville, about 1/2 mile north of I-40, exit 50. Mailing address is 7 Boston Way, Asheville, NC 28803; phone 704/274-2831.

Asheville
Black Dome Mountain Sports

About everything anyone needs to obtain for Carolina mountains recreation—from sound advice to topo maps, reliable gear to weather conditions—can be obtained at either of the Black Dome's two Asheville stores, one in the above historic village. This is also the place to get other maps including those wonderful raised relief maps, suitable for framing. Gear, clothing and accessories are top quality, and so is the staff. More than just friendly salespeople, these men and women participate: they are hikers, campers, skiers and two of the south's leading climbers. (And there's more climbing gear here than anywhere else in the southeast.) If you are planning or would like to plan an Appalachian Trail weekend (or even a through hike), a climb up Looking Glass Rock, a Saturday cross country on Clingman's Dome Road, or a downhill night at Cataloochee, this would be a good place to stop before you start. The stores are located at 144 Tunnel Road (Near I-240 West) and at 2 Biltmore Plaza in the Biltmore Village, about 1/2 mile north of I-40, exit 50. Zip is 28805; phone 704/251-2001 or 274-4280.

Asheville
Richmond Hill Inn & Gabrielle's at Richmond Hill

This 100-year-old mansion is the grand new place in Asheville for weekending, vacationing, conferences, seminars, weddings, receptions, and for dining at a gourmet restaurant called Gabrielle's at Richmond Hill which is open to the public.

Built in 1889 as the private residence of Congressman Richmond Pearson, the doors to the great Queen Anne inn opened to the public in late 1989. The supervising architect of the United States Treasury Buildings during the 1800s, James G. Hill, designed the original 30-room residence. Rehabilitation, including some additions, was under the guidance of North Carolina architect Jim Samsel. Most of the original features were saved including the 10 fireplaces with mantels, bronze door hinges, beautiful paneling, doors, and woodwork of solid oak, cherry, and walnut, a slate roof and two clawfoot bathtubs. The 3,000 square feet of interior space includes the grand Oak Hall, two elegant parlors, and the restaurant that features American and nouvelle cuisine. Restaurant and inn guests can dine in two distinct areas —the Dining Room with its Chippendale furnishings or the less formal wicker-furnished Sun Porch.

Richmond Hill also has a library that houses several collections including rare first editions, a 900-square-foot octagonal ballroom, several meeting and conference rooms, and 12 antique-furnished guest rooms. Each guest room features a luxurious bath (there's a jacuzzi in the Chief Justice Suite), television, telephone, and distinctive decorating. Different features in individual rooms include fireplaces, skylights, and views of the mountains and the Asheville skyline. The inn sits on a 47-acre estate, high above the French Broad River. For an information package, rates and reservations, contact Richmond Hill Inn, 87 Richmond Hill Drive, Asheville, NC 28806; phone 704/252-7313.

Asheville
23 Page Restaurant

This charming little restaurant is located at 23 Page Avenue, a block from the Civic Center in downtown Asheville, but one could easily imagine themselves in an uptown Santa Fe cafe. The adobe-like walls are painted a soft coral and accented with ceiling beams, native American basketry and primitive antique furnishings. Ornamental iron windows in the full service cocktail lounge open directly onto the sidewalk, adding a festive holiday touch to everyday gatherings.

The cuisine includes updated American specialties like Breast of Chicken Old Virginia—stuffed with country ham, grits and peanut sauce. Entrees with a touch of Europe include linguine with smoked salmon and trout. There are old standards like grilled steaks and daily fresh fish and seafood. Lunches offer interesting salads, omelets, crepes and sandwiches, and it's all made with the freshest ingredients available. Service is competent, friendly and unpretentious from proprietors Mark and Amy Ensner and a well trained staff. Prices are reasonable for exceptional quality of food, atmosphere, service and intown convenience. Hours are 11:30 to 2 and 5:30 to 10, Monday through Saturday. Closed Sunday. Reservations are not required but are a good idea; phone 704/252-3685.

Asheville
Cedar Crest Victorian Bed and Breakfast Inn

Within walking distance of the Biltmore Estate and 1 1/2 miles from downtown Asheville, this grand mansion is perched dramatically on a hill over Biltmore Avenue. It's an imposing structure with gables, turrets and verandas. But neither the exterior nor the elegant entranceway of beveled and leaded glass doors prepares the visitor for the interior.

Fine woods were plentiful in the 1890's, and the original owner obviously prized them. There are beautifully carved mantels, entire walls, grand stairwells, even a ceiling or two made entirely of oak and heart pine! Listed on the National Register of Historic Places, the inn offers 10 guest rooms in the main house and two suites in the inn's guest cottage. Each room is uniquely furnished in period antiques including carved oak and walnut headboards and brass beds, adorned with canopies, satin and lace. Baths are private or semi-private. All rooms are air conditioned and phones are provided. Start your day with a deluxe continental breakfast. Take an afternoon break for a stroll through the gardens or a croquet match followed by tea on the veranda, and enjoy evening chocolate or coffee in the parlor, compliments of hosts Jack and Barbara McEwan. The inn is open all year and the convenient location makes it excellent for a winter getaway as well as a summer vacation base for exploring this region. For more information contact the McEwans at Cedar Crest, 674 Biltmore Avenue, Asheville, NC 28803; phone 704/252-1389.

Asheville
Cornerstone Inn

"**I**f Evelyn has two of anything, she starts a collection," claims her husband, Lonnie Wyatt. Which makes one wonder . . . a couple guests here, another there, before you know it, there's a collection of guests . . . and the large stone Dutch tudor-style residence is a full-fledged bed and breakfast inn . . . However it evolved, it's a perfect outlet for the natural hospitality of these two southerners, who, as career military before retirement, had entertained guests all over Europe.

After a warm greeting and perhaps a tour (don't miss the area in back of the kitchen for Evelyn's most unusual collection: old oil and woodburning kitchen stoves), guests may gather with others in the formal living room, or relax in a spacious guest room. All are tastefully and comfortably furnished with family heirlooms and fine antiques from the Wyatt's travels abroad. Each has a private bath and one has a private little balcony above a small walled garden. A full country breakfast is served through French doors on a side porch or in the formal dining room. The inn, constructed of large gray stone, is nestled among grand old hemlocks in the Asheville Historic District near downtown's shops, restaurants, cultural events and many festivals. Guests are welcomed all year. Contact Cornerstone Inn, 230 Pearson Drive, Asheville, NC 28801; phone 704/253-5644.

Asheville
Heritage Hill Bed & Breakfast Inn

The two nicest things about this large old 1900's home (next to the genuine friendliness of hosts, Linda and Ross Willard) is that it's as homey as it looks and it's full of surprises. Third nicest thing is that the surprises get better and better with each visit. An open porch is enclosed to create a solarium —great for Linda's plants, and a favorite napping place for Toby, Sam, Sugar and Smoky, the resident cats. More bedrooms added. More private baths. The round bed has been re-upholstered in floral, and is the most popular of the kingsize beds in the rooms with working fireplaces. Some more "uptown" antique furniture has been added . . . nothing impressive enough to get between the guests and the "homey comfort" they keep referring to in the guest comments book. (Actually the most frequently used words in the comments book seems to be "cozy" although one wouldn't usually refer to a big old house on a hillside acre of parklike grounds as "cozy," so it must be the atmosphere.)

The best things haven't changed. You can still make yourself a cup of tea or coffee at the table in the hallway outside your room. Chill your wine in the kitchen fridge. Discover a good book. Take your bountiful buffet breakfast to the wraparound porch, or join other guests in the dining room. Play the working Victrola in the parlor, or snuggle into a deep chair by the fireplace and watch for a white Christmas to happen in the mountains. Or admire the flower beds in spring and summer. And if the one in back above the stone wall is missing on the next trip, check to see if there is a new, enlarged dining area—with a glass and stone enclosed garden. Ross is considering that for the next surprise. Heritage Hill is located in the Grove Park district, about a mile from I-240 and downtown. Address is 64 Linden Avenue, Asheville, NC 28801; phone 704/254-9336.

Asheville
The Old Reynolds Mansion

This perfect place for bed and breakfast is beautiful, quiet and secluded. The massive, three-story brick house was built in the 1850's by Colonel Daniel Reynolds. Located on a knoll of Reynolds Mountain in a rural setting, the mansion is surrounded by acres of trees with a beautiful view of the mountains. It remained in the Reynolds family until the mid-1970's, but time and years had taken their toll.

Lots of hard work and a perfect place for a bed and breakfast inn was what Fred and Helen Faber saw when they first looked at the house in 1977. A combination of their talents, many years of work, and determination have turned what was once described as a "brick monstrosity" into a majestic, lovely home. It is currently listed on the National Register of Historic Places.

You can sleep in a large, high-ceilinged bedroom with fireplace, bathe in a claw-footed tub in front of the fire in the bridal suite, or choose one of the many interesting rooms on the third floor. Each room has a different feel, but all are furnished and decorated in keeping with an old house. You can choose country, Oriental, elegant, masculine or feminine rooms. Enjoy a continental breakfast by the fireplace, on the verandas or by the old swimming pool, built in the 1930's, and nestled in the pines.

Ten guest rooms are available, some with private baths, some with fireplaces — all are lovely. Call or write for brochure or reservations to The Old Reynolds Mansion, Fred and Helen Faber, 100 Reynolds Heights, Asheville, NC 28804; phone 704/254-0496.

Asheville
The Reed House Bed and Breakfast

Families and children are welcome in this historic restoration-work-in-progress. Restorer and innkeeper is Marge Turcot, one of the founders of the Preservation Society of Asheville. After more than 12 years, she has just begun to make a dent in restoring this 4,000-square-foot 1892 Queen Anne Victorian. The house had been empty and vandalized for years before Marge bought it—and moved in—so all available funds were used for essentials in the beginning: like glass replacement for 62 windows, and 180 bundles of shingles for the roof!

A few simply-furnished, comfortable guest rooms are open. Each has a working fireplace, all laid and ready to be enjoyed on cool evenings. There is a game room with a pool table, used in the wee hours by the house ghost, according to Marge. In addition to the ghost, other unusual features include a tower, secret passageway and a collection of old trunks, rockers and other antiques; many, like the house, are restoration-works-in-progress. But work stops when guests arrive. Then it's time for visiting, talking historic preservation and sometimes, if guests are interested, taking them on walking tours of other historic homes and districts in Asheville.

The Reed House is listed on the National Register of Historic Places, is pictured in the book, *Cabins and Castles,* and was the feature story, with photos, in the December 1987 edition of *The Old House Journal.* For rates and reservations contact The Reed House, 119 Dodge Street, Asheville, NC 28803; phone 704/274-1604.

Asheville
Mountain Spring Cottages-Chalets-Cabins

C lean, clear South Hominy Creek meanders 'round meadows, minirapids its way over small boulders, and scoops out a couple of ol' swimmin' holes as it flows past the 50-acre family farm and the creekside guest cottages of John and Sara Pelteir. Call them cabins, cottages or chalets—each is different, all are delightful. Some have fireplaces, all are beautifully furnished in fine country antiques, and completely equipped from the color cable TV in the living rooms, to the one or two spacious bedrooms with modern bath, to charming country kitchens, to the swings and rockers on porches overlooking the stream. There are flowers in the window boxes, grapes in the arbors and herbs in the garden, even a kitten or two playing around the homestead barn and sheds. 'Midst all this country tidiness there are places for children to play, fisherpeople to fish, romantics to daydream—and just up the road a ways are stables for horseback riding. It's all about 15 miles west of Asheville, four miles from the Blue Ridge Parkway and near the Pisgah National Forest for hiking and waterfalls. This may sound too good to be true, but it's only too good to be missed. For reservations contact Mountain Springs Cottages, P.O. Box 2, Candler, NC 28715; phone 704/665-1004.

Mars Hill/Hot Springs/Spring Creek/Trust/Luck
Mars Hill College/Southern Appalachian Repertory Theater

T his liberal arts college is the cultural center of rugged Madison County, and the little town of Mars Hill seems almost to be an integral part of the 150-acre campus. Many of the college's facilities, activities and events are open to the public including the Rural Life Museum, featuring a collection of tools, furnishings and other artifacts which provide a look at this area's pioneer family life. There is also an excellent handicraft shop operated by the Madison County Crafts Association. During October the college presents a music and dance festival, and throughout the summer there are performances in the college's Owen Theater by The Southern Appalachian Repertory Theater (SART). The professional summer theater group presents a total of six dramas and musicals, rotating nightly, from mid-June through early August. For more information on the museum, shop, festivals and other events, plus a current or upcoming theater schedule and ticket prices, contact Mars Hill College, P.O. Box 53, Mars Hill, NC 28754; phone 704/689-1023.

Mars Hill/Hot Springs/Spring Creek/Trust/Luck
The Baird House Bed and Breakfast

T his turn-of-the-century home has five guest rooms, a parlor for visiting, a porch for rocking, gardens for appreciating—and a vivacious, friendly innkeeper for information about the area. Yvette Wessel can tell you where to go hiking. Or biking. What's to see and do across the street on the Mars Hill College campus. Or just over the mountains in Tennessee.

Where to find wildflowers in the spring and ski slopes in the winter. Or the history of this mountain village, and the history of those who built the Baird House, its "grandest home" and center of community life for many years. Some of the guest rooms have working fireplaces, some have private bath. One has television. A full breakfast, served family style, usually sends people out planning to skip lunch. It features a variety of sweet breads (strawberry, poppyseed, blueberry, etc.) homebaked by the hostess. The inn is open all year except December, and the moderate rates are reduced even more from January through April. Contact the Baird House, P.O. Box 749, Mars Hill, NC 28754; phone 704/689-5722.

Mars Hill/Hot Springs/Spring Creek/Trust/Luck
Hot Springs and Scenic Route 209

Hot Springs sits at the intersection of the Appalachian Trail, the French Broad River, US 25/70 and one of North Carolina's less traveled scenic highways, state route 209. You can't miss Hot Springs. As for Spring Creek, Trust and Luck . . . well they are more states of mind than towns, but you'll find them by following 209 south and you'll enjoy every mile of the way. It's only 36 miles all the way back to Waynesville, and this scenic road winds and twists around rocky bluffs, beside cascading creeks, past rural homes and farms, through miles of the Pisgah National Forest and offers great places for outdoor activities and even some refreshments along the way.

Hot Springs was a thriving resort town back in the 1920's when it was known for its warm mineral springs. The springs are on private property and no longer open to the public. Vacationers come to Hot Springs for other reasons now; to hike (or take a break from) the Appalachian Trail which comes off the mountain here, runs right down Main Street and follows the French Broad River into Tennessee, or they come to raft or canoe the river. There are several rafting company outposts near the bridge offering guided trips for beginners and experienced rafters, and there's a hiker's hostel operated by Jesuit priests at the Catholic Retreat Center on a hill in town. The hostel offers bunk-type lodging and a kitchen where hikers may prepare their own food. (Address is Hiker Hostel, P.O. Box 7, Hot Springs, NC 28743; phone 704/622-3248.) The U.S. Forest Service, French Broad River District Office is located in town on US 25/70. Stop here for hiking, camping and recreation area information and trail maps. The office is open Monday through Friday, 8 am to 4:30 pm. Address is P.O. Box 128, Hot Springs, NC 28743; phone 704/622-3202.

Mars Hill/Hot Springs/Spring Creek/Trust/Luck
Spring Creek Cafe & Trust General Store

You're still going south on 209, admiring the scenery, getting a little hungry and expecting to find, at most, some place where there's a cold drink machine, and suddenly here's an oasis in the forest. A real cafe with a deck and umbrellas, and inside booths and tables with real food! This is *not* a convenience store with a microwave oven, though the cafe shares building space with a general store and gas station.

The Spring Creek Cafe and the Trust General Store were built and are owned and operated by Bill and Beverly Barutio—and a very nice staff. Beverly writes good poetry and makes excellent pies. You can get both poetry and pie here. Bill keeps the nice, modern, general store stocked with everything people in these communities might need, from fertilizer to razor blades. He also keeps picnic and camping replenishments on hand during vacation season. You can get breakfast, lunch, dinner (and pie) from early morning until around 9 in the evening and a country-sized Sunday buffet until 3 which has everything you'd expect on a country buffet. Lunches and dinners offer things like ribeye steak, burgers, deli-style sandwiches, fresh mountain trout . . . and pie. The store has the same hours.

You can get one more thing here that is almost impossible to get anywhere else — correct directions and a rough map to Max Patch Bald, Bill and Beverly's favorite picnic spot. From atop this 4,629-foot meadow, wildflower and grassy covered bald you can see some of the prettiest and highest mountains in the eastern United States. You can reach Max Patch Bald by hiking the AT to its summit, or you can reach it by finding the right gravel road which goes right up to the top. It might be easier to hike it than to find the right road without Bill and Beverly's map. If you don't like gravel roads, keep south on 209. You'll find Luck just down the road. The cafe and store numbers are 704/622-7431 or -7412.

Mars Hill/Hot Springs/Spring Creek/Trust/Luck
Rocky Bluff Campground & Recreation Area

L ocated a few scenic miles south of Hot Springs on 209 is the Rocky Bluff Recreation Area, appropriately named for the high bluffs along the mountains in this section of the Pisgah National Forest, separated only by the state line from Tennessee's Cherokee National Forest. You'll have many views of the bluffs along this highway. This recreation area never seems to be full or even heavily used, possibly because, in addition to this being such a little traveled road, there are no electric or water hookups for RVs' at the campground's 29 tent and trailer sites. There are flush toilets and running water (no showers though), 13 picnic sites and a beautiful easy loop trail along Spring Creek which borders the camping area. Except on holiday weekends, there are usually sites available. For more information call the ranger office above.

Bat Cave/Chimney Rock/Lake Lure

A bout 1 1/2 hours southeast of Asheville the Rocky Broad River cascades and tumbles and splashes around a riverbed of boulders, through the Hickory Nut Gorge and into Lake Lure. The river banks are strewn with private campgrounds, there's a beach and boat rentals at the lake, and a variety of shops along the US 64/74 through the three side-by-side communities. The biggest attraction here is the following park which includes hiking trails and some awesome views.

Bat Cave/Chimney Rock/Lake Lure
The Stonehearth Inn

G o for lunch or a country supper, for one of Susie Scheaffer's luscious desserts, or go for a getaway, sleeping in a pine paneled room so close to the Rocky Broad River you can almost reach out your window and touch the water. If this 1940's inn was any closer to the river, it would be in it. The four guest rooms are comfortably, simply, back-to-grandma's furnished, and each has a private bath with shower. Next morning you may start your day a perfect way; take your complimentary continental breakfast at one of the picnic tables on the banks of this absolutely splendid river. Or you may prefer the warmth of the dining room, the great stone fireplace and hearth.

Lunch and dinner are open to the public. You may order a light lunch of soups, salads and sandwiches, or go for the popular suppertime entrees of roast beef, baked chicken or fish or western style ribs, served with family style bowls and platters of biscuits, potatoes, vegetables, salad and relishes. Brown bagging is permitted. Closed on Mondays and the month of January. Located on Highway 64/74. Contact Susie Scheaffer, Stonehearth Inn, P.O. Box 242, Bat Cave, NC 28710; telephone 704/625-4027.

You can spend an entire day here, and it begins as soon as you cross the Rocky Broad River at the park's entrance deep in Hickory Nut Gorge (The name of the gorge is derived from the falls high atop the cliffs in this park.) The drive to the top is three miles of unspoiled natural beauty. If visitor traffic is light you may see a fox or racoon along the road which winds upward through woodlands thick with fern and wildflowers, songbirds and small wildlife.

The highlight of the park is the towering Chimney Rock with its 75-mile view, and Hickory Nut Falls, one of the highest waterfalls in eastern America. There are picnic areas with tables and grills, a children's playground, and the Sky Lounge with an indoor viewing area, snack bar and gift shop. You can enjoy it all from here or you can continue to the top of Chimney Rock, so named because it is believed that Indians once sent smoke signals from the top.

Access to the chimney level is by elevator rising 26-stories through a shaft blasted through the sheer granite cliff. Or you can go on foot along a trail through a subterranean area, over catwalks from rock to rock, through an authentic moonshiner's cave, with several camera stops along the way. (There is an annual photo contest, open to all, with cash prizes for photos best capturing the spirit of the park.) Two trails lead to the falls; one to the top along rugged cliffs, and a less strenuous trail to the bottom of the falls which start with cascades, drop 400 feet, then continue falling through a series of cataracts for another 1,000 feet into Hickory Nut Gorge.

Several special events are scheduled in the privately owned park throughout the season, including an Easter Sunrise Service for which no admission to the park is charged. The two other major events are auto races; one up, one down. The Hillclimb takes place the fourth weekend in April when members of the Sports Car Club of America race against the clock, one car at a time, up the three miles and 19 curves to the top. The Downhill race is the third weekend in September; a bit less glamorous perhaps but to some a lot more fun—adults race down the mountain in gravity powered washtubs.

The park is open from mid-March through the end of November, weather permitting. An admission is charged and visitors may stay the entire day if they choose. For a free brochure with area map, information on the photo contests and an events calendar contact Chimney Rock Park, Chimney Rock, NC 28720; phone 704/625-9611.

Bat Cave/Chimney Rock/Lake Lure
Lake Lure Inn

T his gracious 1920's inn, which once hosted such personalities as Emily Post, F. Scott Fitzgerald and F. D. Roosevelt, offers lakeside luxury getaways for two and conference and banquet facilities for up to 125. Under the new ownership of Sand Dollar Management Corporation of Hilton Head Island, SC since 1989, the three-story facility is completely renovated and refurbished, from the kitchen to the lobby to all 50 guest rooms and suites. The inn offers the amenities of a small, elegant hotel, including modern private baths, room phones and television, fine dining, a full service cocktail lounge and a garden-setting swimming pool, all directly across the road from the lake and surrounded by some of the prettiest mountains in the Blue Ridge. There's golf nearby, and Asheville's attractions less than an hour away. Contact Lake Lure Inn, P.O. Box 10, Lake Lure, NC 28746, phone 704/625-2525 in state or toll free, 800-277-5873. (For conference, banquet and meeting information call 800-768-2525.)

Bat Cave/Chimney Rock/Lake Lure
The Dogwood Inn

G eorgann and retired naval commander Lamont Davis have added an international flair to this 1930's country inn, accenting traditional furnishings with accessories collected from 22 years of travel.

Each of the 10 guest rooms, some with private bath, has its own interesting pieces to complement country quilts, braided rugs and architectural features such as tongue-and-groove ceilings and heart pine floors. Many of the rooms have balconies or porches right above the Rocky Broad River.

Television and daily newspapers are available in the den, along with early morning juice and coffee. On cooler days there will be a cozy fire behind the glass door in the wood stove. A complete breakfast is served later, in the dining room or on one of the several riverside porches. Picnic lunches are available on request. Dinner can be arranged for groups, and the entire inn is available, at special rates, for weddings, receptions, luncheons and family reunions. Located on the main street, within walking distance of the village shops, restaurants, and attractions. Open all year. Contact the Dogwood Inn, P.O. Box 70, Chimney Rock, NC 28720; phone 704/625-4403.

Bat Cave/Chimney Rock/Lake Lure
Hickory Nut Gap Inn

I t's one mile up to this mountain in Bat Cave from the winding road along the river gorge. After the founder of Trailways Bus Company built his weekend retreat up here in the late 1940's, he used to arrive by chauffeur-driven limousine, but your Chevy, Ford, BMW or Jeep will do nicely.

Follow the gravel road. You'll know when you get there. After gaping at the scenery, close your mouth and go into the screened, shingled, rustic, sprawling inn. You'll find "B" or "Easy", your hosts who are as informal as their names. They have a special way of making you feel like you live here.

Look around, and, if you think the greatroom is great—as in large, wait till you see the basement, with two more fireplaces, a bowling lane, ping pong area, sauna and massage room . . . and six guest rooms with private baths, some with fireplaces . . . and all those different woods on walls, floors and ceilings; maple, cherry, oak, poplar, walnut, wormy chestnut—all milled from trees found on this mountain. There's a piano, games, books, VCR, Native American rugs and artifacts, art posters and oriental prints, fresh cut flowers, an 80-foot long porch, rockers, swings, hammocks, hummingbirds, hawks and miles of mountain woods laced with logging trails for excellent hiking.

Breakfast might be German Apple Pancakes, sour cream coffee cake, bagels with cream cheese, nutbreads or muffins with preserves, fresh fruit, yogurt and herbal teas. If you are looking for heaven, this is at least as close as a lot of people will ever get. But remember, that this heaven has only six guest rooms (with surprisingly modest rates) so make your reservations ASAP: Hickory Nut Gap Inn, P.O. Box 246, Bat Cave, NC 28710; phone (704)625-9108.

Tryon/Saluda
Scenic 176 & Pearson Falls Park

I t's only seven miles between these two small towns, but there is 1,000 feet difference in elevation, and a less measurable but nonetheless tangible difference in the character of these two communities almost bordering South Carolina. Tryon has a Riding and Hunt Club, the Blockhouse Steeple Chase Races, and a Fine Arts Center. The plain little business district gives no hint of the small but cosmopolitan population which includes many retirees attracted to a lifestyle that includes riding to the hounds.

Saluda has railroad tracks parallel to main street with its one caution light, two real old time general stores with real oldtimers on the benches along it's tree-shaded sidewalk, an active resident association of artists and craftspeople, and a lot of visitors poking around shops featuring their works.

The best thing connecting these two villages is little-used US 176—little used because now there's I-26, which is not nearly as enjoyable. This little two-lane unwinds around the base of the bluffs along the Pacolet River, giving one an ear-popping, eye-pleasing seven-mile trip up or down what is known as the Saluda Rise. About halfway between, watch for a small sign on the river side of the road to Pearson Falls Park. Open 10 to 6 daily, the 308-acre park is about one mile off the highway, hidden in a cool glen where the river tumbles over several waterfalls, and wildflowers, ferns and mosses grow in profusion. The Tryon Garden Club owns and operates the park and maintains the riverside trails and picnic facilities. There is a minimal admission, but a trip here is priceless.

Tryon/Saluda
Heartwood

Hand-dyed cotton cords are used to create stunning and comfortable hanging chairs, an exceptional item even in this gallery of many exceptional contemporary crafts. Shelley Dekay created the design for these lovely chairs which she assembles in back of the shop. She also offers hammocks to match, and can custom dye the cords to match fabric swatches. Because she sells her work direct, you will find these chairs are exceptionally priced, so consider one as a gift for yourself while you are shopping for others.

Shelly also has a floor loom in the shop where she creates wearable art; beautiful handwoven clothing and accessories from scarves to jackets. Other popular items in the shop include art jewelry, baskets, pottery and quilts. There are also some unusual wind chimes, birdhouses and feeders—nice porch and garden accessories to the chairs and hammocks. Plan time here to watch an artist at work. Heartwood is located on Main Street and remains open some of the winter. Telephone 704/749-9615.

Tryon/Saluda
The Pine Crest Inn

A tiny log cabin for honeymooners; golf privileges at a nearby championship course; a dining room that offers bountiful breakfasts, continental and American cuisine at lunch and dinner, cocktails and an extensive list of fine wines; family-size cottages, lots of fireplaces with the fire laid out for you, air conditioning, and private baths are just a few of the reasons the Pine Crest Inn has been a Tryon tradition for over seventy years.

The inn itself, on the National Register of Historic Places, is a two-and-a-half story frame structure containing the dining rooms, and several public rooms with eclectic and comfortable furniture grouped around fireplaces, libraries and a grand piano. Porches, patios and three guest rooms (one with a fireplace) make up the rest of the main inn. Nine log or stone cabins and modern frame cottages provide most of the accommodations. Five of these offer a variety of guest rooms and suites, each with a private bath, most with fireplaces. A charming one-room cabin of ancient logs and a stone fireplace is ideal for honeymooners. A two-bedroom, two-bath cottage and a three-bedroom, three-bath cottage complete with kitchen are available for families or small groups. Giant oak, poplar, pine and dogwood provide color, shade and seclusion. Small stone walls ramble throughout the grounds.

The enormous fireplace, beamed ceiling, wood floors and pub-style tables give the dining room a relaxed, informal, old English atmosphere. All meals are open to the public. Country fresh breakfasts are served from 8 to 9:30; lunch and dinner from 11:30 to 2 and 6 to 8:30. Lunch and dinner menus are extensive and offer daily specials, tempting one with freshly prepared entrees, with emphasis on fresh seafood, chicken and pasta. Reservations are a good idea for dinner—the inn's 70-year reputation for gracious dining brings visitors from surrounding villages and cities in North and South Carolina. The inn is located about 45 minutes from Asheville, 3½ hours from Atlanta. For reservations contact Pine Crest Inn, P.O. Box 1030, Tryon, NC 28782; phone 1-800-633-3001.

Tryon/Saluda
The Orchard Inn

South Carolinians Ken and Ann Hough spent years preparing for the day they'd "find just the right place" to open their country inn. Sixteen restorations of great old Charleston residences gave them the structural and renovation experiences. A large personal collection of antiques, oriental rugs, good books, prints, paintings, pottery and sculpture waited to be shared with inn guests. Ken prepared for the title of "chef" by studying gourmet cookbooks, practice and "lots of gourmet eating." In the summer of '81, the Houghs found their perfect place: a gabled, early 1900's structure, originally owned by the Southern Railroad Company and used as a summer retreat for their executives. It has all the right places for all the treasures, plus fireplaces, porches, 12 guest rooms with private baths, and its very own secluded 18 wooded acres.

Entrance to the inn is by a private road off US 176, winding up through the woodlands to the inn atop the Saluda Rise at an elevation of 2,500 feet. From the glassed-porch dining room, guests have a panoramic view of the Warrior Mountain range. The dining room is open to the public by reservation. There are 10 tables, elegantly set with fine china, silver, crystal and fresh flowers, all facing that marvelous view. Each is reserved for the entire evening—dining at the Orchard Inn is meant to be a leisurely experience. In this atmosphere of relaxed elegance, guests may choose from an ever-changing menu reflecting the availability of fresh ingredients and Ken's mastery of the culinary arts. Choices may include sweetbread coquille, leg of lamb with mint sauce or homemade chutney, or broiled mountain trout. Desserts may include a cheesecake with fresh raspberries, gateus and mousses. Luncheon favorites are tomato and herb soup, a paté and artichoke picnic plate or a chicken curry salad. Wine service and cocktail set-ups are available, but you must bring your own stock to this dry county. Breakfast is available only to house guests and is included in the lodging rates. For reservations contact The Orchard Inn, P.O. Box 725, Saluda, NC 28773; phone 704;749/5471.

Tryon/Saluda
The Foxtrot Inn

A 14 room, turn-of-the-century home, separate guest house, swimming pool, nature trails on 10 wooded hillside acres overlooking a small village with a temperate climate and a long cultural tradition. . . . The quest for a perfect location for a bed and breakfast inn was over. Betty Colby and Mimi Daugherty, two northeastern neighbors, both with children grown and nests empty, both long active in historic restoration, pooled resources and talents. The result is a perfect home away from home environment with a variety of accommodations.

The air-conditioned, private guest house has a hanging deck with a mountain sunrise view, large living room with television, eat-in kitchen, roomy bath, and two extra large bedrooms. Mountain views continue at the traditionally furnished main house. Spacious guest quarters with private baths include two suites, one with a sleeper sofa in the sitting room (perfect for a small family); another with a queensized canopied bed; a room large enough for twin and queensize beds; and another with a lovely four-poster double. Guests are treated to evening wine and cheese, and a full gourmet breakfast. The inn remains open most of the winter. For rates and reservations, contact The Foxtrot Inn, 800 Lynn Road, Tryon, NC 28782; phone 704/859-9706.

Tryon/Saluda
Cabin Fever

T his is the kind of place cabin fever dreams are made of; old-timey-style cabins with woodburning stoves, gravity-fed spring water, rockers on the porch, and totally surrounded by oaks, poplars and pines on a secluded hillside with a nearby mountain stream and plenty of room to roam, hike and play. This is nostalgia with comfort, serenity with convenience. The cabins are hidden by the woodlands yet they are only a few yards from scenic US 176, two miles from Saluda. Each has free firewood for the stoves, modern bath with shower, completely equipped kitchen, main bedroom with two double beds, and a loft bedroom with a twin bed. Everything is furnished but the linens—bring towels, sheets and blankets. The rates are far below average. Available May 1 to November 1 by the night, week, month or season. For further information, rates and reservations, contact Cabin Fever, c/o Preston Mintz, 1055 Keith Street, Hendersonville, NC 28792. Telephone 704/692-9500 or 704/749-9811 or 1-800-SOS-RENT.

Hendersonville/Flat Rock

H endersonville is the county seat of America's seventh-largest apple producing county, so apples and tourism promotion are often combined here, offering visitors tours of orchards abloom in the spring and heavy with fruit in late summer. The town has a two-week-long apple festival beginning in mid-August and ending Labor Day. In between the beauty of the blossoms and the tastiness of the fruit and the fresh cider, Hendersonville offers other attractions and activities. The city's unusually designed, very attractive and award-winning Main Street is the setting for Monday night street dances during the summers. The town has a variety of eating establishments, and many lovely old bed and breakfast inns.

Flat Rock sometimes seems like an appendage, a quiet, small suburb of bustling Hendersonville, but the village has been welcoming summer visitors since the 1820's, and has an historic district listed on the National Register of Historic Places. Flat Rock is better known to today's mountain visitors as the home of the following theatre and also the last home of poet Carl Sandburg. For more information on this area contact the Hendersonville/Henderson County Chamber of Commerce, P.O. Box 489, Hendersonville, NC 28793; phone 704/692-1413.

Hendersonville/Flat Rock
The Carl Sandburg National Historic Site/Big Glassy Trail

C arl Sandburg might have just stepped out, leaving clutters of papers, magazines and books, for a stroll about this 240-acre farm. A visitor can imagine the poet somewhere near, perhaps out at the goat barn with his wife Paula, looking over the newest member of her prize-winning herd of milk goats. Or off by himself, walking the Big Glassy Trail, perhaps drawing inspiration from some songbird, tree, wildflower or lovely view. The plain and simply furnished old frame house where the the poet lived the last 22 years of his life appears to be exactly as the Sandburgs left it, and a leisurely, thoughtful trip here can be a moving experience. During the Flat Rock Playhouse season, the Vagabond Players present performance readings of Sandburg's poetry and his American fairytales, the Rootabaga Stories. Performances are given at the historic site at 2:30 daily except Wednesday and Saturday during the above theater season. There is never an admission to the site, which is owned and maintained by the National Park Service.

A minimum of an hour should be allowed for the tour which includes a self-guiding visit to the goat farm and its residents, offspring of the herd tended by Paula Sandburg. Plan an extra couple of hours if you want to take the moderate 2.6 mile round trip Big Glassy Trail. This was one of Sandburg's favorite walks, and has been designated a National Recreation Trail by the National Park System. The trail ends on a rock formation atop Big Glassy Mountain from where the panoramic views include valley farmlands and distant mountain ridges. For additional information contact the National Park Service, Carl Sandburg Home National Historic Site, Flat Rock, NC 28731; phone 704/693-4178.

Hendersonville/Flat Rock
Flat Rock Playhouse

T he Vagabond Players perform at the Flat Rock Playhouse every summer, from late June through early September. This is the State Theatre of North Carolina, and the Vagabond Players—a professional group organized in New York in 1937—are considered one of the top ten summer theater groups in the country. For a schedule of the current or upcoming season's performances of comedies and dramas, write Flat Rock Playhouse, Flat Rock, NC 28731; phone 704/693-0731.

Hendersonville/Flat Rock
Expressions Restaurant

M eticulous preparation of classical continental entrees, using only the freshest ingredients available, is the standard set and maintained by chef/proprietor Tom Young. Impeccable tableside service by a well-trained, knowledgeable staff is the standard set and maintained by partner, Frank Valsecchi. It's the combination that makes dining in this small, sophisticated restaurant an experience to remember. And to repeat. The popularity of Expressions is such that reservations are almost a must, unless your party is willing to wait in the intimate upstairs cocktail lounge until a table is available in the downstairs dining room.

Dinner appetizer favorites are shiitake mushrooms stuffed with spinach and goat cheese, or smoked trout with sour cream horseradish sauce. Entree favorites include rack of lamb prepared with fresh garlic and fresh mustard, or poached salmon with a sauce of leeks, tomatoes and fennel, or a grilled stuffed duck breast served with raspberry sauce. Desserts offer choices like fresh ice cream and sherbets made with seasonal fruits, or tableside preparations of bananas Foster. The extensive wine list of imported and domestic wines includes selections from Asheville's Biltmore Estate. Expressions is located at 114 North Main, directly across from the Henderson County Courthouse. Open all year (except for mid-winter vacations), Monday through Saturday from 6 pm until . . . The lounge opens at 5 p.m. Closed for major holidays except for Thanksgiving when a traditional holiday feast is served all day. For reservations telephone 704/693-8516.

Hendersonville/Flat Rock
Echo Mountain Inn and Restaurant

I t's easy to feel like King of the Mountain at this great stone inn, 3,000 feet above sea level and three miles above Hendersonville. Now you can be king and contemporary too. There are even fireplaces in some of the guest rooms, suites and kitchenettes. All are air-conditioned, have private baths, phones, cable TV including HBO and special program reception via the inn's mobile satellite dish. Rental VCRs and movies, even computer and copy facilities and facsimile transmission are available for a nominal fee. More! Now there's a poolside tiki bar, a new full cocktail lounge, with a large screen TV.

An extensive menu in the gourmet restaurant with that fabulous view includes 18 entrees and over 70 fine wines and champagnes. A full breakfast, lunch, dinner, and Sunday brunch is open to the public. (There's a continental complimentary breakfast for house guests.) And there's live entertainment on weekends. A new gift shop is stocked with items ranging from personal care toiletries to gifts from Carolina. And a large selection of paperback science fiction and fantasy novels has been added to the inn's library.

New Echo Mountain innkeepers, Bill and Cyndi Calvo (and their baby sons, Billy and Alexi) are keeping all the best features of this grand old favorite, including the unobtrusive, but personal, warm, friendly service. They've added a complimentary afternoon tea for guests (with optional coffee or sherry). Recreation on premises includes shuffleboard, ping pong, the pool and a billiards room. Golfing is available on several nearby championship courses. The inn is AAA and Mobile Travel Guide approved. It is now open all year, with lodging rates available by day, week, month or season. Contact Echo Mountain Inn, 2849 Laurel Park Highway, Hendersonville, NC 28739; phone 704/693-9626.

Hendersonville/Flat Rock
Claddagh Inn

Approved by the American Automobile Association (AAA) and listed on the National Register of Historic Places, this newly renovated inn has hosted North Carolina mountain visitors since the turn of the century. The three-story, yellow, country style inn, a few blocks from the heart of Hendersonville, offers a real chance to "Relive an American Tradition" . . . with a bit o' Irish magic and a touch of Italian cooking provided by innkeepers Marie and Fred Carberry.

Actually it took more work than magic to transform the Claddagh with fresh paint, cheerful wallpaper and comfortable antique furnishings into the meticulously clean and sunshine cheerful inn. It's hard to decide which is the most attractive of the 14 spacious guest rooms, all with private bath. Each is air conditioned and has a ceiling fan and a private telephone. A Fax machine is available for guests' use. Complimentary creme sherry is served in the well stocked library, glowing with the warmth of the fireplace on cool afternoons. The parlor is a favorite lounging area for good conversation with new found friends. The all-you-want-to-eat breakfast, served in the beautifully cheerful dining room, is included in the moderate rates.

Throughout the year Marie and Fred are the people to ask about nearby activities, from sightseeing to cultural experiences to sporting and outdoor action including golf and tennis, hiking and whitewater rafting. Winter at the Claddagh is a favorite time for many: making new friends and renewing summer acquaintances in front of a cozy fireplace, enjoying popcorn, hot cider and a spirited game of scrabble or trivia. During the holiday season, the inn fairly glows with the Christmas spirit, decorated from the veranda through the third floor with Marie's beautiful decorations. And everyone agrees that shopping nearby mountain shops and galleries is more fun than city malls. During the regular season, June through October, the inn's daily, weekly and monthly rates are in effect, with discounts offered at other times, between November and May—for many the very best time to visit the mountains. To plan the best getaway for you, contact Fred or Marie at The Claddagh Inn, 755 North Main Street, Hendersonville, NC 28792; phone 704/697-7778 or for reservations, 800-255-4700.

Hendersonville/Flat Rock
Courtland Manor

T his 1850's manor house has 22-inch thick granite walls, hardwood floors and rope masonary from basement to roof. The long front porch, just made for rocking, and a large covered patio are surrounded by a well tended lawn, abloom with seasonal flowers, and graced by a giant Ginkgo tree. The latter is believed to have been planted by England's Lord Courtland, and to be the oldest of these rare trees in America. The setting is perfect for an outdoor wedding, but the interior is equally beautiful.

A grand front hallway opens through French doors on one side to a formal dining room, and on the other side to a living room accented with a large fireplace. A graceful stairwell leads to the second floor. There are four guest rooms, with private and shared baths, and one suite. Decor is lovely—one has a wonderful art deco bedroom suite. Many of the antique furnishings are for sale. Mary Ann and Cy Miller are keepers of this manor which they opened as a bed and breakfast in 1988. Guests are welcome throughout the year. Modest rates include a full breakfast. Located just off Highway 25 at the north edge of Hendersonville. Contact Courtland Manor, #2 Courtland Blvd., Mountain Home, NC 28758; phone 704/692-1133.

Hendersonville/Flat Rock
Havenshire Inn

H orses and hummingbirds are among the residents of this 40-acre country estate. Guests are welcomed year round at the restored English country manor-style home, built in 1882 and operated as a European style bed and breakfast inn since 1982.

Lyra Picard is the innkeeper. You'll like her immediately. She'll serve refreshments on the screened veranda (be here for the sunset!), and take you on a tour, from the oriental carpeted, antique furnished downstairs common rooms to the five guest rooms, two with private bath. Each is comfortably eclectic with antiques and family bric-a-brac. There is also a charming, rustic one-bedroom cottage with kitchen a few hundred yards from the main house.

There's more to tour at your leisure. If the horses see you about, they'll probably come to the fence near the pond, hoping for an apple. For bird watching, including the hummingbirds attracted by the garden flowers, there are benches at various locations on the broad, sloping lawn. Look for the path to the French Broad River for a longer stroll. After dinner at Brevard or Hendersonville (the inn is between the two towns), enjoy one of the inn's movies on the VCR. Next morning Lyra will be baking something for breakfast, including cinnamon apples if the harvest is in. Contact Havenshire Inn, Route 13, Box 366 Cummings Road, Hendersonville, NC 28739; phone 704/692-4097.

Hendersonville/Flat Rock
The Waverly Inn

T he Waverly is ninety-something; new proprietors since 1988, John and Diane Sheiry are thirty-something. It's proving to be a dynamic May/December relationship. The bed and breakfast inn, listed on the National Register of Historic Places, has three stories, two verandas, about half a dozen common rooms, plus seventeen guest rooms and suites, some with fireplaces and four-poster beds with hand crocheted canopies. About 20,000 square feet (counting the lawn) of charm and romance in the best southern tradition. And since the Sheirys became innkeepers, all private bathrooms, cable TV in all the setting areas (including those on all three floors), a great deal of redecorating and refurbishing including some king and queen size beds. And now something special on several off-season weekends; Murder at the Waverly. The murder mystery weekends are professionaly written and staged with the help of professional actors, posing as guests. Real guests are expected to solve the crime by Sunday, with the aid of ace detective, trench coated and brown fedored, Elliot Schwin (alias Bill Finch, mystery writer). The mystery weekends also include one of the oldest of the Waverly's traditions; breakfasts including huge pancakes, french toast and Moravian sugar cake during the winter. "We will feed you til you cry," claims John. The one judged best among the amateur detectives wins a return trip for two. Every mystery weekend has a new script and new actors, and many guests make reservations for the next one before leaving. For the special weekends, private parties, weddings, getaways and full vacation rates and reservations contact the Sheirys at The Waverly Inn, 783 N. Main Street, Hendersonville, NC 28792; phone 704/692-1090 or out of state, 1-800-537-8195.

Hendersonville/Flat Rock
Bent Oaks Cottages

F rom the little one room "Wild Rose" to the spacious two-bedroom "Magnolia," these 12 individual cottages have all the charm of the late 1930's plus today's comfortable furnishings and amenities, including color cable television, modern baths, heating and air conditioning. Most have fully equipped kitchens. Each has its own little porch. Maid service is provided for guests staying longer than a week. Set in a beautifully maintained, garden-like grove of oak trees, dogwoods, azaleas and beds of wildflowers, Bent Oaks has been in the Cordray family for two generations. Libby and Chuck Cordray, formerly of Tuscaloosa, Alabama, have remodeled and updated everything but the rates, which are still reminiscent of days gone by. Located conveniently on US 25 south, near Flat Rock. Open all year. Contact the Cordrays at Bent Oaks, 1522 Greenville Highway, Hendersonville, NC 28739; phone 704, 693-3458.

Brevard/Cedar Mountain/Lake Toxaway

T he county seat of Transylvania County—"The Land of Waterfalls"—is also the summer cultural center of the south, and in the recent past was voted the number one retirement community in the nation by Rand-McNally's retirement guide. Mountain forests cover 80 percent of the county's 378 square miles. More than 150 waterfalls tumble down the Blue Ridge Mountains into Transylvania County. The Blue Ridge Parkway runs along the northern boundary, just part of a National Scenic Byway loop entirely in the county. The entrance to the Pisgah National Forest, practically at the edge of town, offers almost unlimited outdoor recreation and attractions. Nightly cultural events during the summer include performances at the famed Brevard Music Center, the Brevard Little Theatre and the Brevard College Chamber Orchestra. Children can have their own vacation in the Brevard area too, at over 20 summer camps for boys and girls. For a map to waterfalls, a directory of accommodations, and a complete schedule of annual events, contact Esther Wesley, Brevard Chamber of Commerce and Welcome Center, 35 West Main Street, Brevard, NC 28712; phone 704/883-3700.

Brevard/Cedar Mountain/Lake Toxaway
The Brevard Music Center

S ince 1946, the annual Brevard Music Festival has presented several hundred promising young musicians and nationally renowned performing artists during its six-week long festival beginning in June. In addition to performances ranging from operettas to pops concerts, there's also a schedule of lectures, ballets and chamber orchestra evenings, plus a week-long "Festival of the Arts" which includes western, gospel and choral programs. For a complete performance schedule and ticket information contact the chamber, above, or the Brevard Music Center, P.O. Box 592, Brevard, NC 28712; phone 704/884-2019.

Brevard/Cedar Mountain/Lake Toxaway
Pisgah Forest/Scenic Byway/Camping/Recreation Areas

J ust north of Brevard US 276 enters Pisgah National Forest. The National Scenic Byway loop begins at the entrance, continues on 276 to the Blue Ridge Parkway, turns west (left) on the parkway to NC 215, then south to US 64 then east back to 276 at the entrance to the forest. In addition to scenic attractions after the connection with the parkway, this section of the forest served by US 276 probably offers more outstanding attractions, activities and recreational opportunities than any other 15 or so mile stretch of mountain highway. Stop at the Pisgah Ranger Station less than a mile inside the entrance for hiking maps and information on the attractions ahead. (The ranger office telephone number is 704/877-3265.)

The Davidson River Campground/Fishing/Hiking

Some of the 161 level sites in this lovely spot, located almost directly across from the above ranger station, can be reserved between Memorial and Labor Day; phone 1-800-283-CAMP. The rest are on a first come basis. The campground follows the nice flat area long the riverbank, so its a good place for bicycles and tricycles. There is a nice trail following the river bank for scenic and exercise walking, which eventually leaves the river and becomes the North Slope Trail, a good long half-day hike climbing up forested slopes and following ridgelines in a loop back to the campground area. The beautiful, shallow, clear river is stocked with trout. There are some small shoals here and there, and plenty of places for wading and splashing about to cool off on summer days. The campground is very well run and maintained with a friendly staff of mostly volunteers. There's a 24 hour/day staffed gate house, phones, hot showers, tent pads, full hookups and dump stations and a schedule of nature and music programs. Open from late spring through mid-December. Dispersed primitive camping is allowed off many of the unimproved forest service roads (check with the ranger office).

Looking Glass Falls

Looking Glass Falls is about three miles north. There are pullovers for a good look and photo opportunities of the beautiful falls—85 feet high and 30 feet wide, and bordered on both sides by rhododendron which bursts into bloom in late spring.

Sliding Rock

Photo: Courtesy National Forests in North Carolina

Cooling off at Sliding Rock

Sliding Rock is another mile or so north. This is the ultimate sliding rock, complete with a bath house for changing and an observation deck for "just watching" those daring enough to dunk themselves in icy cold Looking Glass Creek via the 60-foot sliding rock.

The Cradle of Forestry

The Cradle of Forestry in America is a few miles further. This is where the nation's first forestry school was established in 1898. A small admission is charged for your visit here where you will see an 18-minute film and various exhibits including restored buildings of the original school, a 1915 logging locomotive and a steam powered sawmill.

Between the entrance and the parkway, you will also have the opportunity to visit one of the nation's largest trout hatcheries, picnic in a number of areas, stop to fish, to photograph and admire the scenery at roadside pullovers, and begin some hikes, from short loops to overnights and sections of the Art Loeb National Recreation Trail.

Brevard/Cedar Mountain/Lake Toxaway
Oh! Susanna's Restaurant and Store Next Door

 ere's a little Oh! Susanna's trivia: this fun place to get something good to eat opened in 1982, seats 110 in fair weather, 72 in foul weather, is located in a West Main Street house built in 1924; the player piano was built in 1914 and there are over 30 items on the menu ranging from super salads to deli-style sandwiches to nightly complete supper specials, and the beverage list ranges from root beer to champagne. Be the first to answer the daily trivia question and win one of the free desserts which includes homemade pies, cakes and Do Dahs. (Do you know the name of the only movie to pair Gable and Lombard? Do you know the ingredients in a Do Dah!?)

Oh! Susanna's is closed on weekends but is open for lunch and supper, weekdays, served inside or on the deck, and features live music on Friday night —bluegrass to blues—except during football season when J.T. and Susanna Taylor and the entire staff go to cheer for the Brevard Blue Devils. Telephone 704/883-3289.

The House Next Door is a store—the Oh! Susanna's gift shop, managed by Pat McGarrahan. Pat will offer you a complimentary cup of the gourmet coffee-of-the-day and cheerfully answer your questions about the incredible collection and variety of gifts, ranging from A to Z. . . . really, from accessories (for self and home) to a zoo of stuffed animals. The gift shop number is 704/884-9823.

Brevard/Cedar Mountain/Lake Toxaway
Sassy Goose Bed And Breakfast

T his fifty acres of pasture, woodlands and a six-acre lake is tucked away like a dreamscape, two miles down a country lane near the Carolinas' state line. Until a few years ago the site was occupied only by a sassy goose. It now includes the retirement home of Bette and Bob Vande Weghe (pronounced Way), and a separate bed and breakfast guest house. Plenty of tranquility. Serenity. And comfort. Three sunny guest rooms with private bath and color television. Creatively furnished in country eclectic and Bette's own handmade quilts. The special buffet breakfast is served in the dining room or on the deck with that wonderful view. This inn is within a few minutes of all the attractions in the Brevard area, and is only four miles from the very popular Caesar's Head State Park in South Carolina. For rates and reservations contact The Sassy Goose, Box 228, Cedar Mountain, NC 28718; phone 704/966-9493.

Brevard/Cedar Mountain/Lake Toxaway
The Red House Bed and Breakfast

S ince it was built in 1851, ten years before Brevard was incorporated, "the red house on Probart Street" has served many purposes, survived years of neglect and even an attempt to destroy it. As trading post, tavern-type guest house and home of its builder, Leander S. Gash, it was the bartering center for county residents and the first railroad station in North Carolina. It served as Brevard's first post office and the county's first court house, and in post Civil War days, it survived torching by marauders passing through the area—the solid timbers simply refused to ignite. For Widow Gash, it served as a boarding house and means of college education for her five daughters. Its two floors plus attic had gone through a period of disrepair— and some say disrepute—before it became a private school for children and predecessor to Brevard College. It was later converted to a multiple dwelling after numerous structural changes.

Restoration took two years, but the Red House has now come full circle (minus the bartering), with lodging accommodations in six spacious and beautiful guest rooms. The Red House could never have looked better. Hand-stenciled floor coverings grace the living and dining room floors. Original mantels frame several fireplaces. There are grand antiques and family heirlooms throughout. Innkeeper Lynne Ong actually *uses* her mother's fine silver and china to make breakfast something really special for house guests. Open porches on both levels and two sides, a first floor sunroom, and a secluded, shaded lawn are inviting places to relax with a book, visit with other guests, or, if you are lucky, catch a glimpse of Brevard's famous white squirrels. (The unusual squirrels escaped from a circus passing through the mountains many years ago and took up residence in Brevard.) The inn is open all year, rates are moderate and there's a nice discount in the off-season. Contact Peter and Lynn Ong, The Red House, 412 Probart Street, Brevard, NC 28712; phone 704/884-9349.

Brevard/Cedar Mountain/Lake Toxaway
The Womble Inn

S teve and Beth Womble have been welcoming visitors to this inn since 1974, with the casual, comfortable friendliness one usually finds only at the homes of relatives, next door neighbors or old friends. But there are some extra treats here not usually found at the neighbor's or even mother's. A private bath and your own big cheerful bedroom, furnished in 18th & 19th century antiques, for example. Or breakfast served on a silver tray. Yes, in your room! Unless you prefer it on one of the porches on in the dining room. Even catered luncheons or dinners can usually be arranged when reservations are made, unless Beth's culinary talents are already reserved. (She provides on and off premises catering for all kinds of special occasions.)

The two-story, air-conditioned inn has seven guest rooms with private baths. Common areas include a large old fashioned parlor for gatherings, games, cards, music and television. Children are welcome—no charge if they are under 10. The Wombles keep the home fires burning all winter, and reduce the already modest rates from November through April. Located a half mile from the Music Center and three blocks from the intersection of Highways 64 & 276 in the center of the summer cultural center of the mountains. Contact The Womble Inn, at 301 West Main, P.O. Box 1441, Brevard, NC 28712; 704/884-4770.

Brevard/Cedar Mountain/Lake Toxaway
Earthshine Mountain Lodge

T ake an energetic, professional couple with backgrounds in outdoor education, recreation, environmental and Appalachian studies. Add a vision of a vacation, recreation and education center for all ages. Make available a 70-acre mountaintop farm adjoining Pisgah National Forest, and the result is Earthshine—exactly the way Marion and Kim Boatwright dreamed.

From Memorial Day to October 31, this epitome of rustic luxury, with its chinked cedar logs, great stone fireplaces, spectacular views and charming furnishings, operates as a vacation or getaway destination for individuals, couples, families and small groups. Three wonderously fresh, bountiful meals, served family and buffet style, are included with lodging—and the total cost is surprisingly modest.

The main lodge has eight ingeniously designed guest rooms with extra sleeping loft space so that each feels just the right size for a couple or a family or six. Each room has a gleaming private bath. A separate cottage has three double occupancy rooms.

There are plenty of activities right on the mountain; eggs to gather, vegetables and berries to pick, goats to feed, trails to hike, fish to catch, games to play and several strategically placed hammocks in hidden spots for solitary relaxation. Evening programs include campfires, cookouts, sing-alongs, square dancing, storytelling and night prowls. Horseback riding, even lessons, are available and well worth the extra expense—an adventuresome way to explore a network of mountain forest trails. Earthshine is also 20–45 minutes to most all attractions in Cashiers, Brevard, Flat Rock and Asheville.

In addition to being a mountain lodge, Earthshine offers outdoor education programs for schools and serves as the Earthshine Human Development Center for small conferences, seminars, special events and retreats. The Center provides food, lodging, meeting rooms, and programs designed to mobilize group resources and to enhance team work, communication and problem-solving skills. For further information, rates and reservations contact Earthshine, Route 1, Box 216-C, Golden Road, Lake Toxaway, NC 28747; phone 704/862-4207.

Brevard/Cedar Mountain/Lake Toxaway
The Greystone Inn

The Greystone Inn is actually an early 1900's restored Swiss revival mansion listed on the National Register of Historic Places. Owner Tim Lovelace coordinated the extensive renovation and opened the inn in 1985—the only public accommodations on private Lake Toxaway, and the only country inn in North Carolina with the coveted AAA Four Diamond Award.

Due to special agreement with its neighbor, the Lake Toxaway Country Club, the Greystone Inn offers a package of amenities uncommon to most country inns. Guests can enjoy golf, tennis, croquet, badminton, volleyball, horseshoes, bocci, picnicking and hiking to the area's waterfalls and mountainous overlooks. On the beautiful 640-acre lake, the inn provides swimming, sailing, windsurfing, canoeing, waterskiing and fishing.

The tarrif includes a full country breakfast, a six-course dinner, afternoon tea, beverage set-ups, twice-daily maid service, a daily sunset cruise on the lake, and all other recreational amenities except golf.

There are 20 guest rooms in the mansion, 12 in the new luxurious Hillmont Building and two in the historic lakeside cottage. Rooms are furnished in antiques and period reproductions. All except one have jacuzzis, some have fireplaces, others a view of the lake. The large Hillmont rooms all have wetbars, fireplaces, oversize jacuzzis and private balconies overlooking the lake.

Located off US 64, the Greystone Inn is 23 miles east of Highlands and 17 miles west of Brevard. Open from late April to early November. The Greystone Inn, Greystone Lane, Lake Toxaway, NC 28747; phone 704/966-4700 or out of state toll free 1-800-824-5766.

Cashiers

Cashiers is, as the old timers have probably been saying since the first summer cottage was built here, "really growing." That was back around the turn of the century, 100 years *after* the first Scots-Irish settlers put up their first log cabins. It took another 40 years before Cashiers' first multiple-unit lodging facility for weekenders and vacationers. Cashiers *is* really growing—as it always has—slowly. Quietly on its way to becoming a favorite mountain getaway, appreciated as much for what it doesn't have as for what it does. There is now a traffic light at the main intersection (US 64 and NC 107) and a Visitor Center in the Chamber of Commerce. Lodging now ranges from a charming old country inn to motels and luxury condos, and there is a variety of places to lunch and dine. You can shop in quaint old houses or country stores. There's an airport—55 miles away. There are no parking meters and no need for them. No hurry. And apparently, no growing pains.

Set between the casual elegance of Highlands and the smooth orderliness of Sapphire Valley's planned resort communities, Cashiers remains a relatively unpolished gem of a getaway destination. At 3,600 feet above sea level, it's a cool mountain-valley village surrounded by the Nantahala and Pisgah National Forests. It is 5 to 10 minutes from three mountain lakes, 90 minutes from Greenville, SC and Asheville, NC; three hours from Atlanta—and a long way from noise and neon.

About the only time you'll find a real crowd in Cashiers is during festival days. There are several of these, including Pioneer Day, celebrating the founding of the village. There's a great deal of history and a great deal of fun all packed into one day and evening that was planned all year long. Whatever else is planned, the day will probably include a wagon train, bluegrass music, various contests requiring more audacity than talent, street dancing, barbecue chicken and other goodies. This one is usually held the first Saturday in August. For a schedule of events and more information, contact Cashiers Area Chamber of Commerce, P.O. Box 238, Cashiers, NC 28717; phone 704/743-5191.

Cashiers
Whitewater Falls And Horsepasture River Scenic Areas

For a nice scenic loop, combined with some hiking or nature walks, start with the trip to the tallest waterfalls in the Eastern US, Whitewater Falls, dropping 411 feet, practically from North Carolina into South Carolina. Then swing back up to the beautiful Horsepasture River Scenic Area for more waterfalls and some lovely nature trails. For the loop, leave Cashiers on 107 south for about 13 miles to SC 130, then left to NC 281 (Whitewater Falls Road — good signage) and another mile to the parking area. From there it's about a quarter-mile paved path to the overlook, with various other steep trails around the area. There are several spectacular lower falls reached by a really tough steep half-mile trail. To reach the trail, go south on Whitewater Falls Road about a mile, turn left on a gravel road and continue about 4 more miles to a bridge. Park before the bridge—the trail is on the right. No blazes but usually easy to follow—if not easy to climb. To reach the Horsepasture

Whitewater Falls in the Nantahala National Forest
Courtesy North Carolina Travel and Tourism

Photo by Clay Nolen

River Area, follow 281 back north to the bridge over the Horsepasture River (about 2 miles south of US 64). The trail begins near the bridge. It's about a quarter-mile moderate walk to Driftwood Falls and Ranibow Falls, with more nature trails and smaller waterfalls for additional hiking. The Welcome Center above can supply you with more information.

Cashiers
Ralph J. Andrews Recreation Park/Camping

This priceless little park, operated by Jackson County, is such a hidden away place it appears to have become almost an exclusive getaway for its regular annual campers and recreational visitors. But you'll find they're a friendly bunch—after you first find the park. Take 107 north from Cashiers for four or five miles and watch for the small Glenville Grocery. Near the store is a park sign and paved State Road 1157 (Pine Creek Road) which will take you back into the forest, up, down and winding around to the 79-acre park on a Lake Thorpe (formerly Lake Glenville) cove where the fishing is good and the scenery is a postcard from paradise. Check in with park hosts Mr. and Mrs. Howard Hooper before you choose a tent or full hookup RV site (and have a real campground hot shower). The Hoopers will help you get oriented and invite you to scheduled activities like covered-dish suppers, picnics, music fests, square dancing and special celebrations on Memorial Day, Fourth of July and Labor Day. In between you can fish (there's a boat ramp), hike and do some creative loafing. The park's phone number is 705/743-3923, or you can contact the Chamber of Commerce, above.

Cashiers
The Laughing Ram

Lynn Garrett is a Wisconsin native who fell in love with this area while visiting Cashiers in 1982 and decided to open a gift shop just so she could live here. Since then, using contacts in Wisconsin and Florida as well as in the area, she's built her shop into an arts, crafts and fine gifts gallery representing an exciting and varied group of artists. From sophisticated hand-woven clothing to fine art and sculpture, the shop offers exceptional and unusual items you may just have to have for yourself or a special person. The Laughing Ram is a small shop, but give yourself time to browse so you don't miss anything. Among the collection you'll find whimsical pottery by Nancy Hicks, the life-like and lovely pottery animals of Aletha Rector, the functional pottery of the Chappelles, exquisite hand-wovens of Lyn Oglesby and Joy Boatwright. Lynn is also the exclusive dealer of Anna Lee collector dolls for this area. So stop and say "hey" to this talkative midwesterner who'll extol the joys of living in the southern mountains as much, if not more, than any native Carolinian. The Laughing Ram is located at Laurel Terrace just east of the main intersection on Highway US 64 East. Telephone 704/743-2595.

Cashiers
Cashiers Country Store

Expect the unexpected here, beginning with split-rail fences and flower beds around the parking lot. This intown-rustic, uptown-country store carries a combination of antiques, collectibles, country and general store items—which doesn't leave much out. There are lots of antiques, including the display cases, counters and cabinets for gourmet coffee, home-made fudge and other goodies. There's an imaginative selection of gifts for men and a collection of Vera Bradley clothing and accessories for women. The decorative accessories, suitable for mountain cabins and seaside cottages, include lamps, pillows and quilts. There is handpainted pottery from the centuries-old Quimper Pottery Works in France, and selections from various North Carolina potters. There are toys and teddy bears, and everyday is Christmas in the Christmas room. Custom made, handwoven, 100% cotton rag rugs are available and can be ordered from the store. Their summer hours last through Christmas; 10 to 6 weekdays, 1 to 5 on Sunday. In winter the store closes on Sunday and at 5 on weekdays. Located on 107, just south of the main intersection. Cashiers Country Store, P.O. Box 860, Cashiers, NC 28717; phone 704/743-3612.

Cashiers
High Hampton Inn and Country Club

S taying at High Hampton, a resort 3,600 feet high in the Blue Ridge Mountains, is like staying on someone's private estate. Which once upon a time it was—the summer home of the illustrious Hampton family of South Carolina. Picture this. Landscaping by nature and by man is magnificent. Mountains all around. Pine and hemlock forests. Lakes and water-falls. Sweeping green lawns, huge specimen trees, flower gardens. Wild-flowers, ferns and birds. In all, 1,200 acres of mountain beauty.

You stay at the inn, which, with its shaggy chestnut bark siding, blends right into the scenery, or at one of the cottages surrounding the inn. Rooms are comfortable with simple, sturdy furnishings. The food is bountiful, featuring vegetables and herbs from the Hampton gardens, homemade breads and desserts, and regional specialties like country ham. Even frail appetites in-crease with that clean mountain air and all the outdoor activities.

Activities. What choices! A famous 18-hole golf course designed by master golf architect George W. Cobb. Eight fast-dry tennis courts. Fishing on the private lake, no license required. Boating, sailing and swimming. Hiking and jogging. And a planned program of activities for children to keep them happy and busy from morning until bedtime. Through High Hampton's three seasons (the resort opens April 1, closes November 1) there is a full calendar of special events. Monthly golf schools. Tennis tournaments. Nature seminars. House parties. And a bang-up Fourth of July. Depending on your interests and the inn's schedule, you may attend a wildflower forum, go bird watching, graduate from a fly-fishing school, learn to quilt, or play in a duplicate bridge tournament all in one short getaway.

One family, the McKees, has owned and operated this very distinguished inn and complete resort for over 60 years. It's a green and private world where nothing changes much except the seasons and where you could call mountain-watching a sport. For more information and reservations, call or write Miss Agnes Crisp, Reservations Manager, High Hampton Inn and Country Club, 700 Hampton Road, Cashiers, NC 28717; phone 704/743-2411.

Cashiers
Oakmont Lodge and The White Goose Cafe

What makes Oakmont so outstanding is its setting: eight acres shaded by great oak trees and park-like grounds accented with old farm implements, split rail fences, and grist mill. A pond full of ducks, a small pony, a tiger cat minus a tail, and Sarge, the friendly shepherd, add to the country atmosphere. This is an especially good lodging choice for families—equally suitable for anyone who wants quietness with accessibility to all nearby attractions. Located about a quarter-mile north of the US 64 and NC 107 junction in Cashiers, it's approximately three hours from Atlanta, one and a half hours from Asheville. Accommodations for two to four people in rustic lodge units are bedroom/sitting rooms with private bath, and one housekeeping unit with eat-in kitchen, two baths, two double beds in the bedroom and a queensize hide-a-bed in the living room. Each unit has in-room coffee makers, complimentary instant coffee, cable television, walk-in closets, electric heat, good cross ventilation, porches with rockers (and old checkerboards) and plenty of hammocks, picnic tables and grills all about the grounds.

The White Goose Cafe is located in a renovated old barn by the duck pond. Get breakfast, lunch or supper featuring quality food as fresh as this unique country setting. Try the crab cakes! Open to the public as well as to guests — a nice place to go and to linger. Better make reservations for the evening meal, especially during the busy weekends.

Oakmont is family owned and operated, and it shows. Very nice. Reasonable rates and additional off season discounts. Open all winter. Contact Bill Boswell, Oakmont Lodge, Cashiers, NC 28717; phone 704/743-2298.

Cashiers
Cottage Inn

This is practically a little resort secluded on nine wooded acres right in the middle of Cashiers, with a heated pool, tennis courts and 13 cottages with lots of extras. Most have fireplaces and free firewood. All have satellite-dish television, air conditioning, kitchens, full modern baths and showers, decks or porches with swings, chairs or rockers, and furnishings that are simple, clean and comfortable. Split-rail fences, native flowering trees, a pavillion with picnic tables and grills, nature trails and a small laundromat add extra conveniences as well as making this an attractive place to unwind.

The one and two bedroom cottages will accommodate two to eight, with individual cottage features ranging from a second bath to queensize sleeper sofas, lofts with kingsize beds, a double deck built *around* a large poplar tree, a *double* fireplace, an enormous bed handmade of six-by-six cedar posts, and a deck with a heated spa! Four of the newer cottages, built since 1987, are constructed entirely of cedar, have full stone fireplaces and 24-foot ceilings.

New owners since 1988, Bill and Lucy Christopher live at the cottage lodge and now remain open for winter getaways. Perfect! Ask them to have a fire laid for you. They've renovated and refurnished a place for gatherings too, a large common area with adjoining kitchen suitable for retreats, family reunions and other small groups. Reservations are accepted for the winter holidays. A two-night minimum is required for reservations, but cottages are rented to overnight guests when available. Rates are average for the area and are drastically reduced for a Sunday-to-Friday-morning mini-vacation. For more information, rates and reservation, contact the Christophers at Cottage Inn, US 64, P.O. Box 818, Cashiers, NC 28717; phone 704/743-3033.

Cashiers
Millstone Inn Bed & Breakfast

S ilver Slip Falls, for which this inn was once named, is a short hike away. Whiteside Mountain can be seen from several of the guest quarters; 8 spacious rooms, two suites and two efficiency apartments, each with private bath and color television. This grand view also comes with the breakfast, to be enjoyed on the glassed porch or patio, served in the European manner by a host who speaks German, Spanish—and southern hospitality. This gracious shingled inn, built as a private residence in the 1930's, sets atop a shady knoll, at 3500 feet elevation, at the end of a woodsy country lane. A great fireplace, a comfortable assortment of antique and traditional furnishings, lots and lots of old and new books, and a collection of lively table games tempt guests to settle in for quiet evenings after dinner in Highlands or Cashiers. For brochure, rates and reservations, Millstone Inn, P.O. Box 949, Cashiers, NC 28717; 704/743-2737.

Highlands

W hether visitors drive up US 64, NC 28 or NC 106, they must drive *up* to reach this resort village near the peak of 4,635-foot Satulah Mountain in the Nantahala National Forest. Just getting here and scenic touring in the vicinity is one delightful activity—among many. Drives not to miss: 64 east to the Macon/Jackson county line where the first sight of Whiteside Mountain will leave you breathless . . . and then astound you again and again, changing with the sun, the rain and the seasons. (Stop at the nearby ranger station for a trail map to Whiteside and information on other forest recreation areas around Highlands. Phone 704/526-3765.) Take

Photo Courtesy National Forests in North Carolina

The Dry Falls on NC 28 just north of Highlands were given the unusual name because visitors can walk down steps and behind the falls without getting wet.

64/28 west through the Cullasaga River Gorge. The river cascades and falls alongside the road all the way down the mountain. Along the way is Dry Falls, reached by a short hike from the parking area; then there's Bridal Veil, cascading 120 feet from above the edge of the highway. Take 106 south for a less demanding but no less beautiful drive with smaller waterfalls and three major overlooks.

Other activities and attractions include the Highlands Nature Center and Botanical Garden, the Highlands Playhouse for professional summer theater and Highland Studio for the Arts for improvisational acting, chamber music concerts at the Episcopal Church, hiking and shopping. This is a shop til you drop kind of place, and when you drop you can drop into a chair at one of the auction houses.

A few miles south of Highlands on NC 106 is the community of Scaly Mountain where you'll find the only ski slopes in this southern part of North Carolina.

For a schedule of events plus other information about the Highlands area, stop at the visitor center just off Main Street or contact the Highlands Chamber of Commerce, US 64 West, Highlands, NC 28741; phone 704/526-2112.

Highlands
Lick Log Mill

T his special spot, four miles from Highlands and nine miles from Dillard, Georgia, on NC Highway 106 has no billboards to beckon you—just flowers. Lickloggers Chris and Karen Waldron maintain several hundred yards of woodlands along the highway, pruning, mowing and trimming up to both sides of the road, carefully preserving fragile wildflowers and the banks of rhododendron and mountain laurel for the enjoyment of all who drive this way. Many wildflowers, native trees and shrubs surround their craft shop—housed in an 1851 log cabin—and the adjacent pioneer structures, providing a parade of color nearly all year long. Old vines of rambling roses trail hundreds of blossoms along split-rail fences, stone walls and the front of the old grist mill during spring and summer. Multicolored marigolds line the entire front in autumn. And all around the old structures there seems to be something in bloom or about to bloom at any given time except in deepest winter.

Inside the shop there is more to please the eye. The Waldron select only the best quality from crafters who are serious about their work, so whatever you choose it will be the best of its kind—whether it's a bouquet of native dried flowers that costs only a few dollars or exquisite carvings costing several hundred dollars. You'll find pottery here you may not have seen anywhere else; there is a large selection of the popular handwoven rag rugs, and the shop may have the biggest and best basket selection in the mountains. There are baskets outside and inside, on floors, walls and totally covering the ceilings. This is a cozy place to do some Christmas shopping when the weather turns cool and the Waldrons have the woodstove going—sure beats the malls. They stay open weekends in winter, and seven days a week, usually from 9 to 6 or later during the rest of the year. Visitors are always welcome to browse, shop, photograph the scene or just "stop and smell the roses" at Lick Log Mill.

Highlands
Southern Hands

Visiting Nancy and Bill Aaron's shop, Southern Hands, is somewhat like visiting the home of an avid collector with eclectic taste, or attending a gallery showing of reknowned southern artisans. Except here it's "Please Touch". There are no glass enclosed cases or other barriers between browsers and the display of quality regional crafts—folk art carvings, blown glass, weaving, pottery from more than 20 artists, wood of all kinds including spectacular turned bowls, brass, tin and iron work, and handcrafted furniture accent pieces —all destined to become collectibles and family heirlooms.

This classic, enduring quality, represented by names such as Glen Harbin, Goodwin Weavers, Jane Peiser, Paul Bendzunas, Berea College, David Westmeier, Churchill Weavers, Blenko, Virginia Metalcrafters and the Brasstown Carvers, is the standard the Aarons use in their buying trips across the southern states. These trips often take them to artists' studios for hours of learning their art and handicrafts which the Aarons are then able to share with visitors to their shop. Located in Wright Square near the intersection of Highways 64 and 106; open 10 am to 5 pm April through December 31 and Friday and Saturday only during January—March. Southern Hands, P.O. Box 1478 Highlands, NC 28741; phone 704/526-4807.

Highlands
The Stone Lantern

Stepping into the door of this shop is like visiting a museum of oriental art, with one important exception: all this museum's displays are for sale. You may spend under $10 or over $10,000, or you may simply browse, progressing slowly through aisles of antique porcelains, screens, bronzes, and cloisonne. One of the most popular browsing points is the jewelry department where you'll find unique creations in jade, lapis, pearls, sapphires and rubies. The Contemporary Room offers antique reproduction porcelain, lacquerware, and general decorative accessories. The Mandarin Room displays Japanese and Chinese folding screens as well as handcarved rosewood furnitures. Each piece has been carefully selected by the Stone Lantern's founder and owner, Ralph DeVille. His attention to every detail is reflected throughout this oriental oasis, including the daily creation of fresh flower arrangements in every area. (And there's a Garden Room filled with every conceivable item to delight the flower arranger you may be tempted to become.) There is even a small Japanese tea garden complete with pond, bamboo, native plants and stones, and — yes, stone lanterns. Have your gift selection wrapped in either their handmade rice-paper gift wrap or their cinnabar and gold paper. The shop is located on Main Street and is open all year, but usually closes on Sundays (except in October) and some holiday weekends. The mailing address is The Stone Lantern, P.O. Box 309, Highlands, NC 28741. Telephone 704/526-2769.

Highlands
Ikebana Classes/Japanese Flower and Arts Festival

C lasses in ikebana, the art of Japanese flower arranging, are offered at the Martha P. Neese/Ohara School of Japanese Flower Arranging from July through September. Mrs. Neese has studied ikebana since the 1950's, received her Master's degree from the Ohara School of Flower Arranging in Japan, continues Mastergrade studies in Japan each year and serves as lifetime advisor of Ikebana International and the Ohara Southeastern Chapters. Both private and group sessions for beginner, intermediate or advanced levels are available. Even one session with this Master teacher, who travels worldwide, demonstrating ikbana and lecturing on the oriental philosophy, provides the opportunity to learn basic designs and develop a deeper appreciation for the beauty of nature and the simplicity and philosophy behind this ancient art form.

Once each summer, in cooperation with the Stone Lantern, Mrs. Neese coordinates the Japanese Flower and Arts Festival in Highlands. The festival features exhibits by advanced students and teachers from across the Southeast and demonstrations by Mrs. Neese and other visiting, high-ranking Master teachers from other schools. For festival dates, class schedules, fees, and reservations, contact Martha P. Neese, Chimney Swift Lane, Columbia, SC 29619; telephone 803/796-4564 prior to June 15. After June 15, call 704/526-2769. Brochures are available at the Stone Lantern.

Highlands
The Wee Shoppe

E ven the shop here was imported: the original Wee Shoppe, once located on the grounds of the Dormey Hotel, was shipped to this new "Home in the Highlands." It truly was and still is a "wee" shop, even with additions, and it's jam-packed with imports from the British Isles—items that reflect the Scots-Irish ancestry of the southern highlands people. There are hundreds of tartan neckties, kilts for men, women and children, caps, hats, scarves, woolen and mohair blankets, throws, and sweaters. The shop stocks tartan blazers and Donegal tweed sports coats, and will also take measurements for jackets, slacks and kilts to be custom-made in Scotland.

Irish linens, Bellek and Irish Dresden china, books and photo calendars with scenes of Scotland, distinctive gifts for golfers, tins of teas and hundreds of other unique little gifts make it a nice place to shop anytime. If you are shopping for Christmas, do it early—the Wee Shoppe closes for the winter season, although mail orders are shipped all year. Located about three miles from Highlands on US 64 East, open from 10 to 5, seven days a week. The Wee Shop, P.O. Box 1659, Highlands, NC 28741; phone 704/526-5357.

Highlands
Frog & Owl Cafe

When Jerri Fifer opened this restaurant on little used, winding Buck Creek Road, nearly 10 miles from Highlands, nearly 16 from Franklin, she was 18 years old and had completed one cooking course. That was in 1971. If you'd like to get to the source of this most unlikely success story, you'd be smart to make reservations first. Patrons from as far away as Atlanta are still taking that mountain road. It goes with the territory, so to speak, a sort of preamble to a memorable dinner or Sunday brunch.

The memories start with the environment: the splash and spray of a mountain stream cascading down a woodsy slope, under an old mill and around rambling levels of decks, glassed in porches and many-windowed dining rooms. The walls are of old lumber, the tables beautifully set, and the handwritten menu, which changes weekly, offers about two dozen items from appetizers to desserts . . . Jerri has obviously continued her culinary education . . .

The liver pate, made from old family recipe, is still a favorite, but the baked brie is a frequent opening feature. The selection of entrees will probably include more than one fish and seafood dish, a beef filet, a lamb specialty, duck, and the popular chicken de la Maison. The restaurant is open for dinner Tuesday through Saturday from 6 to 9:30 and for a four-course, fixed price Sunday brunch from 11:30 to 2. When the season winds down, mid to late November, Jerri continues her education at various cooking schools or offers classes herself at the restaurant. (Call her for information). Closed on Mondays. For directions and reservations, call 704/526-5500.

Highlands
Old Edwards Inn & Central House Restaurant

"A few nice rooms for ladies and gentlemen," as the sign on Main and 4th advertises, is a bit of an understatement. There are 21 guest rooms and suites, each with private bath, many with private balconies, all decorated in the country manner. Each room, indeed the entire inn, seems straight out of pages from the past, and has been featured in several national magazines.

The restoration and renovation began in the early 1980's. The original frame and stone structure was built in 1878, and a three-story brick section was added in 1930. Each guest room has its own special blend of period wallpaper, stenciling, antiques, country prints, patchwork quilts, and iron and brass or 19th century wooden beds. More antique furnishing and artifacts from America's past are to be found throughout the many comfortable common rooms of the inn.

The Central House Restaurant, located in the original section, specializes in a variety of fresh seafood; from blue crab soup to Cajun shrimp and stuffed mountain trout. Reservations are necessary and may be made when you make your room reservations. This is one of the most popular places in the area and with good reason. Innkeepers Rip and Pat Benton have been successful seafood restauranteurs for years and still operate Blanche's Courtyard on St. Simon's Island, a longtime favorite of visitors to Georgia's barrier islands. The Central House is closed for lunch on Sundays, open every evening during the inn's season: April through November 30. For rates and reservations, contact The Old Edwards Inn, P.O. Box 1178, Highlands, NC 28741; phone 704/526-5036.

Highlands
Hildegard's

Since 1977, when "Chef" Hermann and Hildegard Strache, (both from Germany) opened this restaurant in Highlands' oldest cottage, Hildegard's has been pleasing Highlands' natives, summer residents and visitors alike. The menu entree selections range from expected schnitzels and bratens through a couple dozen or more specialties like poached salmon, rack of lamb, Dover sole, monk fish, shrimp en croute and stuffed trout. There's steak, too, and a chateaubriand for two. This is food preparation that has won "Chef" membership in the world's oldest gastronomic society, the Chaine Des Rotisseurs, and has put Hildegard's Restaurant in Guide Gastronomique. Each item is prepared to order, so plan to be patient and enjoy an evening in one of several delightfully decorated dining rooms at tables set with handhemmed Austrian linens and beautiful china from Germany.

The wine list includes German whites, French reds and a wide range of domestics. The appetizer, soup and salad accent is on a few rare choices. And after dinner consider one of "Chef's" desserts—all extra special. These temptations include a vanilla fluff, hazelnut and chocolate torte, raspberry mousse, mocca parfait, strawberry Romanoff, cheesecakes, and an apple strudel made by Hildegard herself. Look for the restaurant in a little cottage back off Main Street, next to the Blue Ridge Pharmacy. Open Monday through Saturday, 6 until 9:30. For reservations, phone 704/526-3807.

Highlands
The Phelp's House Inn and Restaurant

This large white clapboard house on the quiet end of Main Street has been a home away from home for visitors to Highlands since 1885. Many of the guests proudly count the number of years they've been visiting the Phelp's House and insist they "wouldn't stay anywhere else." Newcomers are delighted to discover the homey atmosphere, the full country breakfast included with the reasonable lodging rates, and the comfortable old-fashioned guest rooms, luxuriously fresh and clean—no cigarette or cigar odors here as the Phelp's House has *always* invited guests to enjoy their smoking outside.

Along about dinner preparation time, the wonderful aromas wafting from the kitchen tempt even the most sophisticated Highlands' visitors to ask if the dining room is open to the public. It is. The family style dinner begins at six. Tables are set with crisp linens and company china. The menu changes daily but always features classic southern cooking, beginning with variety of salads and relishes, followed by bowls and platters filled and refilled with two entrees, four vegetables and hot biscuits accompanied by beverages and completed with dessert, all homemade and all included in one price. House guests receive a discount on dinner and are encouraged to sit together in the country inn tradition. Individual tables are available for other dinner guests. Lodging accommodations include 13 rooms with private baths in the main house and a newer, two-story lodge with eight rooms and private baths. Open all year. For rates and reservations, contact innkeeper Carol Williams, The Phelp's House, Main Street, Highlands, NC 28741; phone 704/526-2590.

Highlands
Skyline Lodge and Restaurant

T here are "Rooms with a View" and "Top of the Mountain" dining atop this lodge's very own mountain. It's a rare find, only four miles from downtown, hidden at the end of its private paved road on 55 scenic acres of woodlands, lake, stream and waterfalls. The lodge, built in the 1920's, is a Frank Lloyd Wright design, constructed of native granite, blending in perfect harmony with its magnificent landscape. In this naturally romantic getaway, romantic doesn't mean giving up today's amenities: the baths are private, the television is in color and both it and phones are in the spacious guest rooms.

Skyline has 40 of these newly remodeled, luxuriously appointed rooms, each with a private balcony or terrace. The views are ever changing from sunrise to sunset, spring through autumn. Evenings are really special, featuring the breathtaking pinks, mauves and golds of mountain sunsets. And you won't miss the show if you are inclined to dine at sundown. Just off the greatroom with its leather furnishings and *two* massive fireplaces is the Top of the Mountain dining room—facing west—with ceiling-to-floor windows on three sides. After the sunset there is gourmet dining by candlelight for house guests, summer residents, mountain travelers, local residents and anyone in the area who wants a special night out.

Dinner reservations are required (even for house guests) for dining at The Top. Specialties include mountain trout and selected veal scalloppini prepared in a variety of ways. The trout sauteed with fresh ginger and wine sauce is considered the all-time favorite, although there are some very popular pasta entrees too. An appreciation of a healthy lifestyle is reflected in the preparation of the food and in the choice list of non-alcoholic beverages. The dining room is also open to the public for breakfast from 8 to 10 each day. It is not open for lunch but house guests may order a picnic lunch from the kitchen for sightseeing trips or for spending the day exploring and enjoying all there is to see and do on the premises.

There is plenty to see and do, starting with a large swimming pool and tennis courts in a garden-like setting. Plenty of nice trails for brisk walks, jogging, berry picking and photographing scenery and wildflowers. The Big Creek Lake has its own waterfall. Fishing, reserved exclusively for house guests, requires no license. All this casual elegance, natural tranquility, healthy activity and romantic setting is available from May 1 to November 1. If you can arrange a weekday getaway, you'll also get a discount here. Skyline Lodge, P.O. Box 630A, Highlands, NC 28741; phone 704/526-2121.

Highlands
The Chandler Inn

A central courtyard, decks, porches and catwalks tie this rambling barn-board structure into luxuriously rustic lodging accommodations. Located at the eastern edge of town, the inn was originally the Burlap Bag Shops. Conversion was done by R. Chandler Power and friends, and so was the furnishing and decorating—country comfort with the emphasis on comfort. All private baths, deep carpeting, Sealy bedding, color television and, in some rooms, gas log fireplaces. The Chandler has rooms to suit every taste: two-room suites with trundle beds, rooms with window seats and kingsize beds, rooms with iron and brass twin or queensize beds, rooms with lace curtains, rooms with waterfowl motifs, rooms with pretty eyelet coverlets and a very special room with a private deck overlooking the woods in back of the inn. All the decks are lined with rockers. There's a place to gather for the complimentary continental breakfast and for evening socializing. Open all winter for Highlands's quieter getaway times. The Chandler Inn, P.O. Box 2156, Highlands, NC 28741; phone 704/526-5992.

Highlands
Colonial Pines Inn

T he veranda on this bed and breakfast inn may be the widest in the southern highlands. The view of mountains from its porch swings and rockers, and its two acres of lawn, shaded by great spruce, hemlock and pine, give it an air of seclusion, although it's only a half-mile to Main Street. One cottage is located on the grounds, available for weekends, month or season. The cottage sleeps four to five, has its own kitchen and is completely furnished. The main house has five guest rooms with private baths, a big parlor with fireplace, color TV and grand piano, and a country dining room where the deluxe breakfasts are served.

Innkeepers Chris and Donna Alley, of the Atlanta area, opened the old guest house (originally a farmhouse) after a total renovation in the mid-eighties. Donna, an interior space design specialist, has refurnished and decorated using a combination of contemporary and antique furnishings and accessories. Laura Ashley fabrics, L.L. Bean comforters, primitive museum prints, contemporary art and braided rugs have been combined to create unique rooms that help guests feel instantly and comfortably at home. Modern, private baths with tub and shower, and large, walk-in closets make them especially appealing to those who want spaciousness, privacy and convenience along with the charm of a country inn. Open year round. For reservations, contact Colonial Pines Inn, Box 2309, Highlands, NC 28741; phone 704/526-2060.

Highlands
Cricket's Corner

R uth and John Fox offer a variety of lodging experiences, all delightful, in a picture book setting on Mirror Lake. The original Country House becomes a bed & breakfast when Ruth and John are available to play hosts. At other times it can be all yours. From the country kitchen to the wicker furnished porch (with a view of the lake and a gaggle of geese), it's wonderfully cozy with lots of antiques and afghans—even a goose down chaise lounge. It has three bedrooms as pretty as the wildflowers for which they are named and two modern baths. The Guest House has two apartments, complete with lake views, porches with grills, complete kitchens, living/dining rooms with sofabeds, one bedroom and one bath each. The Cottage has a different view of the lake (more wild things here: mallards, muskrats and beavers) from a screened porch with a dozing sofa, rocking chairs and a gas grill. Inside are two bedrooms, one bath, living room with sofabed and an eat-in kitchen. All units have phones and cable television.

There are bicycles, a canoe, a fishing boat for use by all guests, and even a playhouse for the kids, stocked with toys, books and games. Between a morning stroll to feed the geese and an evening campfire on the lawn with Ruth and John there are all the Highlands' attractions just a 20-minute walk (there's a lovely backwoods walk by the lake and up the hill into town) or a five minute drive away. Contact Cricket's Corner, P.O. Box 2141, Highlands, NC 28741; phone 704/526-4733.

Highlands
Kalmia of Highlands

These cottages with fireplaces (and firewood) are located on spacious grounds, practically in the heart of Highlands. Set well back off NC 106, surrounded by hemlock, pine and a flowing stream, they offer a rare combination of quiet country privacy and village convenience—and at moderate daily or weekly rates. The one-and two-bedroom cottages are complete with living/dining area, efficiency kitchen and modern tiled bath. Adjacent to the cottages are the "motel" units which are actually duplex cottages with twin, double or two double beds and on the same garden-like grounds there is the "Country Home," which features spacious guest rooms with king and queensize beds and large baths. All units, rooms and cottages have color cable television, and are as clean and fresh as the mountain air. And there's a well-maintained road through this little bit of country for jogging or nice brisk walks. Open all year. Kalmia of Highlands, 165 NC Highway 106/Dillard Road, Highlands, NC 28741; 704/526-2273.

Scaly Mountain
Ski Scaly

North Carolina's southernmost ski area is family oriented with all slopes in view of the lodge so children are never out of sight. It's an excellent place for beginners or for those who want to limber up before heading for the more challenging trails. A double chair lift and rope tow serves the 1,800-foot beginners, 1,600-foot intermediate and 1,200-foot advanced trails. Rental equipment and instruction are available, and the slopes are lighted for night skiing. The base lodge has a viewing deck, and ceiling-to-floor windows for indoor viewing. It's kept warm by what may be the world's largest wood stove, made especially for Ski Scaly. Hot food and beverages in the cafeteria add to the coziness. Moderate rates are even lower for groups of 25 or more, combining rental equipment, instruction and lift tickets. Located south of Highlands on NC 106 (which becomes GA 246 connecting with US 441/23 just north of Dillard, Georgia). Contact Ski Scaly, Box 339, Scaly Mountain, NC 28755; phone 704/526-3737.

Scaly Mountain
Middlecreek Barn

John and Sandra Fowler, from Marietta, Georgia, rebuilt this old 1910 barn on the bank of rushing Middlecreek in the mid-eighties. Seems they'd just collected too many antiques and needed some place to store them and maybe sell a few things. They sold a few, bought some more and things kept growing 'til they now have around 4,000 items at any given time, all listed on their computer. So if you can't find what you're looking for in the way of old tools or toys, primitives, collectibles, curios, mountain crafts or hard to find antiques, just ask John if he has it stashed, stocked or piled somewhere on the barn's three levels. He'll check the computer. And if he doesn't have it, chances are he knows where to get it.

If you aren't looking for anything in particular, but just like to browse, this is a good place to do it. You never know what you'll discover but it could be mule collars, pie safes, crosscut saws, maybe an Amish carriage, copper wash tub, handmade baby cradle, American flyer wagon, English perambulator, a Red Rider BB gun or carnival glassware. Or it could be some simple and inexpensive mountain crafts like cornshuck flowers and dolls, or authentic handmade Indian baskets. Located about midway between Highlands and Dillard, Georgia on NC 106—which becomes GA 246 and connects with US 441/23 just north of Dillard. Open seven days a week except during the winter months, from about 9 (or 10) to 6. For an item search or more information contact the Fowlers at Middlecreek Barn, Box 441, Highway 106 South, Scaly Mountain, NC 28775; phone 704/526-4587 or 404/782-3912.

Franklin

Two rivers, several good-sized streams, three US highways and one state road converge in this valley town in the shadow of the Smokies, surrounded by the Nantahala National Forest. Rockhounds converge here too, to "mine" for gems once mined commercially in the Cowee Valley where Tiffany's once owned an emerald mine. There are several places to try your luck searching for the emeralds, rubies, garnets, sapphires and amethyst, and if you find a treasure (and it still happens) or even just a small gemstone, you can take it to one of the many gemstone shops in town and have it made into a memento of your visit and effort. If you don't find anything in your "gembuckets" you can always choose a treasure at the one of the gemshops and have it custom set. Probably the best time to go gem hunting is during the annual gem and mineral show in late summer—its really big, and you can find everything from giant-sized crystals to tiny rubies. There is a brand new Visitor Center on the US 441/24 bypass just south of town. Contact the Franklin Chamber of Commerce, Georgia Highway, Franklin, NC 28734; phone 704/524-3161.

Franklin
Wayah Bald Scenic Area

This 5,336-foot peak is a natural "heath bald" and what it lacks in trees it more than makes up for in flowering shrubs: azaleas, rhododendron and mountain laurel cover the mountain in spring and early summer. A number of other wildflower species can be found from pre-spring to almost winter. Bring your camera for this trip—there's more to see than just flowers. There's a 360 degree view—one of the most spectacular in the mountains—atop a great rock tower built by the Civilian Conservation Corp back in 1933. The tower is easily accessible by a foot path about one-fourth mile each way from the parking area, where there's a nice large and shady picnic area.

The area has a number of hiking trails, many of them connecting with the Appalachian and Bartram Trails which intersect on Wayah Bald. For trail maps stop at the Wayah District Ranger Station on US 64 West where you begin your trip to Wayah Bald. Take Wayah Road, paved, (State Road 1310) and turn right on gravel Forest Service Road 69 to reach the picnic area and parking for the path to the tower overlook. You may want to stop on the way at the historic Wilson Lick Ranger Station, built in 1913, the first ranger station in the Nantahala National Forest. There are still some old cabins (boarded up) remaining and an interpretive information booth offering glimpses into into the conditions under which forest rangers lived at the time.

For more scenic touring, go back to the paved road and continue north on 1310 through the forest and down the mountain until it connects with US 19 on the Nantahala River at the powerhouse, boat launch area just north of

Topton. The entire drive is serenely beautiful, often following cascadaing streams. Except for a few cottages near Nantahala Lake, about the only sign of civilization is the narrow paved road itself, which most likely you will have all to yourself most of the way. You may even see deer and other small wildlife and there'll be lots of places you'll want to stop and try to capture on film. Without stops, the entire trip across the mountain takes about an hour. For more information on this Nantahala Forest Area, contact the Wayah Ranger District Office, Route 10, Box 210, Franklin, NC 28734; phone 704/524-6441.

Franklin
Maco Crafts Cooperative

When the original "World's Largest Quilt" is not on tour, you can see it here in one of North Carolina's oldest craft cooperatives. The quilt, made of 116 separate patterns to form an 18-by-21-foot sampler, was made by 96 of the cooperative's 250 members. There's a cotton fabric and quilting supply section, but what most people come for are the crafts: over 10,000 items on three levels and 8,000 square feet of space, include everything from hand-crocheted Christmas ornaments to handmade toys, from glass art to custom designed quilts. Items include the oldest and newest examples of mountain handicrafts, all made by members and priced direct to the mountain visitors. And there's a bench and porch swing for resting between choices. Don't forget this craft cooperative when planning holiday shopping trips. It's open all year (including Sundays, June through October) from 9 to 5:30. Located about three miles south of town on US 441/23. Maco Crafts, 625 Georgia Highway, Franklin, NC 28734; phone 704/524-7878.

Franklin
Ruby City Gems Museum and Mineral Shop

This free museum keeps visitors enthralled for hours, even those who aren't rockhounds. On display is the priceless, 30-year-long personal collection of Mr. and Mrs. Ernest Klatt. Everything is clearly labeled and identified. The collection, from all over the world, includes hundreds of geodes, small and large—some over 500 pounds—embedded with minerals and gems in brilliant colors and soft pastels. There is an entire case of spheres ranging from one inch to eight inches in diameter—a display of color variations polished to perfection by Mr. Klatt. The whimsical "titles" he has given to some of his collection indicate a sense of humor as well as an artist's eye, titles such as a geode named "Brainwashed". The collection also includes two large polished rhodochrosite specimens, one weighting 185 pounds, the other 234 pounds. In addition to gem and mineral specimens, the museum also has on exhibit fossils, millions of years old, in petrified wood, teeth and bones of ancient dinosaurs, an extensive arrowhead collection, the largest jade carving in the US (from Mainland China) and the world's largest sapphire—weighing 385 pounds! from the Franklin area. The Klatt's have recently added The Florescent Black Light Room to their museum.

The gem and mineral shop offers custom gem cutting, mounting and jewelry repair, using the latest technology and finishing equipment available. Virtually all work, from designing to finished jewelry, is accomplished expertly and quickly, right on the premises. Mr. Klatt's son, Al, with the firm since its beginning, has 30 years experience plus formal training in all phases of jewelry making, enabling him to offer the highest quality workmanship at the most competitive prices. The shop has thousands of cut gemstones, 14-karet gold mountings and some exquisite finished jewelry. Boxs of small inexpensive polished stones suggest the creation of bolla ties, pendants and other unique but simple to do handmade gifts. There is a good selection of books and magazines of interest to rockhounds, plenty of uncut mineral specimens and lapidary supplies. The shop and museum are located at 44 Main Street, Franklin, NC 28734. Telephone 704/524-3967.

Franklin
Rainbow Springs: Cabins, Hostel, Camping

T he Applachian Trail is a mile hike away; the Nantahala River flows by terraced tent and RV sites, cabins and a hiker's hostel. Highway 64 is out of sight and out of sound, and Franklin is about 12 miles away. There's a well-stocked general store and a well-stocked trout pond just waiting for your bait, and more trout in the river waiting for a real challenge. And always available on the premises are your genial hosts, Jensine and Buddy Crossman. So if you like your surroundings serene, and your creature comforts basic, you could call Rainbow Springs paradise. There are no luxuries except for electricity, plumbing and propane heat for cool nights. (The hostel has a wood stove.) Cabins are country clean and completely furnished with the basics from linens to dish soap. There are friendly people, pets on leashes, plenty of firewood and plenty to do whether you are a hiker, photographer or fisherperson—and plenty not to do if you want to retreat—just set on the porch at a cool 3700 feet elevation, listen to the birds, watch the flowers grow and the river roll by. Depending on the weather, you can usually find this natural paradise open from sometime in March 'til near the end of November. For a brochure, rates, reservations; Rainbow Springs, 1626 Old Murphy Rd., Franklin, NC 28734: 404/524-6376.

Franklin
The Franklin Terrace Inn & Antique Shop

P erched atop a knoll on beautifully landscaped grounds, the Franklin Terrace Inn, built as a school in 1887, is listed on the National Register of Historic Places. Wide porches on both levels of the inn provide cool places to enjoy the mountain views. Nine spacious guest rooms with color cable television, private baths and lazy paddle fans are furnished with period antiques enhancing the old time charm of the inn. There is also a separate guest cottage, equally appealing, which will accommodate up to four people. Old-time southern hospitality is provided by innkeepers Helen and Ed Henson who also provide guests with such an ample, wholesome breakfast.it can hardly be called continental. The lower level shop is open to the public and offers some very nice antiques, crafts and an assortment of gifts. Stop, browse, rest awhile and enjoy the view. The inn, which is located on NC 28, is within a short walk to Main Street. Open May through October. For rates and information contact The Franklin Terrace, 67 Harrison Avenue, Franklin, NC 28734; phone 704/524-7907. For reservations only 1-800-633-2431.

Franklin
Olde Mill House Cottages and Inn

F ifty cottages, apartments, luxury country villas and a country inn are set on acres and acres of land just off US 441/23 a few minutes south of Franklin, where pretty Cowetta Creek winds its way through the quiet woodlands. There are country lanes to stroll here, and berries to pick, wildflowers and small wildlife to amuse and please the eye and opportunities for fishing and tubing. If you are looking for a place that still has the charm and warmth of the best of the "Olden Days," you'll like this pastoral setting, with sheep, a pony and rolling meadows framed by split rail fences and surrounded by mountain vistas. The accommodations, however, are complete as today's modern conveniences.

Most of the cottages have fireplaces, dishwashers, decks and porches. They range in size from one bedroomers perfect for honeymooners to super cottages that sleep up to 12, perfect for family reunions. Furnished for comfort and relaxation complete with television. Available by the night, weekend, week, month or season, with moderate rates even for overnighters, compared to motel rates.

The inn sets on its own several acre hillside. It has three fireplaces (one in the master suite), patios and porches and a player piano in the parlor, and a large complimentary contiental breakfast especially for the inn guests.

This lovely place is family owned and operated by Dottie and Bill Brokow, daughter Lori and son-in-law Dan. (And they keep it open all winter with a special welcome for skiers.) You'll find them friendly and helpful. They have complete information brochures with descriptions and rates for each cottage. Stop to see them at their office and gift shop on US 441/23 just north of Otto and south of Franklin or contact them at The Olde Mill House, 1247 Georgia Highway, Franklin, NC 28734; phone 704/524-5226.

Franklin
Lake Laurel Woodlands Cottages

T here's luxury in the woodlands for those whose idea of roughing it for a week or more means furnishings from around the world, super kitchens, skylights, king, twin and antique double beds, air-conditioning, color TV, beautiful baths (one with a hot tub in the shower) and fireplaces. There's a paddle boat for guests and a private beach on a small lake stocked with crappie, bluegill and bass. Guests may bring a johnboat for fishing. It's a lovely place for a canoe, too. Hike or jog or just stroll along the woodland trails and roads on 69 private acres in this quiet cove only three miles from Franklin.

Floor-to-ceiling windows bring in the outdoors in the five octagon-shaped vacation homes. All have decks which are well-furnished for lazy days and moonlit evenings. There is one very luxurious and large log cabin which can accommodate a family of four. It has a big fireplace and a wide porch with a swing. Especially woodsy and peaceful. For more information contact the hosts at Lake Laurel Woodlands Cottages, Gail and Don Jerz, 65 Wide Horizon Drive, Franklin, NC 28734; phone 704/524-7632 or 3380.

Franklin
Wayah Creek Cottages

F ireplace cottages in a country storybook setting are located eight miles from Franklin, just off the paved country road to Wayah Bald. Cross the creek on a wooden bridge—there's a wooden footbridge too—and enter a natural garden-like setting at the foot of a steep slope covered with mountain laurel. A few benchs and garden chairs are strategically placed under shade trees along the banks of the shimmering stream.

The cottages, just across the driveway from the stream, are nestled among dogwood, oak and pine. Far enough apart for privacy, they are simple and rustic but comfortable. Paneled in pine or wormy chestnut, each has a small kitchen, and plain furnishings in the living/dining area, dominated by a stone fireplace, and one or two bedrooms with twin, double or kingzise beds. (Bring your own linens, blankets and towel for a discount or request they be furnished for you.) Each cabin has a small porch facing the creek, and there's a barbeque grill for each. There is also a large picnic pavilion on the grounds, making this a good place for groups and family reunioms. A group of 40 can be accommodated without sleeping bags, using all the cabins.

Nantahala Lake with 70 acres of shoreline, bass and trout fishing, boating and swimming is 12 miles away; Wayah Bald, the Appalachian, Bartram and other trails are minutes away, and the gem mines of Cowee Valley are on the other side of Franklin. Reservations by the week or longer with weekend getaways when available. For more information, rates and reservations, contact Robert DuBose, Wayah Creek Cottages, 625 Wayah Road, Franklin, NC 28734; phone 704/524-2034.

Franklin
Whisper Mountain Chalets

There's a 60-mile view from this 70-acre mountaintop where one- and two-bedroom chalets are available by the weekend, week, month and season. Bring food and drink—everything else is furnished. Retreat, hole up, getaway. Get up for the dawn and sunrise when peaks float on an ocean of valley fog; walk or jog on three miles of private roads. Have breakfast with a view on the deck or inside the many windowed, beamed ceilinged chalets, each on a private half-acre, and each individually and beautifully furnished. TV is network, there's a choice of twin or kingsize beds, and there are modern appliances in the fully equipped kitchens. There is also one efficiency (with a stunning kitchen) available at the chalet of hosts Gloria and Al Bass. A sofa bed and trundle day bed can accommodate up to four. The view through the sliding glass doors in this ground-level great room includes Al's rose bushes, climbing along a split-rail fence. Al and Gloria host a cocktail party on Sunday at 4 pm for arriving guests so plan to arrive by then if possible. Located about halfway between Highlands and Franklin at 3,800 feet. Contact Whisper Mountain Chalets, 43 Whisper Mountain Road, Franklin, NC 28734; phone 704/369-6834, out of state, 1-800-528-0395.

Dillsboro/Sylva/Cullowhee
Historic Dillsboro

Smoky Mountain Railroad tours, departing from the old depot, are the latest attraction in this attractive village made up almost entirely of cottages converted to arts and crafts shops. There is also the Jarret House built in 1884 by W. A. Dills for whom the town is named, and now famous for its family style meals. There are other eateries and there's lodging at the inn and in village bed and breakfast accommodations. Situated on the Tuckaseegee River, about half an hour from the Great Smoky Mountains National Park and about an hour from Asheville's attractions, Dillsboro's other main asset is its small size and lack of traffic congestion. Find a parking space on the streets or near one of the shops and walk the entire village, browsing in about 40 shops in a four-block area. Most of the shops have a street map noting the names and locations of the various businesses. There are several working artists' studios, a number of authentic arts and crafts shops, some boutiques for men and women, gift shops, and Christmas shops, and various other establishments.

The train departs for round trip tours daily (see under Bryson City for more details). Call for departure schedule, reservations (especially during peak visitor periods) and fares: 704/586-8811 or out of state toll free at 1-800-872-4681. For more information on Dillsboro shops and accommodations telephone 1/704-743-2241.

Dillsboro/Sylva/Cullowhee
Western Carolina University & Mountain Heritage Center

There is always something interesting for mountain visitors to see, do, hear, learn and be involved in at Western Carolina University at Cullowhee. A year round schedule of activities and events open to the public includes lectures, workshops and seminars on such topics as mountain ecology. Concerts, dance and theater offer frequent cultural experiences. If you have a need to do any research, the university library is one of the best in Western North Carolina. Also on the university campus is the Mountain Heritage Center, free and open to the public, offering multi-media exhibits on mountain culture. For more information call 704/227-7211.

Dillsboro/Sylva/Cullowhee
Squire Watkins Inn and Cottages

This 1880's Victorian bed and breakfast inn couldn't have looked any better when it was the new home of J.C. and Flora Watkins. Innkeepers Tom and Emma Wertenberger and their young son have restored, refurbished and redecorated to perfection. Soft, light tones in the paint, wallpaper and curtains, and uncluttered antique furnishings "open up" the already-large three guest rooms and two suites (some with private bath). Hardwood floors in the wide upstairs hallway and guest rooms have been scoured, scrubbed, bleached, waxed and polished to a warm glow and accented with braided rugs. Off the parlor, with its inviting fireplace and relaxing furnishings, is the small but elegant dining room. Deluxe continental breakfasts are served here or in the informal solarium. There are porch swings and rockers on both porches, and hammocks on the lawn. The inn does not accommodate children under 12, but a cottage with fireplace and efficiency units on the grounds are suitable for families, or for couples who want more privacy than the inn affords. The grounds are three acres of flowering and shade trees, terraced gardens, lily pond and small manmade waterfall. Secluded among the trees just a block west of Dillsboro's only stop light. It's a good location as a base for exploring the national park, about half an hour away, and for warm and tranquil winter getaways. Open all year. For rates and reservations contact Squire Watkins Inn, P.O. Box 430, Haywood Road, Dillsboro, NC 28725; phone 704/586-5244.

Dillsboro/Sylva/Cullowhee
The Jarrett House

This North Carolina landmark, famous for good food and lodging, will soon be celebrating its 110th birthday. Southern hospitality has been served since 1884 here at this three-level inn with rocker lined porches where house guests and other visitors gather to await the mealtimes. The dining room serves breakfast from 7 to 10, lunch from 11:30 to 2, and dinner from 5 to 8:30 every day, April through October, with reduced hours in the off-season, and closed for a while during winter months. The meals are family style, of course, although there are some entree choices. For lunch and dinner, there's usually fresh mountain trout or fried chicken, or baked country ham with hot biscuits and honey and red eye gravy, and always candied apples, coleslaw and all the traditional vegetables and beverages. There is an extra charge for their famous vinegar pie, which does *not* taste like vinegar, and is a special southern treat.

All the 18 guest rooms (each with a private bath) are furnished in an assortment of fine antiques in walnut, chestnut, cherry and brass, and decorated to make them as bright and cheerful as they are spanking clean. There are more rocker lined porches on the two upper levels, so guests can rock and visit and enjoy the view and rock some more til the next meal. Rates are exceedingly moderate, so make your reservations early before all the rooms are taken. Contact innkeepers Jim and Jean Hartbarger, The Jarrett House, P.O. Box 219, Dillsboro, NC 2875; phone 704/586-9964.

Dillsboro/Sylva/Cullowhee
Mountain Brook

T his is a honeymooner's dream, but you don't have to be a newlywed to enjoy a one-night getaway or a full vacation in these quaint log, stone and brick cottages, all with fireplaces and some with private bubble tub and sauna. Has it been a long time since you told someone you love them? Take them to Mountain Brook for their special "Romantic Lovers' Weekend," a perfect getaway for lovers of any age.

Located on a secluded woodland hillside with flowers, brooks and waterfalls to delight you throughout the seasons. (So pretty with winter's frostings and so cozy too). Porch swings invite you to take a day from touring and visiting all the nearby attractions and just enjoy this environment which includes a "spa and sauna" in the woods, combining the pleasure of pampering with the beauty of nature. Games, as well as outdoor sports equipment and reading material for a quiet brookside afternoon, can be found in the game room. The trout in the stocked pond won't require a fishing license—or very much fishing skill either. Prepare them in your own kitchen or freeze them to take home to friends and family.

In addition to the aforementioned amenities, these one-and two-bedroom cottages and vacation homes have fully equipped electric kitchens, towels, linens, blankets, showers in modern baths, comfortable beds and old-time furnishings throughout and are AAA approved. There is a television antenna mounted on each cottage so you can bring a portable if you wish, otherwise you'll not be tempted with the mundane—or have your tranquility disturbed by the ringing of a phone. There is a restaurant within walking distance in case you tire of the kitchen. If there is anything else one could want in a mountain getaway, it would probably be good, friendly hosts who provide you with suggestions and directions when and if you want a day away your Mountain Brook retreat. That's Michele and Gus McMahon (and daughters Addison and Maquell). Write or call them for rates and reservations. (And do it early—this is only three hours from Atlanta and all those overnighters and weekenders.) Mountain Brook is located about midway between Franklin and Dillsboro/Sylva just off US 441/23. The address is Route 2, Box 301, #1 Mountain Brook Road, Sylva, NC 28779. Telephone 704/586-4329.

Skiing in one of the High Country's several ski resort areas

NORTH CAROLINA
PART II

T he North Carolina mountains section of this book is in two parts, with the following map covering Part Two. The map generally indicates only those towns under which information is listed in the book (plus major cities and towns for reference points) and should be used in conjunction with a state map. Towns covered are not listed alphabetically, but as they appear on and off main travel routes. In this Part Two section of North Carolina the route begins north of Asheville and generally follows the area and towns near the Blue Ridge Parkway, north, in the following order: Little Switzerland/ Spruce Pine/Linville Falls, Linville/Pinola, Blowing Rock, Beech/Banner Elk, Valley Crucis/Boone, Todd/West Jefferson/Jefferson, Glendale Springs/Laurel Springs/Sparta.

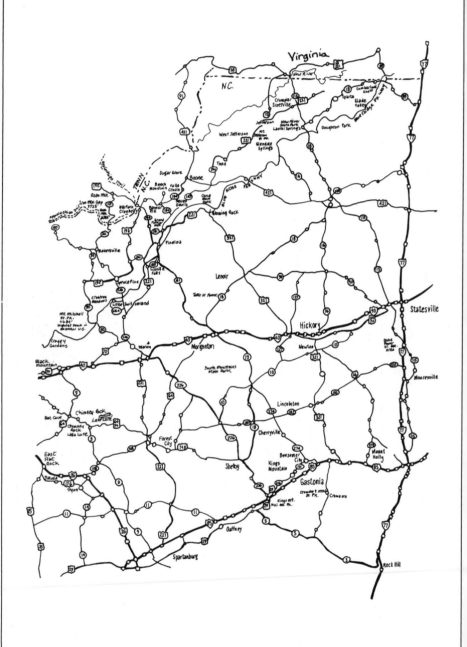

North Carolina: Part 2

· · · · · · · · · · · · ·

Photo Courtesy—N.C. Travel and Tourism Division

The New River (actually the second oldest river in the world) in North Carolina's Ashe and Allegheny Counties is a National Wild and Scenic River, popular for canoeing and fishing.

North Carolina, Part 2, An Introduction and Sources for Additional Information.

Up through Blowing Rock and Boone, through the highest average elevation of the Blue Ridge Mountains, most of this area is covered with the Pisgah National Forest surrounding long-popular four-season resort towns and areas. Almost immediately north, it seems like another country, where tourism is not as evident, and high forested mountains give way almost immediately to spectacularly broad and beautiful vistas of great rolling foothills, dotted with family farms and laced with two forks of the world's second oldest river, flowing northward on a near parallel course with the Blue Ridge Parkway.

Two travel associations serve this area: the High Country Hosts and the New River Country. The former's unique offering is skiing at the many ski areas in the Blowing Rock to Beech Mountain area, while the focus on the latter is the variety of recreation on and along the New River, particularly the 26-mile long section designated a National Scenic River, and the 26-mile long New River State Park.

For scenic touring, the Blue Ridge Parkway winds its way through this entire area, from north of Asheville to Virginia. (See the table of contents for extensive coverage of camping, lodging, hiking and the many other attractions offered along this scenic park and byway.) There are hundreds of miles of scenic all weather backroads, some lovely and little used winding state roads through historic communities, and several US Highways to get you to this area which has no interstates, and no commercial airline service.

Hiking trails are plentiful and varied, from south to north in this area. Some to consider would include a section of the Appalachian Trail along the TN/NC state line across Roan Mountain; trails on privately owned Grandfather Mountain; sections of the Mountains-to-the Sea Trail; 35-miles of former carriage roads on the Moses Cone Memorial Estate at milepost 295 on the parkway; the Linville Falls area trails; the Jefferson State Park and the New River State Park; and 20 miles of easy to moderate trails on the parkway's 6,430-acre Doughton Park area.

For additional general visitor information, contact New River Country Travel Association. Route 1, Box 13, Scottville, NC 28672, phone 919/982-9414; Ashe County Chamber of Commerce, 20 Buck Mountain Road, West Jefferson, NC 28694, 919/246-9550; Alleghany County Chamber of Commerce, P.O. Box 1237, Sparta, NC 28675, 919/372-5473; High Country Hosts, located in the Visitor Information Center on US 321 in Boone, 264-1299 for local calls, 1-800-222-7515 for North Carolina toll free calls, and out of state 1-800-438-7500.

For more national forest information, contact Pisgah National Forest: Grandfather Ranger District, P.O. Box 519, Marion, NC 28752, phone 704/652-2144. For more information on the Blue Ridge Parkway, see table of contents for national lands section.

Little Switzerland/Spruce Pine/Linville Falls

I f you start from near Little Switzerland on the Blue Ridge Parkway's milepost 331, you can go south a few miles to the highest mountain in the Eastern United States, or you can go north for a few miles to the deepest gorge in the Eastern United States. Or you can get off the parkway onto NC 226 and take a scenic drive north to largest natural rhododendron garden in the world.

Side Trip to Mount Mitchell State Park

Although not strictly on the Blue Ridge Parkway, this state park at the summit of 6,684-foot Mount Mitchell can only be reached by a paved spur off the parkway at milepost 355.4. Since you're already on what looks and feels like the highest point on the parkway (you aren't—that's south at milepost 431.4 at Richland Balsom) the five-mile spur to the summit doesn't seem like such a climb. There is no timberline in the Southern Appalachians and the summit of Mount Mitchell is forested. In recent years, however, ice and wind storms and air pollutants including acid rain seem to be damaging much of the summit's woodlands. The 1,469-acre state park includes campgrounds, picnic areas, trails, a restaurant and an observation tower with a 360-degree view. For more information, contact Mount Mitchell State Park, Route 5, Box 700, Burnsville, NC 28714; telephone 704/675-4611.

Side Trip to Roan Mountain

Take NC 226 to Bakersville, then NC 261 for a mountain climbing drive to the summit of the highest "bald" mountain in the east, 6,316-foot Roan, astride the NC/TN state line, traversed by the Appalachian Trail and crowned with the 600-acre Catawaba Rhododendron Gardens usually in peak bloom late May through early July. "Bald" mountains are not actually bald—or above a timberline. Infrequently they are grassy balds, more often are heath balds as in "The Roan," covered with shrubs in the heath family such as laurel and rhododendron, or with ornamental size fir trees such as the Fraser Fir, (popular as Christmas trees). There are 850 acres of Fraser Fir among the 7,000 acres of flora atop this heath bald. There is no charge to visit the gardens, and stroll the trails.

Little Switzerland/Spruce Pine/Linville Falls
North Carolina Mineral Museum

S pruce Pine is the center of mineral mining in North Carolina and this museum, operated by the Blue Ridge Parkway, displays state and area mineral specimens including quartz mined in Spruce Pine and used in the world's largest telescope at Mt. Palomar Observatory. Exhibits also include many gem stone specimens. Perhaps one of the most interesting exhibits features radioactive minerals mined in the area which are shown in comparative displays in both regular and ultra violet lighting. The museum is open 9 to 5 from Easter through Thanksgiving weekend, daily during summer, closed on Tuesday and Wednesday during spring and fall. No admission. Located at the intersection of the parkway (milepost 331) and NC 226. Telephone 704/765-2721.

Little Switzerland/Spruce Pine/Linville Falls
Linville Falls/Gorge/Brown Mountain Lights/Camping

T here is a visitor center and campground with tent and RV sites at this Blue Ridge Parkway area, milepost 316.4. The 2,000-foot-deep, 12-mile-long gorge is the deepest in the earth's crust east of the Grand Canyon. The river plunges into the gorge to form the 90-foot falls. Trails near the visitor center lead to easy to moderate hikes along the rim of the gorge for views of the two levels of falls. Hiking into the gorge (which is lined along some of its 12 miles with sheer 1000-foot cliffs) and the 7,650-acre wilderness preserve of virgin timber requires a permit and should be left to the most experienced hiker. Another spectacular look into the gorge is from Wiseman's View. To reach this viewing area take NC 183 from the Linville Falls community for .7 miles, then follow the marked gravel road for four miles to the parking area. A short paved trail makes the overlook handicapped accessible. This is considered the best place, both to view the gorge, and to look for the mysterious Brown Mountain Lights: bright orange lights which appear suddenly, usually on a clear evening after rainfall, from where no one knows—even scientists who have investigated their orgin for several decades—and disappear just as suddenly. For more information on the Linville Falls recreation area, contact the visitor center at 704/765-1045.

Photo Courtesy Grandfather Mountain

Wiseman's View, Linville Gorge, off the Blue Ridge Parkway at Linville Falls

Little Switzerland/Spruce Pine/Linville Falls
The Chalet Switzerland Inn and Restaurant

At an altitude of 3,500 feet, this small resort community and its center, the Chalet Switzerland Inn, are aptly named. The Swiss-style architecture of the inn and adjoining shops seems natural here, where panoramic vistas of mountain ranges resemble those in the foothills of the Swiss Alps. Even the summer evenings up here are cool—enough for a sweater usually, and for gathering around the great lobby fireplace. From the lobby's floor-to-ceiling windows the view is always splendid, whether it's of brilliant fall colors, early morning clouds floating over the valleys, or in the evening when lights from distant mountain villages twinkle like jewels.

Lodging accommodations include a honeymoon cottage, parlor suites and mountain-view rooms with balconies and chalet cottages. Dining in the spacious and elegant dining room is open to the public and is a special treat. Entree choices include filet mignon, veal, seafood and chicken specialties, Louisiana pan-blackened prime rib and swordfish. Bring your own liquid refreshments to the cocktail lounge which serves set-ups for brown-bagging and nonalcoholic beverages.

There are tennis courts and a spring-fed swimming pool on the lovely landscaped grounds, and inn guests may golf at a nearby course. Hiking trails lead to streams and waterfalls, across mountain slopes and meadows where wildflowers bloom from early spring through late fall. A row of small shops on the grounds offers a variety of treasures including some outstanding woodcarvings, pottery and other handicrafts by local craftspeople. Whether you stop for a meal, lodging, to browse in the shops, or just to take a short stroll and enjoy the view, this is a convenient and beautiful stop about halfway between Asheville and Blowing Rock right at the edge of the parkway and NC 226-A. For a brochure, rates and reservations, contact The Chalet Switzerland Inn, P.O. Box 399, Little Switzerland, NC 28749; phone toll free 1-800-654-4026.

Little Switzerland/Spruce Pine/Linville Falls
Big Lynn Lodge & Restaurant

Dinner and breakfast are included with the modest rates at this old-fashioned country inn. So is the astounding and ever changing view from 3,109 feet—all 40 miles of it! Range after range of mountains stretching to the horizon. Located a hundred yards from the Blue Ridge Parkway, the rambling frame lodge seems to hang on the side of the mountain above a broad wooded valley. Many of the inn's 38 guest rooms have porches or balconies facing this view. Others have decks facing the woodlands, and all have private entrances, telephones, radios, individual controls for heat, and modern baths. Common areas include a television lounge, library with a player piano, game areas, the lodge porch with still more view, and plenty of easy hiking trails, colorful with wildflowers or autumn leaves. The view continues in the dining room where excellent home-style meals are served at individual tables. The emphasis is on freshness and variety. There's no fried food at dinner, and entrees range from trout to meatloaf, to chicken cacciatori to roast beef. The three vegetables are steamed, the salad is cool and fresh, there's a choice of beverages, the bread and dessert is homemade, and you may order as many servings as you wish. Breakfast offers the standard country works or you may choose specialties such as Belgian waffles, hot or cold cereals. The restaurant is now open to the public, with both the inn and restaurant open most of the winter. (A continental breakfast only is served during winter months.) Make reservations, or stop by and enjoy, even if you aren't a lodge guest. Dinner is 6 to 7:30 and breakfast from 7:30 to 9. The inn is under the capable and friendly management of new owners (transplanted from Ohio and Michigan) Gale and Carol Armstrong, and Carol's mother, Elizabeth. You'll usually find Elizabeth at the gift shop (she's also the turn down hostess). Gale, with lots of experience, knowledge and love of good food, is usually working his magic back in the kitchen, and you may contact Carol for rates, reservations and more information. Big Lynn Lodge, Box 459, Little Switzerland, NC 28749; Phone 1-800-654-5232, or in NC 704/765-4257.

Little Switzerland/Spruce Pine/Linville Falls
Linville Falls Cottages, Motel and Restaurant

S top here for lunch and dinner, or stay for a getaway. You can walk to the Linville Gorge Wilderness area from this charming oasis, located just off the Blue Ridge Parkway, milepost 317. Two generations and over 40 years of the Huskins' family pride is noticable in hundreds of little details, from a nicely set dining room to the window boxes and baskets of flowering plants, lawns with split-rail fences and more flowers. There are decks and covered porches with chairs and rockers, updated interiors, pleasantly and comfortably furnished. All the cottages have fully equipped kitchens, sofa beds for extra guests, and some have fireplaces. All units have b/w TV with good reception.

The restaurant specializes in their own outdoor pit-cooked barbeque chicken, pork and babyback ribs. There's a lightly breaded catfish, and real mountain rainbow trout. Other specials include prime rib, and country ham, plus soups, salads and sandwiches for the lighter appetites. The restaurant is closed on Mondays and from November through April, but lodging is available all year. For information: P.O. Box 182, Linville Falls, NC, 28647; phone 704/765-2658; for reservations only, 1-800-634-4421.

Little Switzerland/Spruce Pine/Linville Falls
Pinebridge Inn and Executive Center

O verlooking the little town of Spruce Pine, this unique hotel and conference center facility was built on the campus of the old Harris School. The inn itself is actually the old 1940's school building which now boasts forty-five beautifully decorated rooms and suites. The high ceilings and broad windows of the old school have been preserved and restored, making the already large rooms and suites feel even more spacious and grand. Each is equipped with modern conveniences of telephone, cable television and climate control air and heat.

Across the courtyard, the Executive Center has an additional 12 rooms, plus a restaurant and facilities to accommodate conferences and private parties of up to 500 people. The adjacent Pinebridge Center features a year-round indoor pool, sauna, whirlpool and exercise center—one of the best equipped centers in the south—highlighted by the south's largest indoor ice skating arena, open throughout the winter season.

Located only minutes from the Blue Ridge Parkway, at the intersection of US 19E and NC 226, it is also only a short drive to Mitchell County's gemstone mines and a scenic drive to Roan Mountain's Rhododendron Gardens. For more information, rates and reservations, contact Pinebridge Inn & Executive Center, 101 Pinebridge Avenue, Spruce Pine, NC 28777; phone 704/765-5543 in state; out of state, toll free 1-800-356-5059.

Little Switzerland/Spruce Pine/Linville Falls
Richmond Inn

Y ou'll find real southern hospitality at this bed and breakfast inn. Lenore (Lee) Boucher, a retired legal secretary, and Bill Ansley, a retired police officer, are ex-Floridians, having a great time as mountain innkeepers. Lee is the muffin baker and country breakfast maker. Bill keeps the grounds and the 1941, many-dormered and bay-windowed, rambling frame home-turned-inn in company-ready condition. There are seven large guest rooms with private baths, beautifully and individually decorated and furnished, with a commitment to at-home comfort. There are spacious common areas, shady nooks and sunny crannies for get acquainted gatherings and getaways with a good book. The village shops are a short walk from this quiet residential street, and the Blue Ridge Parkway is minutes away. Contact Richmond Inn, 101 Pine Ave, Spruce Pine, NC 28777; phone 704/756-6993.

Linville/Pinola
Grandfather Mountain

I ncredible beauty and panoramic vistas from its many rugged peaks are just some of the attractions here on one of the world's most unique mountains. Wild animal environmental habitats, a new nature museum, a swaying suspension footbridge, 25 miles of hiking trails and a variety of special events enhance the appeal of "Carolina's Top Scenic Attraction."

Named "Grandfather" because the north slope resembles the profile of an old man looking skyward, the 5,964-foot mountain is the highest in the Blue Ridge range, with rock formations dating back over one billion years. Follow the paved road to the summit for the most spectacular visitas. Here the famous Mile-High Swinging Bridge spans an 80-foot chasm between its Linville Peak and Visitor Center. Named for its 5,280-foot elevation above sea level, a stroll across the bridge is second only to the thrill of the view from the other side. On clear days, surrounding mountain ridges continue to the horizon, visible over a

Hiking Grandfather Mountain

hundred miles away into Virginia and Tennessee. At other times, when thick clouds of fog linger in the valleys, the only peak visible will be Mount Mitchell, 40 miles to the southwest.

Half way down the mountains is the new Grandfather Nature Museum which houses a restaurant, a gift shop, an auditorium with free movies, and a large museum exhibit hall. Displays cover minerals and gems, wildflowers, native animals, geology, weather, pioneer history and more.

Take a short walk down the hill to visit and photograph some of America's native animals from close range in natural habitats. Mildred the Bear can be photographed in her two-acre enclosure, as well as cougars, deer and rare Bald and Golden eagles—part of the Audubon propagation program—probably the only chance you'll ever have to view and photograph eagles at close range.

The remaining 5,000 acres are your's to explore via a system of carefully managed hiking trails, ranging from very easy to extremely difficult, winding among native wildflower gardens, huge boulders, and quiet wooded areas, with plenty of areas for picnicking and relaxing.

Special events like the oldtime gospel "Singing on the Mountain" in late June and the gala Highlands Games and Gathering of the Scottish Clans in mid-July mean that you'll likely find something happening whenever you visit, and always plenty of enjoyment for the entire family. Open daily, (including winter, weather permitting). Privately owned, admission charged. The entrance is located on US 221 at Linville, one mile south of the Blue Ridge Parkway. For more information contact Grandfather Mountain, Box 995, Linville, NC 28646; phone 704/733-2013.

Linville/Pinola
Linn Cove Viaduct/Tanawha Trail

C onsidered an engineering marvel and believed to have been the most difficult bridge in the world to build, the Linn Cove Viaduct, part of the 7.7 mile stretch of the Blue Ridge Parkway around Grandfather Mountain, rivals even the mountain itself as an area attraction. In addition to mountain vacationers, it has attracted engineers from all over the world and received national attention on *CBS News With Dan Rather*.

The quarter-mile-long bridge was started in 1979, completed in 1983 and the entire 7.7 mile "missing link" was opened to parkway traffic in 1987. The $8 million viaduct was constructed of 153 segments weighing 50 tons each, of which only one is straight and no two are alike. And it was built *from the top down* because of the rugged terrain and to protect the fragile ecosystem of Grandfather Mountain. Constructed over billion-year-old rock formations, the "S" shaped structure rests on seven supporting tiers 150 feet apart. There is an information and parking area at the southern end of the viaduct, from where visitors can take the following trail *under* the viaduct for a close-up view of the construction.

The 3.5 mile Tanawha Trail parallels the parkway on Grandfather Mountain, with several access points for shorter hikes. It offers the opportunity to hike along privately owned Grandfather Mountain where a permit is required on all except this trail which is within the parkway boundary. The trail can be accessed from the Linn Cove Viaduct parking and information area (get a trail map here) where it crosses under the viaduct offering the unique opportunity for a closer view of the construction. From there north, the trail climbs steeply for a short distance, then levels off up above the parkway, paralleling it around the mountain for some easy to moderate hiking across incredibly beautiful and varied terrain. The first three or so miles of the trail offer unobstructed and spectacular views. There is another short, steep climb to the Rough Ridge overlook which can also be accessed from a parking area. A 200-foot boardwalk here high above the parkway provides the best overlook of the trail. To this access point from the viaduct it is 2.6 miles. It's another mile to the next access point at Raven Rocks Overlook. From there it's 3 to 4 miles to the next access point and, for some, the trail loses its charm along here with views mostly obstructed by a narrow green belt, which does not obstruct the sights and sounds of the traffic on the parkway. After the Boone Fork parking area, the trail does move farther away from the parkway and offers some more wonderful wooded and meadow hiking before ending at the Price Lake parking area. Even if you aren't much for long hikes, do take the trail at the viaduct to the next access point—it's not really difficult and you'll never forget being on this grand mountain, or the views from it if it's a crystal clear day. The trail is overused on heavy travel and peak weekends and you'll not have a lot of opportunity for solitude unless you can hike it on weekdays or in the off-season. After the trail leaves the viaduct area, you will encounter fewer hikers even at the busiest times.

Linville/Pineola
Old Hampton Store, Grist Mill & Cornbread Cookoff

A n annual cornbread cookoff on the third Saturday in June is cooked, judged and enjoyed by visitors at this old store and grist mill near Grandfather Mountain. Anyone can enter. There is live blue-grass music for the event, and the fresh hot bread is available to visitors, while it lasts, served with soup made with the store's bean soup mix. Proprietor of this 1921 store, Jeff McManus is also working on a marble project. (Possibly the first marble contest in the area . . . region . . . south . . . nation?) The store has thousands of old fashioned marbles, and is chock full of other neat stuff. The grist mill has cornmeal, grits, whole wheat, buckwheat, and pancake mixes, freshly milled, free of chemicals and pesticides. Located at Highway 181 and Ruffin road, 1.8 miles west of the Highway 105/221 intersection. For more information, contact Old Hampton Store, P.O. Box 57, Linville, NC 28646; phone 704/733-5213.

Linville/Pineola
Huskins' Court & Cottages

The setting, well kept grounds with lovely flower gardens on a country hillside, suggests that this is not your ordinary motel. It may, in fact, be the only motel in America where there is a handmade quilt on every bed. There is also handmade rhododendron living room furniture in one of the cottages, purchased by Mr. Huskins from a craftsman in Burnsville in 1930 for $35.

The Huskins family built and have operated this lovely oasis since 1951. Hanging flower baskets and flower carts adorn the porches of the 11 spotless and airy units. Each has television, shower baths, some have cribs and roll-aways. The cottages have completely equipped kitchen, bath with tub and shower, double bedrooms and sofa beds. The grounds include a grill and picnic pavillion and playground area with equipment for the children. Located just off highways 221 & 181, about 3 miles from Linville, close to all area attractions. Open May 1 to November 1. Contact Huskins' Court & Cottages, P.O. Box 86, Pineola, NC 28662. Phone 704/733-2564.

Blowing Rock
Ski Area/Summer Theater/Charity Horse Show/Arts In the Park

Photo: Courtesy Appalachian Ski

Enjoying a winter holiday at Appalachian Ski

This is one of the most charming and oldest "resort" villages in these mountains—a summer residence and vacation destination since the 1800's. The village sits on the continental divide at 4,000 feet, and at the edge of the 2,000-foot John's River Gorge and is named for a rock which protrudes over the gorge. When lightweight objects are thrown from the rock area they are caught by wind currents and carried back toward the "blowing rock."

Among its attractions and special events is a professional summer stock theater, the Blowing Rock Stage Company; the early August Blowing Rock Charity Horse Show, one of the most prestigious and oldest continuous horse shows in America, entering its seventh decade; the Arts in the Park series which takes place several Sundays during the season in a pleasant little park on Main Street in the heart of the small village; and nearby Appalachian Ski Area. The downtown area is filled with interesting, quality shops and galleries. There is a Welcome Center near the park on Main, open daily until 5 and on Saturday until 4. Phone 704/295-7951.

Blowing Rock
Tweetsie Railroad

H ave a great time by going back in time on the same steam locomotive that whistled its way from mountain town to mountain town a hundred years ago. Bring the family—a day at Tweetsie is more than just a three-mile train ride in the mountains. Tweetsie Railroad is a theme park, a fun park, packed with all kinds of entertainment, mostly focused on the sights, sounds and sensations of old time North Carolina. There are country crafts to celebrate the Appalachian Mountain heritage, and mountain entertainment including live shows of country music and clogging, a Gospel Jubilee—and something that is not quite so old time Carolina: a can-can show. There's enough to see and do to spend a day and one admission price covers everything at Carolina's Number One family fun park. Located on US 321 between Blowing Rock and Boone north of the Blue Ridge Parkway. For more information contact Tweetsie Railroad. P.O. Box 388, Blowing Rock, NC 28605; phone 704/264-9061.

Blowing Rock
Parkway Craft Center/Moses Cone Park/Julian Price Park

L ocated on the Blueridge Parkway just south of Blowing Rock these two parks, each with different features, are major attractions for this area. The Moses H. Cone Memorial Park, named for the industrialist who gave the land to the park service, is a 3,500-acre estate with lakes, miles of carriage trails now used for hiking, horseback riding and cross country skiing, and the 20-room Cone summer manor house. The latter now houses a craft center operated by the Southern Highland Handicraft Guild, an association of mountain craftspeople dedicated to preserving the skills and traditions of southern mountain craftspeople.

Weavings, paintings, sculpture, baskets, pottery, toys, carvings and more are available at the Craft Center which also houses a Pioneer Museum of tools and implements from the farms and homes of early mountain settlers. The National Park Service also maintains a Blue Ridge Parkway information center in the mansion. There is no admission to the park's recreation areas—or to the Craft Center which is open May through October. For more information, phone 704/295-3782.

Camping is available at the Julian Price Memorial Park just south of the Cone Park. This 4,000-acre wilderness-like recreation area has a 47-acre lake, a hardwood forest, miles of hiking trails, beautiful campsites and picnic areas. The land is named for an insurance tycoon and was donated by the insurance company to the Blue Ridge Parkway. For information, phone 704/963-5911.

Blowing Rock
Blowing Rock Stables

Carl Underwood is the man to see in this area for horses, whether it be for boarding, buying, selling, or for trail rides on the 27 miles of bridle trails on the Cone Estates section of the Blue Ridge Parkway. Mr. Underwood has owned and operated this facility for 15 years, and has a stable of 18 horses for riders of all ages and levels of experience. Rides along the wide bridle paths meander through secluded wooded coves and out onto open meadow with great vistas of the Blue Ridge Mountains. Rides are one to three hours, by reservation only. The stables are open 8 am to 6 pm. Closed in winter. Parkway access near the Cone Manor, just south of Blowing Rock. Telephone 704/295-7847.

Blowing Rock
Country Farmhouse Antiques & Crafts

Deer antlers from Montana, buffalo skulls from the west, a large selection of duck and fish decoys, quilts from the old south, farm wagons and tools from Appalachia, all these are usually among the always interesting items to be found at John and Joan Hastings' two shops. During their annual four-month "hunting trip," the Hastings track American artifacts —unique pieces that tell us what we were, what we are, and hint at what we may become.

Although "Antiques and Crafts" are part of the Country Farmhouse name, that description is too limited. There are also hundreds of other items: jams and jellies, greeting cards and guidebooks, dolls both old and new, embroidered and crocheted linens, brass and copper gifts, and two Christmas shops. The basket collection, perhaps the largest in the High Country, includes, but is not limited to, baskets made in the region. There's a large quantity of good quality regional crafts, from pottery to potpouri, twig furniture to "wearable" art. Open 10 to 6, seven days a week, May—December in both locations; across from the Mast store in Valle Crucis, 704/963-4748, and across from Chetola on Highway 321 in Blowing Rock; 704/295-9914.

Blowing Rock
The Dulcimer

Rogers Magee claims that "it takes 10 minutes for most people to learn to play a dulcimer; 15 minutes for the exceptionally backward." Even with that risk to your ego, you'll enjoy meeting Rogers and wife, Jo, at this shop for music lovers both talented and un, located in the Martin House on Main St. And if it does takes you longer than 15 minutes, ask Rogers to demonstrate an instrument he designed especially for those who can't even pick out a tune on a dulcimer; his OONEE-CAN. This one-stringed instrument is guaranteed to make you the most interesting, if not the most musically talented, person at any party. In addition to dulcimers, ranging from an inexpensive plywood kit for youngsters to exquisite handcrafted walnut McSpadden dulcimers, the shop also offers a mini-hammered dulcimer, harmonicas, Zither Music Makers—a sort of play-by-number instrument for children of all ages—and a variety of other music related items for all ages including tapes, music and song books, ranging from classic mountain ballads to campfire songs for boys and girls. (The Magees close this shop after the holidays and can be reached during the winter months at 612 Laurel Dr., Aiken, SC 29801; phone 803/648-1791.) For an order form, contact the Magee's The Dulcimer, Rt. 1, Box 571, Blowing Rock, NC 28605; 704/295-3367.

Blowing Rock
Goodwin Guild Weavers

Begun in England in 1812, this enterprise is now operated by fifth, sixth and seventh generations of the Goodwin family. The same looms that were powered by water over a hundred years ago are still producing coverlets, afghans, place mats, napkins and tablecloths.

The only concession made to modern technology is the use of electricity to run the antique looms. Natural fibers of wool and cotton are still used exclusively, and nimble fingers still weave a story into traditional patterns such as Lover's Knot, Whig Rose, Morning Star and Honeycomb, creating durable woven goods that will become the prized heirlooms of future generations. Finished weavings are available in the adjacent gift shop on US 321 Bypass. A catalog and price list are available by mail. Contact Goodwin Guild Weavers, P.O. Box 314, Blowing Rock, NC 28605; phone 704/295-3577 or -3394.

Blowing Rock
The Green Park Inn

In 1882 guests arrived in horse and buggy to enjoy the cool mountains and gracious hospitality of this fine inn. Although much has changed, much is still the same. The famous Green Park wicker rocking chairs still line the veranda, where tea is still served, and where guests still enjoy lazy afternoons, lively conversations and lovely sunsets. There's still the chime of silver and crystal and the soft sounds of live music as guests dine on the inn's fine culinary creations. And nowadays the wonderful meals including the scrumptious Sunday Brunch can be enjoyed if you make reservations even if you aren't a registered guest. Guests can now enjoy tennis and golf privileges at the adjoining country club. And there's the inn's own heated swimming pool, bicycles available for guests in spring, summer and fall, and ski packages available for winter fun on nearby slopes. There are cocktail parties on the house, high tea at 3 and all the Carolina hospitality that the Green Park Inn has epitomized for about 110 years. And there's all of today's amenities in the 74 spacious guest rooms and suites: color television, private baths and comfortable furnishings.

The Green Park, a rambling white-with-green-trim, three-level Victorian inn actually straddles the continental divide at an elevation of 4,300 feet near the John's River Gorge on US Highway 321 South. Contact The Green Park Inn, P.O. Box 7, Blowing Rock, NC 28605; phone 704/295-3141.

Blowing Rock
The Nutcracker & Glockenspiel

This truely unique toy store is the creation of owner and former teacher, Sharon Keese, and reflects her background, knowledge and interests. You won't find a single Saturday morning cartoon toy here. But you will find pure joy and delight in the selection of superior and durable, quality educational toys from around the world. Sharon studied abroad, including music (she still tutors piano) at the University of Heidleburg, and you'll find many toys from Germany, plus the best from other countries and America. Don't miss a visit here even though your children, grandchildren, nieces and nephews may seem too old for toys. You'll find wonderous things for children of all ages, infancy through adulthood; maybe something for the kid in you. The shop is in a rear section of the Martin House on Main Street and is open all year. Sharon offers many special extras including a children's party service, gift shipping, and a layaway plan which allows out of state guests to take their selection with them. For more information, contact her at P.O. Box 2367, Blowing Rock, NC 28605; 704/295-4671.

Blowing Rock
Stone Pillar Bed and Breakfast Inn

There are gas log fireplaces in two of the six guest rooms in this 1920's residence, and a private bath for each. Except for the latter, achieved through extensive renovation, a visit here feels pretty much as it might have back then; it's much more like a home than an inn. Side by side with its well-kept neighbors on a tree-lined street, a half block from the heart of the village, the Stone Pillar has porch rockers for neighborliness (and smoking—outside only) a charming little rock garden, and a deck on the second level for "taking the air" on a soft summer night. Twenties and thirties furnishings, "gleaned from family antiques, early attic and recent St. Vincent de Paul," according to innkeepers, George Van Nuys and Ronald Tharp, have been used upstairs and down, for comfort as well as charm.

There's a great room for fireside gatherings, games, and for enjoying real breakfasts like French toast or pancakes, eggs, and breads hot from the oven. Each bedroom has its own character and special touches. One has a double iron bed, another has a slant roof and twin beds, two have a setback area for reading and writing; the first floor guest room is handicapped accessible. And for winter getaways, there are those two with fireplaces. For rates and reservations, contact Stone Pillar Bed & Breakfast, P.O. Box 1881, Blowing Rocking, NC 28605; phone 704/295-4141.

Blowing Rock
Roaring River Chalets

In the High Country where there's no end to condos, finding anything resembling romantic cottages is a real find. These are exactly that, even if they are called chalets. In thick woodlands on the banks of the middle fork of the New River, they seem romantically remote, yet are only a few hundred yards from US 321/221, and a half-mile from the Blue Ridge Parkway. Except for a split rail fence along the private road, the landscaping is by Mother Nature: dogwood, rhododendron and large boulders along the banks of the river that's a sparkling clear and clean habitat for mountain trout.

Each chalet has an upper and lower level, one-or two-bedroom units, very private, with separate entrances and separate balconies overlooking the river.

Each is comfortably furnished and completely equipped, from kitchen to color television, queen or double beds. Ideal for honeymooner hideaways, big enough for a small family or ski group. Rates are low for the area and are not increased during the ski season. Up to six can be comfortable in the two-bedroomers and save enough in lodging to pay for lift tickets at the nearby slopes. For reservations, contact Donald and June Barket, Roaring River Chalets, Route 1, Box 200, Blowing Rock, NC 28605; phone 704/295-3695.

Beech Mountain/Banner Elk
Ski Areas/Lees-McRae College/Festivals

Skiing in the High Country at Sugar Mountain
Photo: Courtesy High Country Hosts

There are three major ski areas with advanced to expert slopes in the Beech Mountain and Banner Elk area: Ski Beech, Sugar Mountain Resort and Ski Hawksnest. The village of Banner Elk is almost literally overshadowed by Beech Mountain which bills itself as the highest incorporated town in Eastern America, at 5,056 feet. A trip to its summit and ski area is quite an experience for flatlanders. Opportunities to attend concerts, theater and a variety of other cultural events throughout the year are also available in Banner Elk at Lees-McRae College where an extensive schedule of programs is open to the public. Banner Elk also hosts the Woolly Worm Festival along about mid-October, complete with woolly worm races, woolly worm forecasts of the coming winter weather, and even "woolly worm sandwiches." For more information on Banner Elk, phone the Chamber of Commerce at 704/895-5605. The big festival at Beech Mountain is, of course, ski related: Winterfest, during the first 10 days in February, complete with a torchlight parade. The Beech Mountain Chamber of Commerce number is 704/387-9283.

Beech Mountain/Banner Elk
Blue Ridge Hearthside Crafts

This association of regional craftspeople has 400 members representing 20 local counties. Formed in 1965 to promote the production and sale of goods by area craftspeople, its members sell their art and crafts at four annual fairs, through 500 wholesale accounts and at the Blue Ridge Hearthside Crafts retail shop in a large log cabin on Highway 105 between Banner Elk and Boone. Member craftspeople produce an extensive variety of fine arts and contemporary, traditional and folk crafts, ranging from oils and watercolors through weavings, basketry, pottery, photography, carvings and more. All priced moderately, and attractively displayed at the shop which is open all year, daily 9 to 6 in summer, from 10 in the off-season. The craft fairs are held on the grounds of the shop one weekend each month during June, July, August and October. For dates and more information contact Blue Ridge Hearthside Crafts, Route 1, Box 738, Banner Elk, NC 28604; 704/963-5252.

Beech Mountain/Banner Elk
The Blue Ridge Blueberry Farm

Sample all the sun ripened blueberries you want as you pick your own on Jack and Betty Kelsey's 37-acre farm. Or just sit on a hillside and soak up the view if your prefer; there are pre-picked blueberries at the barn, plus raspberries, garden vegetables, shiitake mushrooms, homemade jams, and baked goods, all fresh, all affordable, all mouth-watering good, and all produced with the Kelseys' emphasis on natural farming. You may store your goodies in the barn cooler until your vacation or getaway is over. Picking containers with shoulder straps are provided but take your own take-home containers. If you still want to do some more picking, you may pick your own or a gift Christmas tree from the Kelsey's Fraser Fir Farm, and have it shipped after Thanksgiving. The Kelseys also have a mountain pond available to the fly-caster. And should you long to see the sun rise over the blueberry patch, the Kelsey's offer bed and breakfast for two to four adults at their unique farmhouse where the amenities include an indoor pool. The harvest season begins around mid-July. The farm is located less than two miles from town, off Highway 194 North. Address: Route 3, Box 529, Lee Gwaltney Road, Banner Elk, NC 28604; phone (barn) 704/898-4747, (home) 898-5885.

Beech Mountain/Banner Elk
Archer's Inn

Here's a bed and breakfast inn, a restaurant, and an annex where each guest room has a fireplace, refrigerator, microwave and porch with rocker overlooking the valley, and it's all stacked way up on the side of Beech Mountain, two miles from the ski slopes. The view is awesome and equalled only by the architecture of the inn. Whoever built this structure was certainly not intimidated by the magnificent mountains. A gigantic stone support column in the greatroom is four feet in diameter. Steps made with large stones lead from the entrance and the greatroom to the upper level. Railings and bannisters are good-sized logs. There is huge stone fireplace in the greatroom and a fireplace in most of the bedrooms. What was originally the master bathroom in this once private home features a large sunken tub. There is a total of 14 guest rooms, each with private bath. Furnishings are comfortable and luxurious. The restaurant is open for dinner and features a breathtaking view along with its good home cooking. Hours vary with the season, so it is best to call first. The complimentary breakfast for house guests is prepared by innkeepers Joe and Bonny Archer who also make their own delicious jams and jellies. Lodging is available year round. For rates and reservations contact Archer's Inn, Route 2, Box 56-A, Beech Mountain Parkway, Banner Elk, NC 28604; phone 704/898-9004.

Boone/Valle Crucis

Boone is probably better known as the home of the dynamic Appalachian State University than as a center of vacation activity, but the largest town in the High Country does offer a variety of places to eat, a number of national chain motels, a shopping mall and a schedule of cultural events open to the public at the university. There is an interesting older district around the campus, the US 421, King Street area. The town is named for Daniel Boone, a resident of the area in the years between 1760 and 1769.

Valle Crucis, which means Valley of the Cross, is around eight miles from Boone and from Banner (the most scenic route) on NC 194. This hidden valley is a real treasure which, in spite of changes and growth in the late 80's, still seems to belong to another time and place. Some historic and new shopping places are available here, and several outstanding bed and breakfast and country inns. And if you want a simple little place to pitch your tent in a grassy meadow beside a stream, check out the Valle Crucis Campground.

For more information on this area, call the Boone Chamber of Commerce, phone 704/264-2225 or the High Country Hosts travel association. Their Welcome Center is located on US 321 south of its intersection with 105; phone 1-800-222-7515 in state, out of state, 1-800-438-7500.

Boone/Valle Crucis
The Mast General Store

A must-visit place in the High Country, but not one you'd be likely to discover by yourself unless you like small winding state roads. NC 194 is such a road, leading to many interesting out-of-the-way places, Valle Crucis (Valley of the Cross) being one that still seems to belong to another time and place, even though it's only eight miles from Boone or Banner Elk.

For nearly a century, the Mast General Store, listed on the National Register of Historic Places, has retained the best examples of traditional general store merchandising: old oak counters, antique glass and oak display cases, candy cabinets, pot-bellied stove and rotating ribbon dispenser. Its old chestnut walls (pre-wormy) are still adorned with their original advertising posters placed there during the last century. But this is more than a museum. Continuing the general store tradition, it and the old annex next door still stock almost anything a body could need, from old-time housewares to boots, shoes and clothing suitable for mountain work or play, to groceries, including stone-ground cornmeal and buckwheat flour. You can even find tents and other outdoor gear. And gift items for about anyone you could possibly want to buy a gift for, and there's even a sack area serving hot and cold sandwiches.

Directly behind the Mast Store is the Little Red School House, built in 1907 by the residents of Valle Crucis. Recently restored, the Little Red School House now houses a gallery featuring North Carolina artists, and a shop with a unique selection of gifts, handcrafted furniture and books. Open all year. For more information contact Mast General Store, NC 194, Valle Crucis, NC 28691; phone 704/963-6511.

Boone/Valle Crucis
Mast Farm Inn

This inn, 18-acre farm and 13 outbuildings are listed on the National Register of Historic Places. Innkeepers are North Carolina natives Sibyl and Francis Pressly, who began restoration on the 1815's farmhouse and other buildings in 1984 and opened the inn in 1985. The Mast Farm Inn was included in the prestigious *Country Inns and Back Roads* the following year.

Located just down the road from the Mast General Store, the original 13-bedroom home now has 12 guest rooms and 11 baths. Rooms are furnished with plain, simple antiques similar to those used in mountain farmhouses in the late 1800's and early 1900's. Rich in history, the main house has served as an inn before—for a time in the early 1900's, operated by Finley and Josephine Mast. The two-room log cabin of their grandfather, David Mast, still stands. Other buildings include a wash house, spring house, smokehouse, apple house, blacksmith shop and barn.

A deluxe continental breakfast and the evening meal are included in the modest lodging rates. The evening meal is available with reservations to non-registered guests. The menu includes homebaked breads and desserts, and fresh vegetables and fruits from the Mast Farm. For further information, rates and reservations, contact Mast Farm Inn, P.O. Box 704, Valle Crucis, NC 28691; phone 704/963-5857.

Boone/Valle Crucis
Outdoor Drama: *Horn in the West*

This historical drama experience is enhanced by the outdoor setting. Nearing it's fourth decade of performances, this Kermit Hunter play is about the early families of this region, especially those "Regulators" who fled to the mountains to escape British tyranny. During the decade covered between the opening and closing curtain, there's intrigue, battles, a wedding, a smallpox outbreak, interaction with friendly and hostile Indians, heroism, laughter, and most of all, history. The production runs eight weeks each summer, nightly except Monday, from late June through mid-August. Admission includes a tour of an 18th century living museum. For more information contact Horn in the West, P.O. Box 295, Boone, NC 28607; phone 704/264-2120.

Boone/Valle Crucis
The Dan'l Boone Inn

Family-style breakfasts, lunches and dinners are served here at this turn-of-the-century rambling, frame inn located at the edge of the Appalachian State University. Noon and evening meals *include* three entrees, two of which are always fried chicken and country ham biscuits, and are accompanied by five vegetables, preserves, more biscuits, and a choice of beverage, followed by homemade dessert and preceded by a salad in the summer and a kettle of soup in the winter. You may order complete box lunches to go or just their delicious ham biscuits. For parties of 15 to 120 there's a choice of the family-style or a buffet. Open all year for breakfast on weekends from 7 to 11, with lunch and dinner continuously in summer and fall from 11 to 9. In winter and spring, dinner is 5 to 9. No reservations needed except for large groups and parties. Located at the junction of US 421, 321 and 221 at 105 Hardin Street (with free parking). Telephone 704/264-8657.

Boone/Valle Crucis
Bedside Manor

This 1880's gingerbread farmhouse has two full stories topped by a coupala with lookout windows. There's a barn and various barnyard creatures, a garden, a meadow, a gazebo, fruit and nut trees. There is one up-to-date exception to all this traditional Victorian charm: a garden deck with a large hot tub for the guests. Otherwise this bed and breakfast inn looks as it might have looked as the home of a country squire at the turn of the century. All rooms have the original fireplaces, including the guest rooms and the kitchen. The dining room and parlor have period furnishings including a Grammophone and Victorola. The four guest rooms are furnished with simple country antiques. (If all four rooms are occupied, guests share the two modern baths.) There are bay windows curtained in white and a porch from where you may survey the broad lawn shaded by century old trees, and watch the occasional car or pickup pass down the country road. After a breakfast served by hosts Dwight and Etta Helm, guests may return to the real world via 321 or 421. . . . Boone is just minutes away. . . . or you might linger a bit, exploring this once upon a time and far away kind of valley. The inn is open all year.

Contact Bedside Manor, Rt. 1, Box 90A, Sugar Grove, NC 28697; 704/297-1120.

Boone/Valle Crucis
Bluestone Lodge

A t the top of Bluestone Hollow, 3,000 feet closer to the heavens than the sea, Bluestone Lodge lets you enjoy panoramic mountain views from several balconies and picture windows. A full-course, nothing-ordinary breakfast is served to start your day in the mountains. Each comfortable room welcomes you with fresh flowers and antiques. Guest rooms include kitchenettes and full, private baths. There's a cozy loft room with a half-bath and a skylight over two single beds. Entering the third floor suite, you'll see why it's the perfect honeymoon retreat. It has a full bath and whirlpool tub, a stone fireplace to enhance the romantic environment, even a full kitchen in case you want to get in some domestic practice. You can watch the stars out the skylight over the bed or view the mountain tops from the balcony surrounding your "tree-house" suite. The recreation/common areas include fireplace conversation areas, a wet bar, redwood hot tub, sauna, solarium, pool, seven acres of mountain top and a 360 degree view. Innkeeper Merry Lee will make you feel like a special friend in her home, whatever season you care to enjoy this four-season area and lodge. Contact Bluestone Lodge, P.O. Box 736, Valle Crucis, NC 28691; phone 704/963-5177.

Boone/Valle Crucis
The Inn at the Taylor House

C hip and Roland Schwab, proprietors of one of Valle Crucis' newer bed and breakfast inns, are not new to the art of hospitality. They are partners, along with Roland's brother Heinz, in the five-star Hedgerose Heights Inn of Buckhead in Atlanta, considered by many to be the best restaurant in Georgia. Roland is a native of Switzerland and fifth generation innkeeper. Chip operated the Truffles Cooking School in Atlanta before Hedgerose Heights opened in 1981. She had had a summer home in the Valle Crucis area for the past 20 years, before the Schwab's opened their Valle Crucis inn in 1988 in this house they had admired for many years.

The 1911 Taylor House, originally the Taylor family's private residence, is a three-story white frame house encircled by a spacious porch, complete with porch swings and antique wicker furniture. Renovation in the house provided seven large guest rooms with individual baths. There are original fireplaces in the living room, library and updated kitchen. The comfortable furnishings are a collection of the Schwab's personal antiques, art, oriental rugs and newer purchases to complete what Chip describes as "an eclectic French country look." Individually decorated guest rooms have large windows and lovely views of the grounds bordered by the Watauga River and surrounded by the still operational Taylor Farm. The inn is located on that wonderfully scenic NC 194, eight miles from Banner Elk, one mile from the Mast Store. For rates and reservations contact the Taylor House, P.O. Box 713, Valle Crucis, NC 28691; phone 704/963-5581.

Boone/Valle Crucis
Overlook Lodge

View Sugar, Beech and Grandfather Mountains from the decks. Walk a few yards up the road and pick up a trail connecting with the 35 miles of National Park trail on the Blue Ridge Parkway's Moses Cone Estate. Then kick off your boots and curl up on the comfortable sofa in front of the greatroom fireplace. It's OK if you sneak in a snooze—informality and hospitality are the operative words here. If you get too relaxed to go out to dinner (Boone is six miles away), innkeeper Nancy Garrett might be coaxed into preparing you a light supper. Or come prepared with steaks for grilling on one of the three levels of decks or your own private balcony if you have the secluded-enough-for-a-honeymoon suite. Next morning you'll find a pot of coffee outside your door, and later a full country breakfast. The lodge can sleep 12 in three comfortably furnished guest rooms with private baths and a two bedroom suite with shared bath. Or bring the troops with sleeping bags and create your own ski hostel—the lodge is open all winter. Contact Overlook Lodge, P.O. Box 1327, Boone, NC 28607. Phone 704/963-5785.

Todd/West Jefferson/Jefferson
Scenic Drive on 194/New River Country Attractions

You're now in New River Country, and if you came in via the Blue Ridge Parkway from the Boone area, consider returning on NC 194, from here back to Valle Crucis, one of the most scenic roads in the mountains. The little used road goes roller-coasting up and around these rolling hills, dipping down into tiny rural communities. You'll drive through lovely valleys laced with mountain streams spanned by small wooden bridges to country homes and small farms landscaped with crops of Fraser Firs or grazing herds of dairy cattle. You'll even pass a waterwheel powered hammock on the grounds of one retiree's country home—watch for it between Todd and Baldwin.

Mount Jefferson is the highest mountain here among these gentle hills, rising to 4,900 feet with a 541-acre park at its summit and views into Virginia and Tennessee. The park has hiking and nature trails and picnic areas. Telephone 919/246-9653.

The annual Blue Grass and Old Time Fiddlers convention is held in the Ashe County Park in August and it's the real thing—no electric instruments are allowed. Instead you'll hear music the way the early mountaineers heard it on traditional instruments: banjos, mandolins, fiddles and guitars. For specific dates and times, call 919/246-9945.

For more information on this specific area, call the New River Country Travel Association, 919/982-9414, the Ashe County Chamber of Commerce, 919/246-9550 or the Alleghany County Chamber of Commerce, 919/372-5473.

Todd/West Jefferson/Jefferson
The New River/New River State Park & Campgrounds

Only the Nile is older than this 100 million year old river, named for a surveyor of this area, the father of Thomas Jefferson. Beginning on the northern side of the continental divide at Blowing Rock, the river flows north into Virginia and through West Virginia, flowing eventually into the Gulf of Mexico via the Ohio and Mississippi Rivers. Declared a National and State Scenic and Wild River, it's ideal for short or extended canoe trips, with camping along a 26-mile long, 500-acre State Park. Its gentle flow is also ideal for tubing, rafting and family or novice canoeing. The fishing is good —

and considered great for small mouth bass; the scenery is beautiful with river banks abloom with wildflowers or ablaze with autumn color, and above the gentle river sounds, you can hear the song of birds and catch glimpses of small wildlife which make this river environment home. For more information on the the state park and the spaced river camps, contact New River State Park, 919/982-2587.

Todd/West Jefferson/Jefferson
Todd General Store/Bicycle Trail

L ocated on wonderfully scenic NC 194, this authentic and historic old store, established in 1914, can easily be missed—as can the entire community of Todd. Watch carefully for the small sign about halfway between Boone and West Jefferson. Todd was once the largest town in Watauga and Ashe Counties, but that was back when railways, not highways, kept a town alive and growing. You can still visit the old depot here, see memorabilia from the early 1900's and shop for items ranging from real farmer overalls to Bob Cole's sourwood honey, made famous by Willard Scott of the *Today Show.* You can have a nice deli sandwich, get some gourmet coffee and discover some lovely crafts and antiques in the shop in an old house next door. Or you can bring your bicycle for a lovely 10-mile scenic bike and motor road which begins in front of the store and meanders along the South Fork of the New River on serenely beautiful Railroad Grade Road which connects back with 194. The store is open 7 to 7 Monday through Saturday, 12:30 to 5 on Sunday; phone 919/877-1067.

Todd/Jefferson/West Jefferson/Glendale Springs
New River Outfitters/New River General Store

T his experienced company, the oldest outfitter on the New River, founded in 1976, will outfit you for any length trip to canoe the New, from a one-hour sampler to a six-day camping trip, supplying all you need from quality canoes to shuttle service, even camping equipment, box lunches and experienced New River guides if desired.

The New River Outfitters are located on the banks of the South Fork of the New River in the historic New River General Store. This is the oldest continually operating store in the area, serving this rural community for three generations. Most of the food you'll need for a canoe trip, (including cheese from the local Ashe County Cheese) as well as supplies for fishing and camping are available at this picturesque and authentic old-time country store. It is still actually serving the area, and still stocking such diverse items as salves, linaments, toys, hardware, molasses and more, with some antiques just for good measure. Located 9 miles north of Jefferson at the US 221 bridge over the South Fork of the New River. P.O. Box 433, Jefferson, NC 28640; phone 919/982-9192.

Todd/West Jefferson/Jefferson
Zaloo's Canoes, Rafts, Tubes, Camp & Lodge

F loat or paddle for half a day or a full vacation, with all equipment and shuttle service provided (even camping and lodging if desired) by Jeb Farrington and his crew. Based camped on the family farm, Zaloo's has had 20 years experience in providing safe, environmentally protective and enjoyable experiences along the New River.

Their rafts and canoes are state-of-the-art and their custom built tubes have two separate chambers to assure flotation even if one chamber loses air. For overnight or longer trips, camp in outposts along the river or treat your group to a night or two at Jeb's lodge. Just above the river, this rambling four-bedroom home will actually accommodate up to 24, and has an additional new, large bathhouse for men and women (plenty of hot showers, too) at the river's edge camping area a few feet below the lodge. The lodge is also available for hikers, and it's only 20 minutes to the Appalachian Trail Three Corners area of North Carolina, Virginia and Tennessee. For information on any or all the above, contact Jeb at Zaloo's Canoe's located about 8 miles south of Jefferson on NC 16. Zaloo's Canoes, Route 1, Jefferson, NC 28604; phone 919/246-3066.

Todd/West Jefferson/Jefferson
Ashe County Cheese

The lay of the land here is much like southern Wisconsin, and there's even a cheese company (the only one in North Carolina) where you may visit a viewing room to see how it's made and sample the wares in their retail cheese shop. If you've never tasted newly made cheese curd (supermarket packages aren't the same) ask for a sample of the golden nuggets. After you've sampled several varieties of cheese, you may buy some to take along, order some sent home, or shipped as gifts anywhere at specified times. You can choose among the company's own bright yellow cheddars, mellow colbys, monterery jack, mountain jack and from about 50 other varieties of domestic and imported cheese, plus fancy relishes and preserves. There is no admission to the viewing room, airconditioned and with floor-to ceiling window which allows visitors to see clearly the various steps involved in converting milk into cheese. Open 8 to 5, Monday through Saturday, and conveniently located in the middle of the small town at Main and Fourth. Ashe County Cheese Company, P.O. Box 447, Main & Fourth Streets, West Jefferson, NC 28694; phone 919/246-2501.

Todd/West Jefferson/Jefferson
Mount Jefferson General Store

This old country store is now on its third name, third phase and third generation in the Ambrose Bare family. It could be called a crafts, herbalist and quilting center in this phase, with Margaret Bare and daughter, Amelia Burns the quilter and herbalist respectively. Margaret has her quilting frame set up at one end of the store where you'll usually find her and maybe a neighbor or two working on a quilt in progress. The quilts are sold in the store, which also stocks fabrics, notions, handwoven rugs, hand forged iron works, handmade furniture, pottery and baskets among the crafts sections. Amelia's special section features herbs and spices (with information sheets on their historic and current uses), organic gardening supplies, gourmet coffee beans, organicaly grown flours, grains, beans and assorted baking mixes. It's a wonderfully aromatic place to visit, and on cooler days there's a big old wood stove to add to the warm and friendly atmosphere. Located on Highway 16/88 between Jefferson and West Jefferson, phone 919/246-5835.

Todd/West Jefferson/Jefferson
Greenfield Restaurant/Cabins/Camping

This looks like a large family farm, spread out across meadow and woodlands at the base of Mt. Jefferson, near the entrance to the state park at the summit. It *is* family owned and operated—by the Woody family for nearly three decades. But it is not a farm, although there are horses in the nearby neighbor's pasture. Greenfield is a popular destination of visitors seeking a variety of mountain activities. The most commonly shared activity is enjoying the food that has earned Greenfield the reputation as one of the state's finest—featuring country food, served family style. *Pan* fried chicken. (Honest, pan fried slowly to perfection in great cast iron skillets.) Country ham (for breakfast, lunch or dinner) with red eye gravy. A tableful of bowls of vegetables—seasonal when available. Biscuits. Homemade desserts. For the more uptownish tastes, the menu offers steaks, seafood, nightly specials with all the fixings, and a salad bar. In the big sitting room with the oversized fireplace (this was once a farmhouse), Bill Woody's extensive collection of Indian artifacts is on display. Give yourself time to look and learn. Many are museum quality pieces you may never have seen before and may never see again.

The cabins are new, rustic sleeping cabins, with a double bed, double mattress in the loft, more room for sleeping bags, modern bath, air conditioning, electric heat, cable television, and rockers on the porch. The campground offers everything an RV traveler needs, and it offers a discounted fee for the tent camping section.

There's a swimming pool too. And trout ponds which require no fishing license. And trails connecting to the state park. And a country store for supplies, sundries, ice cream, crafts, gifts, homemade food and country hams. So go to eat. Lodge. Hike. Swim. Camp. Fish. Shop—and from there, explore all the nearby attractions in Ashe, Alleghany and Watauga Counties. Contact the Woodys for more information, rates and reservations at Greenfield, Route 2, West Jefferson, NC 28694, phone 919/246-9671.

Todd/West Jefferson/Jefferson
Shatley Springs Inn

If you are inclined to drink only bottled water, bring your empty Perrier bottles here for the free mineral water believed to have cured whatever ailed Martin Shatley in 1890. You may have to get in line. Many diners and local residents fill their jugs and bottles at the Shatley Springs. However it's not really the water that brings most visitors to Shatley Springs today. It's the family-style meals, morning, noon and night.

The rambling old building housing the dining rooms also contains what is referred to as the "music room" with a floor so warped from the spring waters beneath it that Saturday night musicians have to prop and steady their instruments. The live country and gospel music is not to draw crowds; the meals do that only too well. The music is to soothe the hungry guests, overflowing the porch lined with rockers. They begin arriving early, sometimes by the busload even for breakfast. By 7:30 the dining room is full and so are the porch rockers. Breakfast service stops at 9:30, lunch is served from 11 to 3, and dinner from 3 to 9. You may order from the menu but most order the family style which includes platters and bowls of such southern favorites as county ham with red eye gravy, fried chicken, biscuits, cornbread, and an array of vegetables, relishes, beverages and desserts. Reservations are recommended for all meals except breakfast and are almost essential on Saturday evenings and Sundays. But if you arrive without them, join the waiting crowds on the porch or wandering about the grounds where there's a large pond and some rustic rental cabins which are more and more being used to house various craft and gift shops.

The man behind or, more precisely, in the midst of all this is Lee McMillan, an Ashe County native who keeps his staff and guests happy, his kitchen Grade A and still finds time to ship free jugs of water to long-time out-of-state visitors. The inn is open every day from May through November and is located on NC 16, a few miles north of Jefferson. Telephone 919/982-2236.

Todd/West Jefferson/Jefferson
Ransom's Bed & Breakfast

Norma Ransom likes people, especially children. She grew up with 11 brothers and sisters in her Pennsylvania Dutch family. Myron Ransom likes people too, especially those who appreciate a well-tended orchard and garden, and a comfortable place to watch televised ballgames. Both are incurable romantics, in love with the mountains, with retirement, and with their new, traditional style bed and breakfast dream home. The two-level, five-dormered house has three guest rooms with private baths. Honeymoon and anniversary suites have sunken jacuzzi tubs, and canopied queensize beds. There are ideal family suites too, with double and day beds and extra alcove space for kids. There's a real front porch with rockers, a sprawling back deck overlooking the garden, orchard and berry patch, and a close up view of Frenche's Knob rising up out of the wooded foothills. And of course, there is a good place to watch the ballgames in front of the family room fireplace, lighted at just a hint of chill. Breakfast is country style, complete with homegrown fruits and vegetables. Open April 15 through November, located just off US 221 on NC 163, just minutes from the village. Contact the Ransoms at Route 2, Box 847, West Jefferson, NC 28694; phone 919/246-5177 (off season phone 407/851-5059).

Todd/West Jefferson/Jefferson
Smith Haven Bed & Breakfast

Staying here is kind of like having your own comfortable home along with you on vacation, only better. Someone else keeps it spotless, makes the breakfast, lays the fire in the fireplace, even researches area events, attractions and restaurants, and provides a booklet of the information for each guest room. All you have to do here is relax and enjoy yourself. Smith Haven provides robes, color cable television, games, books and comfortable, country furnished guest rooms. There are three; two doubles, each with private deck and view of Mount Jefferson, and a cozy single. Two baths are shared when all guest rooms are occupied. The two level brick home provides plenty of privacy (the Smiths have a separate basement apartment) and, with the exception of the kitchen, is open to use by the guests. Phones are available; there are rockers on the porch, a picnic area on the grounds, and a swing under a grand old oak tree. Nightly rates are exceedingly modest, weekly and winter rates even lower. No smoking, no pets. Children over 10 are welcome. Contact Smith Haven, 203 W. Main St. Jefferson, NC 28640; phone 919/246-5149.

Glendale Springs/Laurel Springs/Sparta

This remaining portion of the North Carolina mountains is mostly in Alleghany County. "Alleghany" is an Indian word meaning endless stream, and possibly referring to the New River and its many tributaries flowing through these fertile farmlands, dotting a landscape of steep hills rising abruptly from almost dream-like valleys. NC 88/18 unfolds around the landscape, wondering into and out of small communities, paralleling and connecting with the Blue Ridge Parkway at its last exit before entering Virginia. From the Parkway overlooks, this part of North Carolina bears little resemblance to the rugged forested mountains a few miles back in Watauga County. It does, however, offer outstanding places to visit, eat, shop, hike, lodge, see and enjoy, beginning with one of the Parkway's most beautiful recreation areas.

Photo: Courtesy North Carolina Department of Tourism

Catching the Clouds on the Blue Ridge Parkway near Doughton Park

Glendale Springs/Laurel Springs/Sparta
Doughton Park (Blue Ridge Parkway)

Y ou'll find some of the friendliest people on the parkway at The Bluffs Lodge and Restaurant here, as well as absolutely some of the best food, and a setting for lodging and camping you'll find hard to equal.

This 6,000-acre Parkway area was named for Congressman Robert L. Doughton, a staunch supporter and neighbor of the parkway. And what a neighborhood! Sweeping meadows and heath-covered hillsides are adorned with great, almost white boulders, and in spring and summer splashed with the bright pink and white blossoms of laurel and rhododendron. A perfect place for a picnic. Twenty miles of irresistible (and mostly easy to moderate) hiking trails beckon the walker across green meadows into woodland slopes up to rock overlooks and the sheer cliffs of Bluff Mountain, across small streams, to an 1880's cabin and back to the parkway. This is one of those places that may make you want to burst into a chorus of the *Sound of Music* even if you didn't like the movie and can't sing a note. For more information on the camping and lodging facilities and the restaurant, phone 919/372-4499. For more extensive coverage of the parkway, see that section under national lands listings.

Glendale Springs/Laurel Springs/Sparta
Stone Mountain State Park

I f you're familiar with a state park by the same name in the Atlanta area, don't think you're confused if you see signs around the Sparta area directing you to this state park. You can see the 600-foot granite mountain from the parkway, and if you look very closely perhaps you can see the "dove" on its face, or at least the resemblance of one, formed naturally by the rock's indentations, protrusions, shading and foliage. You'll find challenging hiking here, camping, waterfalls, picnic areas and trout fishing streams. Phone 919/957-8185. For additional information on this area and especially Alleghany County, contact the New River Country Travel Association, 919/982-

9414 or the Alleghany Chamber of Commerce in downtown Sparta, 919/372-5473.

Glendale Springs/Laurel Springs/Sparta
Blue Ridge Mountain Frescoes

A fresco is an almost forgotten art form, first used by early Egyptians and perfected during the Italian Renaissance. The most celebrated is Michaelangelo's work on the Sistine Chapel ceiling in the Vatican. Two quaint mountain churches in this area have frescoes by Ben Long, a native of North Carolina who studied under Italian master, Pietro Annigoni. Long's *Mary, Great with Child,* in the St. Mary's Episcopal Church at West Jefferson, won the Leonardo Da Vinci International Award—the first time it has been presented to a contemporary artist. At Glendale Springs in Holy Trinity Church, Long's *The Last Supper,* a 17-foot by 19½-foot work, is the largest fresco in America. Both churches are open every day, all year, with worship services conducted each Sunday. A guide service to view the frescoes and explain their significance is provided daily 9:30 to 4:30. There is no admission fee. For more information, telephone 919/982-3076.

Glendale Springs/Laurel Springs/Sparta
Greenhouse Crafts, Books & Music

F resh herbs, folk art and crafts, and books and music are the three distinctly different interests of the three people involved in the operation of this shop, across the street from the above church.

Betty Stiles is the herbalist. Stroll around her herb garden for a mini-course in these aromatic, historical, medicinal and culinary plants. Betty offers about fifty different herb plants for sale, and this visit will tempt you to start your own herb garden.

Joanie Bell is the manager of the crafts shop, which features folk arts and crafts from various cultures, from the southern Appalachians to Guatemala. Thousands of items in all price ranges include handwoven coverlets, toys, woodcarvings, art cards, baskets and pottery.

Michael Bell keeps the book section well stocked with a good back list of field and travel guides, children's classics, poetry and fiction by or about local people, places and history. He also has a fine selection of tapes and CD's, and stocks (and plays) hammered dulcimers, bowed psalteries and other unusual folk instruments. The shop is open seven days a week. Telephone 919/982-2618.

Glendale Springs/Laurel Springs/Sparta
Glendale Springs Inn

L isted on the National Register of Historic Places, this lovely 1890 three-story bed and breakfast inn and restaurant offers five guest rooms with private baths. Innkeeper Gayle Winston has furnished the rooms simply, almost starkly, with her family heirlooms, country antiques, quilts and hooked rugs. The result is a wonderful example of not gilding the lily, and a restful, unpretentious place that will linger in your memory for years to come. If you can't stay overnight, you can enjoy an elegant lunch or dinner while you are in the area or traveling the almost adjacent Blue Ridge Parkway.

For more information and reservations contact Glendale Springs Inn, Glendale Springs, NC 28629; phone 919/982-2102.

Glendale Springs/Laurel Springs/Sparta
Marion's Old Home Place Restaurant

W hether it's family-style or from the menu, dining here is down home in high style, Sunday best, served Wednesday through Saturday evenings, and Sundays from 12 noon until 8:30. You'll find it well worth a visit from anywhere in the mountains. The 12-room, 1921 farmhouse sets on a spacious lawn a few hundred yards off NC 21, about 4 miles east of Sparta and 2½ miles west of the Blue Ridge Parkway. If you arrive early, there are chairs on the lawn and rockers on the porch, and a lovely view to enjoy. This is really the old Marion homeplace and you'll usually be greeted by Newton C. (Bud) Marion II, Watana Marion or their son, Buddy. and you'll be seated at tables set for company, with pretty dishes, glassware, flowers and linens.

The family-style menu includes platters and bowls of *pan fried* chicken and gravy, Marion's country ham and red eye gravy, heavenly biscuits, salad, four vegetable specialties, dessert and tea or coffee. The same items may be ordered individually from the menu. Prices are are below average for family-style meals, although the food, setting and service are all above average, with minimal to half prices for children through age eight. Reservations are not accepted except for parties of 20 or more. Open from May 1 through October 31. Telephone 919/372-4676.

Glendale Springs/Laurel Springs/Sparta
Mountain Hearth Inn

E xit the parkway at milepost 231.5, turn east on SR 1109 for 200 yards for a must visit to this restaurant, bed & breakfast inn, gift and antique shop. Five guest rooms with private entrances and baths are cheerfully comfortable with country antique furnishings. There are more of these accessories and furnishings in the gift shop; handmade quilts, local potter and arts, and carefully chosen antiques. You can also buy loaves of the home baked bread which is served with the restaurant's breakfasts, luncheons and dinners.

Eleanor Rancourt is the baker and homemade soup maker; otherwise Ernie Rancourt is in charge of the kitchen, preparing breakfasts (these are for house guests only, served 8 to 10) which might include Belgian waffles or a French herbed omelette; luncheon entrees as hearty as an herbed burger with wine sauce on oatmeal bread, or as light as a Waldorf salad; dinner (five course on weekends!) entrees such as an herb crusted pork tenderloin with onion gravy and sherried sweet potatoes. This family owned and operated oasis includes daughter Sherry Babish, who will see that your visit to the dining room (cheerful with country linens, fireplace and lots of windows for that lovely country view) or you stay at the lodge is the highlight of your mountain getaway. Their season runs from April through December. The restaurant is open Tuesday through Saturday, with lunch 12–2 and dinner 6–8. Reservations are a good idea on weekends. Contact Mountain Hearth, Route 1, Box 288E, Sparta, NC 28675; phone 919/372-8743.

Glendale Springs/Laurel Springs/Sparta
Bella Columns Bed and Breakfast

I f you've ever wondered why anyone would put a house on a completely cleared hilltop, you'll understand when you visit this inn. From here, it's a glorious — visibly glorious—world, spreading out in all directions. Tidy farms, wildflower meadows, pastures with horses and spotted cows, breezes stirring clusters of hardwood trees dotting the unfolding landscape—too steep to be called hills, too gentle to be called mountains.

Everything is beautiful and everything is visible from this hilltop which is crowned by a country home over a hundred years old, but only moved to this perfect spot in 1984. The large stately house has a broad wraparound veranda graced by nine white columns. Inside is just as grand, beginning with a baby grand piano in the music room. There are oriental rugs on hardwood floors and antique furnishings from the library to the dining room to the four over-sized guest rooms-with-a-view (two with private baths). There's a game room, a sun room, a screened porch, patio and a lovely flower garden. Take your pick of where to take your complete southern breakfast—there's a view from everywhere.

All this and trails to the New River (if you canoe, bring it along), a public golf course nearby and the Blue Ridge Parkway only minutes away. Open April through December. Contact innkeeper Debbie Weaver, Bella Columns, Route 2, Box 228B, Sparta, NC 28675; phone 919/372-2633.

Glendale Springs/Laurel Springs/Sparta
Burgiss Farm Bed and Breakfast

Your family, or family of friends, will be the only guests when you make reservations at this 200 acre family farm near the Blue Ridge Parkway. The newer addition of this lovely old 1899 farmhouse has two guest rooms which will accommodate up to four in one party—more if some are children. There is a recreation room, equipped for all ages, a large hot tub, and plenty of room to roam, inside and out. There are lawns and gardens, swings and hammocks, orchards, even a kennel for the family pet, and a private pond for catfish fishing. Your hosts, the third and fourth generation on this farm, Tom and Nancy Burgiss, and son Brant, will be happy to prepare your catch for dinner—or even for your breakfast, although you'll have plenty of other choices for that country morning feast. There are more recreation opportunities on the premises, plus the parkway, the nearby New River, and miles of backroads to explore with your camera for wildlife and waterfalls. Contact Burgiss Farm Bed & Breakfast, Route 1, Box 300, Laurel Springs, NC 28644; phone 919/359-2995.

Glendale Springs/Laurel Springs/Sparta
Turby-Villa Bed & Breakfast

Mimi and R.E. "Turby" Turbyville live in large contemporary brick home two miles out in the country, near the new public golf course. Set on 20 pastoral acres at the end of a long tree lined private road, Turby-Villa has a 360 degree view of Blue Ridge Mountain farmlands. This is real relaxation, sitting under a shade tree, watching the cloud shadows move across the meadows, sipping on some iced tea, shelling fresh garden peas with Mimi, and listening to Turby's tales of Alleghany County history. Mimi's needlepoint and other handicrafts are on display throughout the cheerful home. There are cool and quiet or sunlit places to relax with newspapers, books, television, your own needlework—or paperwork if you are in the area on business. Each of the three guest rooms has a gleaming private bath, and each is furnished to comfortable perfection by this ultimate homemaker. Your complimentary breakfast, to be enjoyed along with the view from a glassed in porch, will be prepared to order—from a menu listing everything Mimi has available. All this, all year, at rates so low no one will believe you, and so there will still be a room for you when you return, again and again. Contact Turby-Villa, East Whitehead St., Sparta, NC 28675; phone 919/372-8490.

Autumn in the mountains

Epilogue to an Episode

This book has been growing since 1984, thanks in no small part to readers who have sent information about their favorite places, both old and new. Your comments and suggestions are always welcome. They will be put on file, checked out, and some year, when it's time for the book to have another growth spurt, you may find your recommendations included in the next episode of On the Road . . .

If *Mountain Getaways* is not available in your local bookstore, or if you wish to order additional copies for yourself or mailed directly to others, please send $5.95 plus $1 postage for each separate order. Address all correspondence to the publishing address on the inside page.

Happy highways, byways and backroads.

Rusty Hoffland

Once upon a time on the Blue Ridge Parkway...Exact time, place and photographer unknown.

NOTES TO REMEMBER